RICHARD MATHESON'S

THE

SHRINKING

MAN

"*The Shrinking Man* is a dark masterpiece. Ted Adams weaves magic in his faithful and unflinching comic book adaptation of Richard Matheson's brilliant novel."
–Jonathan Maberry, *New York Times* bestselling author of *Patient Zero* and *Captain America: Hail Hydra*

Adaptation: **Ted Adams**

Art: **Mark Torres**

Colors: **Tomi Varga**

Letters: **Robbie Robbins**

Assistant Editor: **Michael Benedetto**

Editor: **Chris Ryall**

Dedicated to the great **Richard Matheson**

Facebook: **facebook.com/idwpublishing**
Twitter: **@idwpublishing**
YouTube: **youtube.com/idwpublishing**
Tumblr: **tumblr.idwpublishing.com**
Instagram: **instagram.com/idwpublishing**

COVER ART BY
MARK TORRES

COLLECTION EDITS BY
JUSTIN EISINGER
AND ALONZO SIMON

COLLECTION DESIGN BY
CLYDE GRAPA

978-1-63140 -519-8   19 18 17 16   1 2 3 4 5

THE SHRINKING MAN. JANUARY 2016. FIRST PRINTING.
The Shrinking Man © 1956 Richard Matheson; renewed 1984
by Richard Matheson. All Rights Reserved.
Introduction © 2016 Peter Straub. All Rights Reserved.
Afterword © 2016 David Morrell. All Rights Reserved.
© 2016 Idea and Design Works, LLC. All Rights Reserved.
The IDW logo is registered in the U.S. Patent and Trademark Office.
IDW Publishing, a division of Idea and Design Works, LLC. Editorial
offices: 2765 Truxtun Road, San Diego, CA 92106. Any similarities
to persons living or dead are purely coincidental. With the exception
of artwork used for review purposes, none of the contents of this
publication may be reprinted without the permission of
Idea and Design Works, LLC. Printed in Korea.
IDW Publishing does not read or accept unsolicited submissions of
ideas, stories, or artwork.

Originally published as THE SHRINKING MAN issues #1–4.

Ted Adams, CEO & Publisher
Greg Goldstein, President & COO
Robbie Robbins, EVP/Sr. Graphic Artist
Chris Ryall, Chief Creative Officer/Editor-in-Chief
Matthew Ruzicka, CPA, Chief Financial Officer
Dirk Wood, VP of Marketing
Lorelei Bunjes, VP of Digital Services
Jeff Webber, VP of Licensing, Digital and Subsidiary Rights
Jerry Bennington, VP of New Product Development

Special thanks to Paula Adams, Susan Ramer, and Lauren Gennawey
for their invaluable assistance.

Library of Congress Cataloging-in-Publication Data

Names: Adams, Ted (Writer) author. I Torres, Mark, illustrator. I Varga,
   Tomi, illustrator. I Robbins, Robbie, illustrator. I Matheson, Richard,
   1926-2013. Shrinking man.
Title: Richard Matheson's The shrinking man / adaptation, Ted Adams ; art,
   Mark Torres ; colors, Tomi Varga ; letters, Robbie Robbins.
Other titles: Shrinking man
Description: San Diego, CA : IDW Publishing, 2016. I "Originally published as
   THE SHRINKING MAN issues #1-4."
Identifiers: LCCN 2015046016 I ISBN 9781631405198 (pbk.)
Subjects: LCSH: Graphic novels. I Science fiction comic books, strips, etc.
Classification: LCC PN6727.A35 R53 2016 I DDC 741.5/973--dc23
LC record available at http://lccn.loc.gov/2015046016

Peter Straub on

The Shrinking Man

This introduction was originally published online for the Library of America.

Richard Matheson, at this writing still publishing in his ninetieth year, is the most varied and intellectually agile of the community of fantasy/sci-fi/horror writers that gathered in Los Angeles in the mid-fifties to create, along with a great many *Twilight Zone* episodes, a body of short stories and novels that brought a sleeker, more refined and efficient aesthetic to the *Weird Tales* model they had absorbed from H. P. Lovecraft. Ray Bradbury, who by the mid-fifties had lived in Los Angeles for two decades, was in some sense the alpha dog of those writers—Charles Beaumont, Bill Nolan, Harlan Ellison, George Clayton Johnson—who provided scripts for Rod Serling's adventurous new television series. But if these men set Bradbury apart by almost literally revering him, Richard Matheson was their point man, an equal who nonetheless had more on the ball than the rest of the pack. Robert Bloch, a close friend to all parties, once explained his absence from *Twilight Zone* by saying that it was safe "in the hands of . . . the Matheson Mafia—Beaumont, Nolan, Johnson, and other friends." That is, their work could by summed up by the mention of his name.

These men, along with Bloch, had perfected a clean, craftsmanly sub-genre that could be called California Gothic. Their stories were as carefully engineered as haikus and as intolerant of wasted motion. Every line of dialogue, every observed detail, hastened the story forward toward a conclusion that upended all we had imagined them to mean. Trick endings, twist endings, shock endings, if you make them the core of your aesthetic you create a literature of steely, ironic misdirection narrated to bamboozled readers by unreliable characters. Digression, self-indulgence, and pretension are disallowed, strenuously.

No one was better than Matheson at demonstrating the many uses of this variety of minimalism, but it did contain one unshakeable limitation, that it was designed for the production of short fiction. However, in the right hands the method did allow for a cautious expansion. The rest of "the Matheson Mafia" succeeded in writing no more than two or three novels each. (Some of them had zero interest in novels.) Matheson, however, who started novelizing early on and just kept going, has now written twenty-eight. *The Shrinking Man* was the fourth of these, and like its immediate predecessor, *I Am Legend*, it brilliantly aerates the minimalist aesthetic of its time and place by linking it to an episodic structure in which each of the episodes serves further to tighten the narrative noose.

Episodic narratives never work like this, that's what makes them episodic. A narrative consisting entirely of episodes and connective tissue generally careens all over the map like Odysseus and Don Quixote, gathering and losing steam as it goes. As in *Rogue Male*, Geoffrey Household's masterpiece, *The Shrinking Man* begins with its First Cause, then traces the unfolding consequences of that event in a close-up, one-to-one, unswerving manner that sweeps us ever closer to what may not after all prove impossible in a first-person novel, the protagonist's extinction. It might not be death, exactly, but it should be the next closest thing, total disappearance. In 1953, Matheson had not yet moved beyond the desire to finish a tale with a surprise ending, but what he found here is a real surprise, filled not with deadpan professional cynicism but serenity and optimism—a fresh, wide-eyed step into a world both beautiful and new.

Peter Straub has published almost twenty novels including The Talisman *(1984; with Stephen King),* Koko *(1988), and most recently* A Dark Matter *(2010). For the Library of America, he has edited* H. P. Lovecraft: Tales *(2005) and* American Fantastic Tales *(2 vols., 2009).*

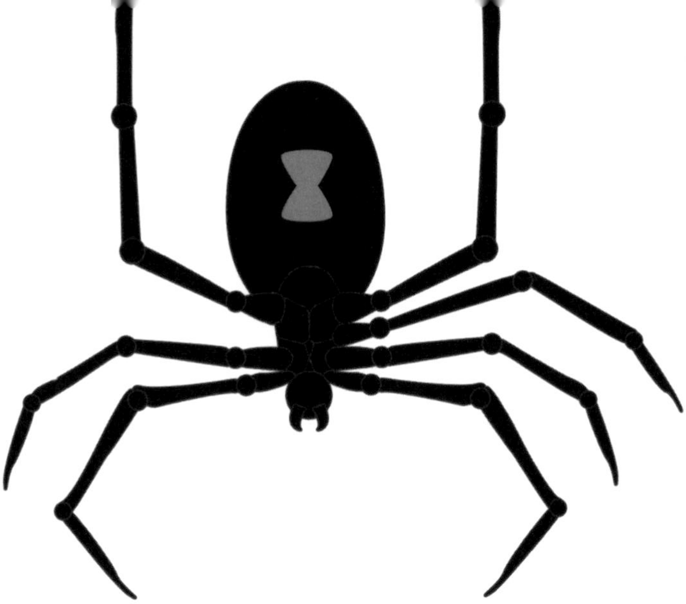

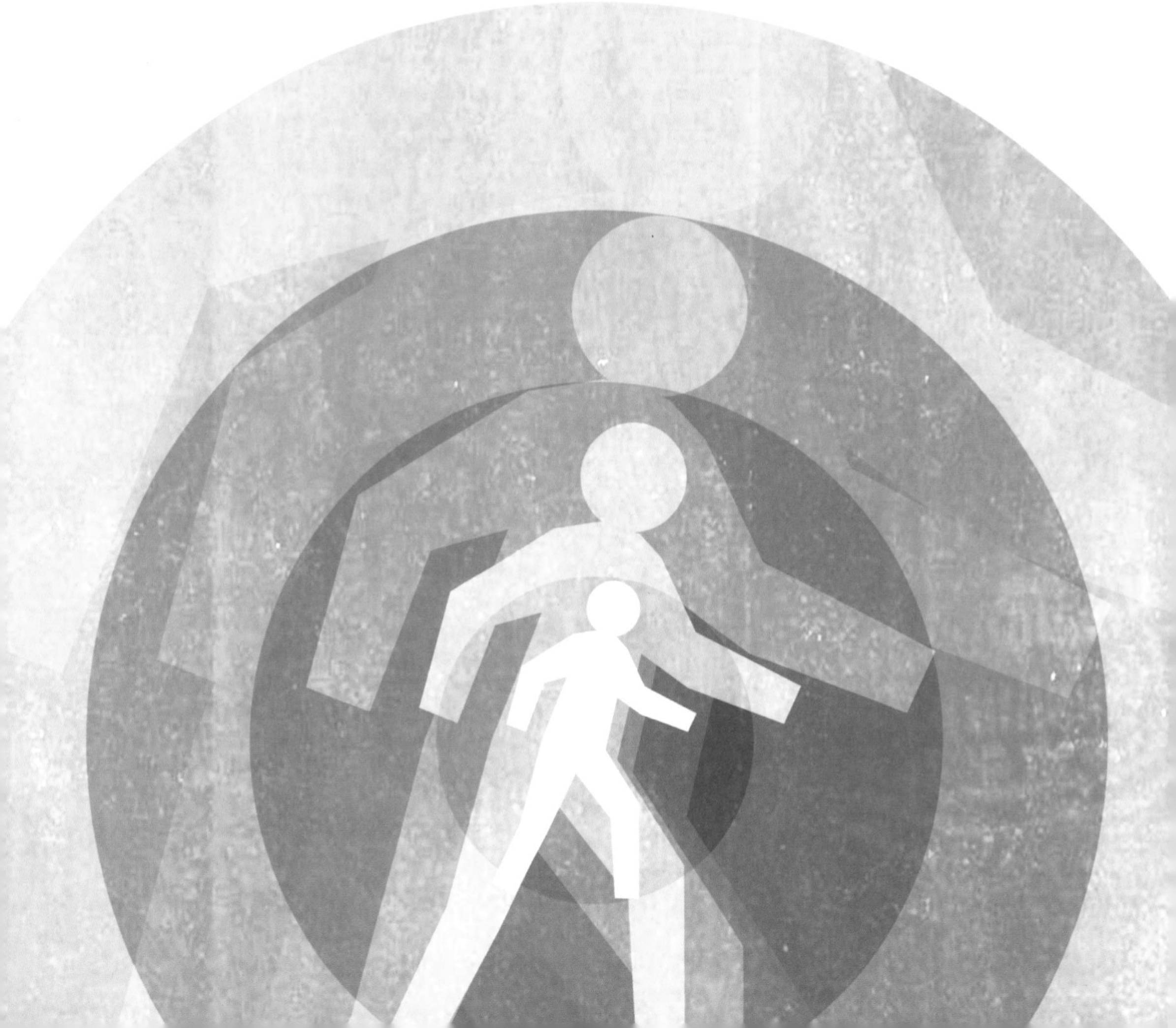

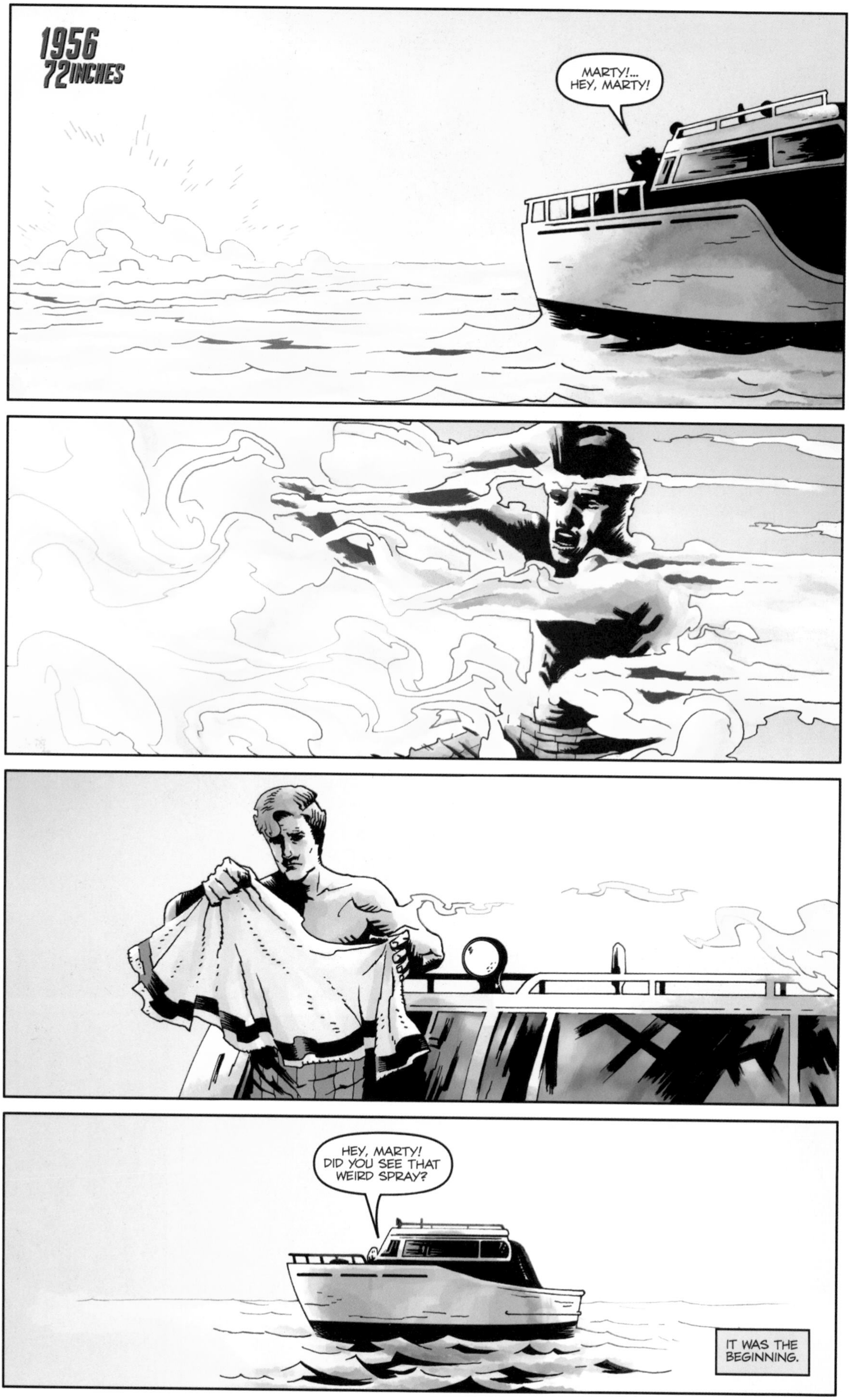
1956
72 INCHES
MARTY!... HEY, MARTY!
HEY, MARTY! DID YOU SEE THAT WEIRD SPRAY?
IT WAS THE BEGINNING.

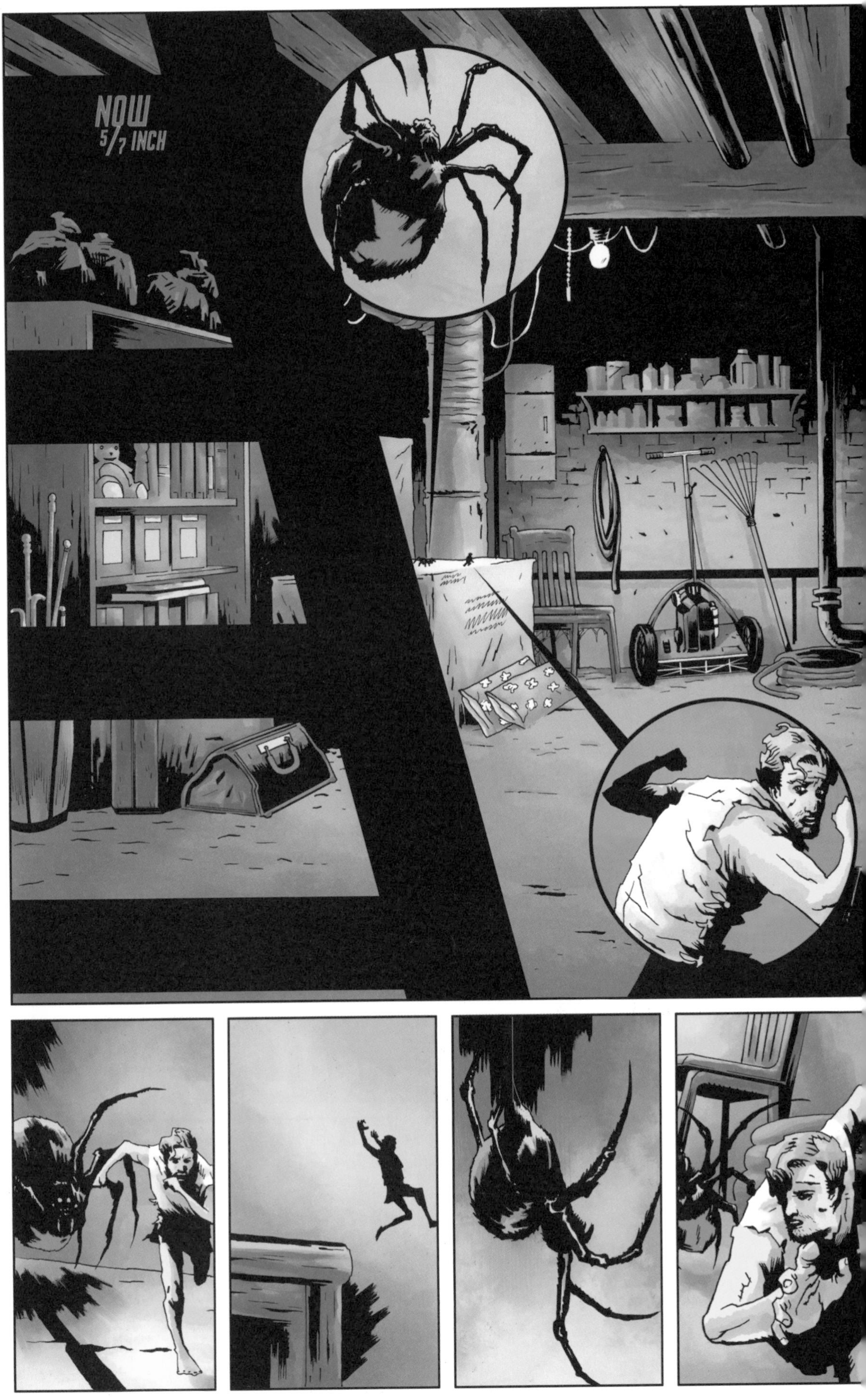
NOW
5/7 INCH

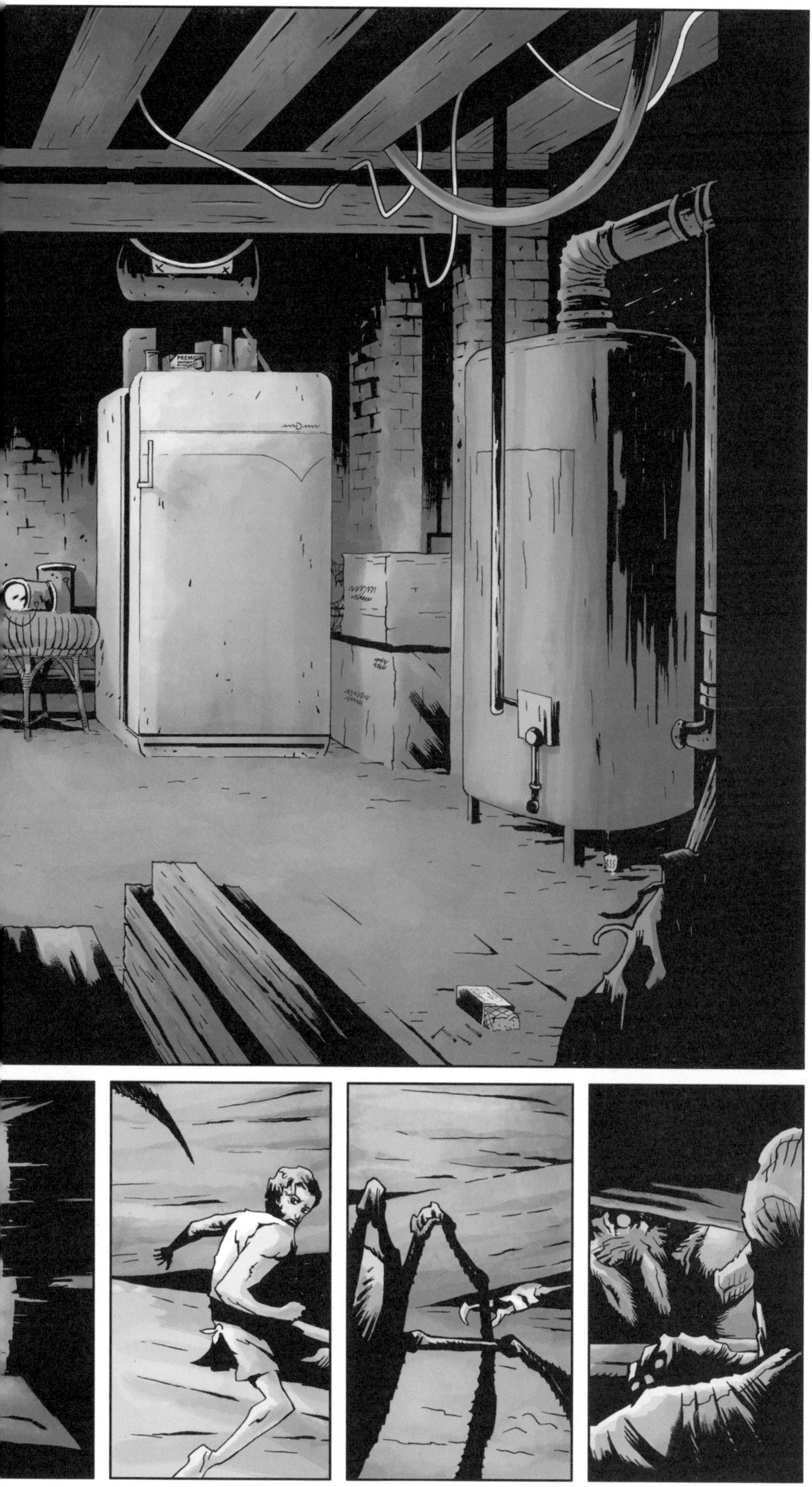
PREMIUM

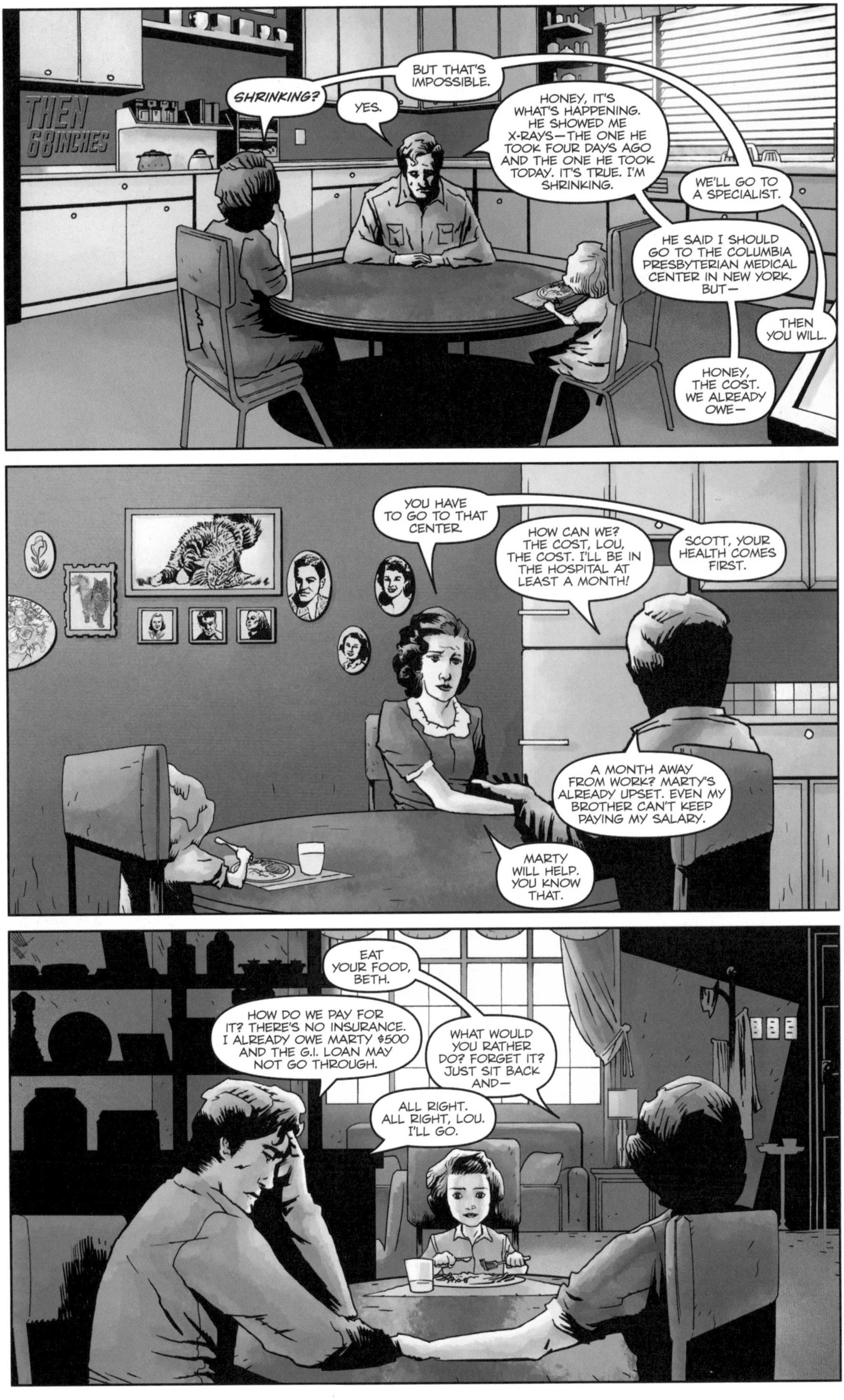
THEN 68 INCHES
SHRINKING?
YES.
BUT THAT'S IMPOSSIBLE.
HONEY, IT'S WHAT'S HAPPENING. HE SHOWED ME X-RAYS—THE ONE HE TOOK FOUR DAYS AGO AND THE ONE HE TOOK TODAY. IT'S TRUE. I'M SHRINKING.
WE'LL GO TO A SPECIALIST.
HE SAID I SHOULD GO TO THE COLUMBIA PRESBYTERIAN MEDICAL CENTER IN NEW YORK. BUT—
THEN YOU WILL.
HONEY, THE COST. WE ALREADY OWE—
YOU HAVE TO GO TO THAT CENTER.
HOW CAN WE? THE COST, LOU, THE COST. I'LL BE IN THE HOSPITAL AT LEAST A MONTH!
SCOTT, YOUR HEALTH COMES FIRST.
A MONTH AWAY FROM WORK? MARTY'S ALREADY UPSET. EVEN MY BROTHER CAN'T KEEP PAYING MY SALARY.
MARTY WILL HELP. YOU KNOW THAT.
EAT YOUR FOOD, BETH.
HOW DO WE PAY FOR IT? THERE'S NO INSURANCE. I ALREADY OWE MARTY $500 AND THE G.I. LOAN MAY NOT GO THROUGH.
WHAT WOULD YOU RATHER DO? FORGET IT? JUST SIT BACK AND—
ALL RIGHT. ALL RIGHT, LOU. I'LL GO.

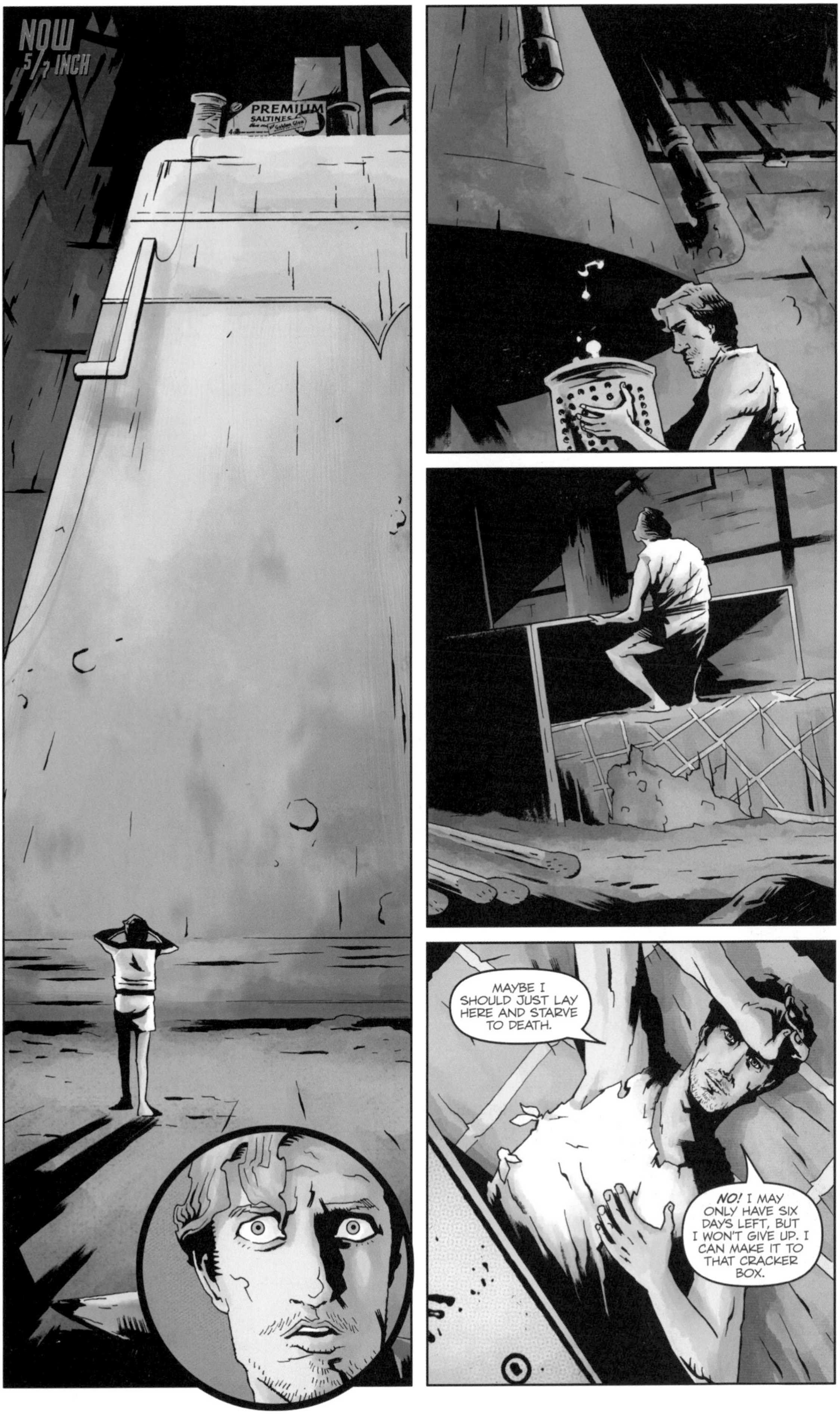
NOW
5/7 INCH
PREMIUM
SALTINES
MAYBE I SHOULD JUST LAY HERE AND STARVE TO DEATH.
NO! I MAY ONLY HAVE SIX DAYS LEFT, BUT I WON'T GIVE UP. I CAN MAKE IT TO THAT CRACKER BOX.

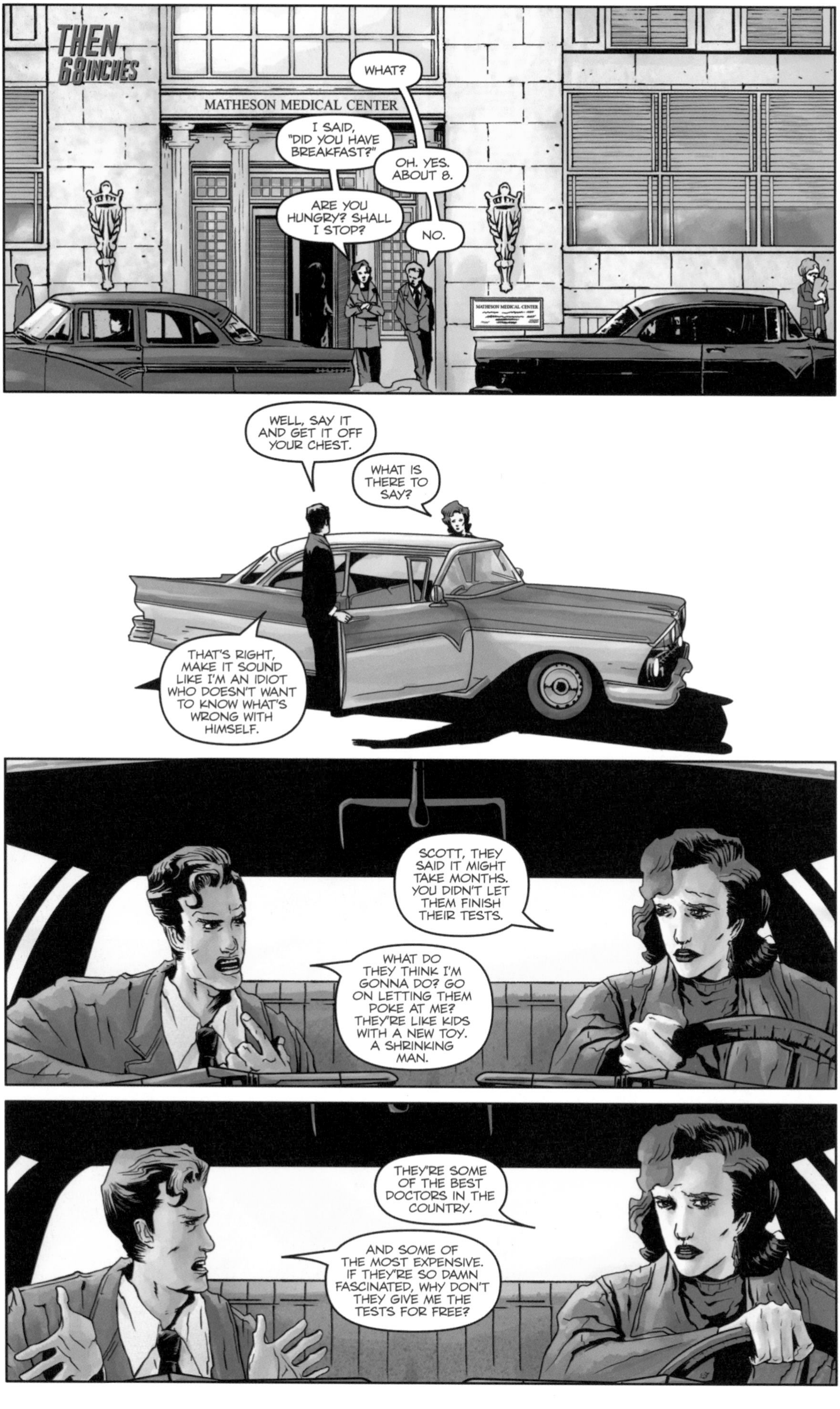
THEN
68 INCHES
MATHESON MEDICAL CENTER
WHAT?
I SAID, "DID YOU HAVE BREAKFAST?"
OH. YES. ABOUT 8.
ARE YOU HUNGRY? SHALL I STOP?
NO.
MATHESON MEDICAL CENTER
WELL, SAY IT AND GET IT OFF YOUR CHEST.
WHAT IS THERE TO SAY?
THAT'S RIGHT, MAKE IT SOUND LIKE I'M AN IDIOT WHO DOESN'T WANT TO KNOW WHAT'S WRONG WITH HIMSELF.
SCOTT, THEY SAID IT MIGHT TAKE MONTHS. YOU DIDN'T LET THEM FINISH THEIR TESTS.
WHAT DO THEY THINK I'M GONNA DO? GO ON LETTING THEM POKE AT ME? THEY'RE LIKE KIDS WITH A NEW TOY. A SHRINKING MAN.
THEY'RE SOME OF THE BEST DOCTORS IN THE COUNTRY.
AND SOME OF THE MOST EXPENSIVE. IF THEY'RE SO DAMN FASCINATED, WHY DON'T THEY GIVE ME THE TESTS FOR FREE?

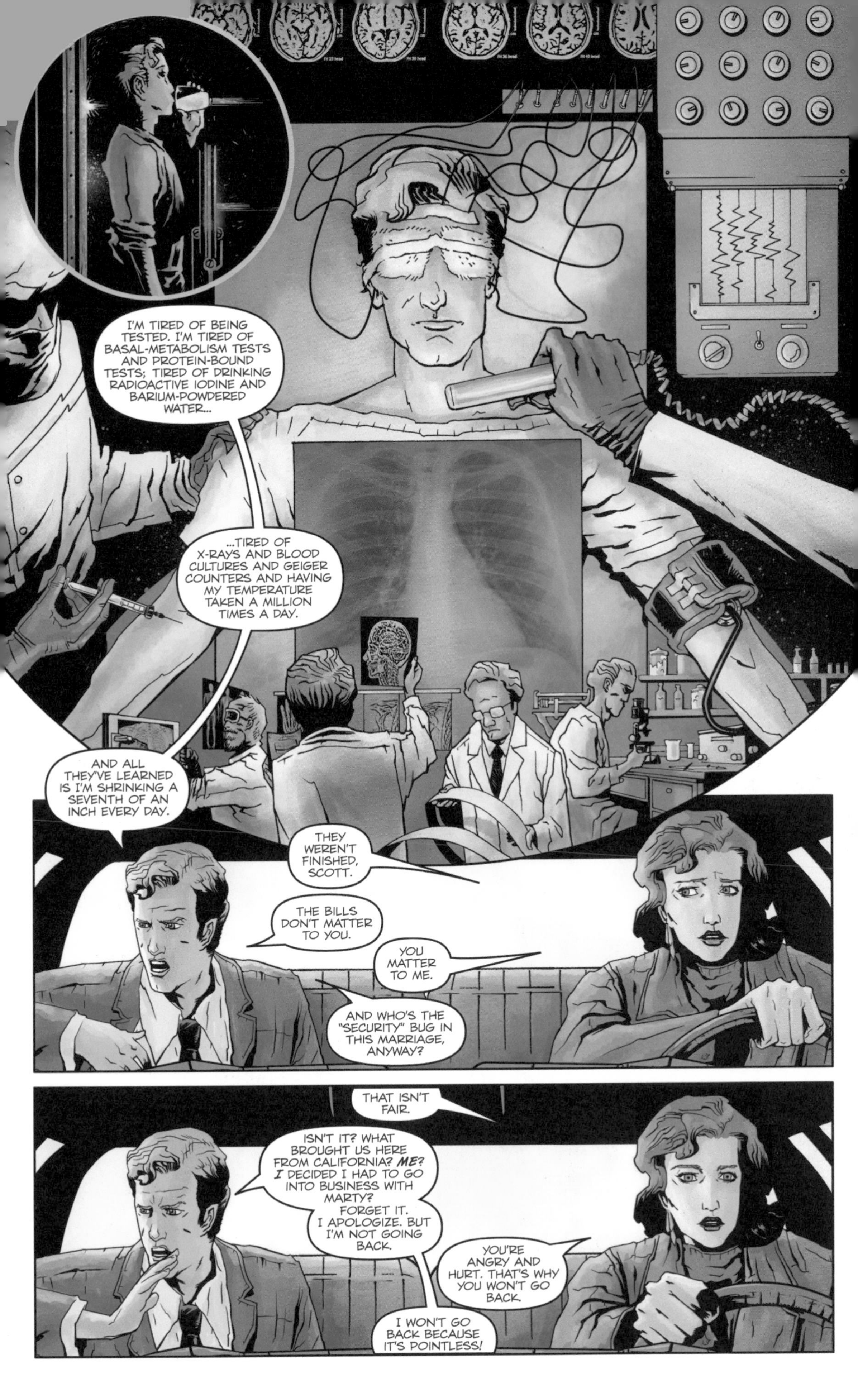
I'M TIRED OF BEING TESTED. I'M TIRED OF BASAL-METABOLISM TESTS AND PROTEIN-BOUND TESTS; TIRED OF DRINKING RADIOACTIVE IODINE AND BARIUM-POWDERED WATER...
...TIRED OF X-RAYS AND BLOOD CULTURES AND GEIGER COUNTERS AND HAVING MY TEMPERATURE TAKEN A MILLION TIMES A DAY.
AND ALL THEY'VE LEARNED IS I'M SHRINKING A SEVENTH OF AN INCH EVERY DAY.
THEY WEREN'T FINISHED, SCOTT.
THE BILLS DON'T MATTER TO YOU.
YOU MATTER TO ME.
AND WHO'S THE "SECURITY" BUG IN THIS MARRIAGE, ANYWAY?
THAT ISN'T FAIR.
ISN'T IT? WHAT BROUGHT US HERE FROM CALIFORNIA? *ME*? *I* DECIDED I HAD TO GO INTO BUSINESS WITH MARTY?
FORGET IT. I APOLOGIZE. BUT I'M NOT GOING BACK.
YOU'RE ANGRY AND HURT. THAT'S WHY YOU WON'T GO BACK.
I WON'T GO BACK BECAUSE IT'S POINTLESS!

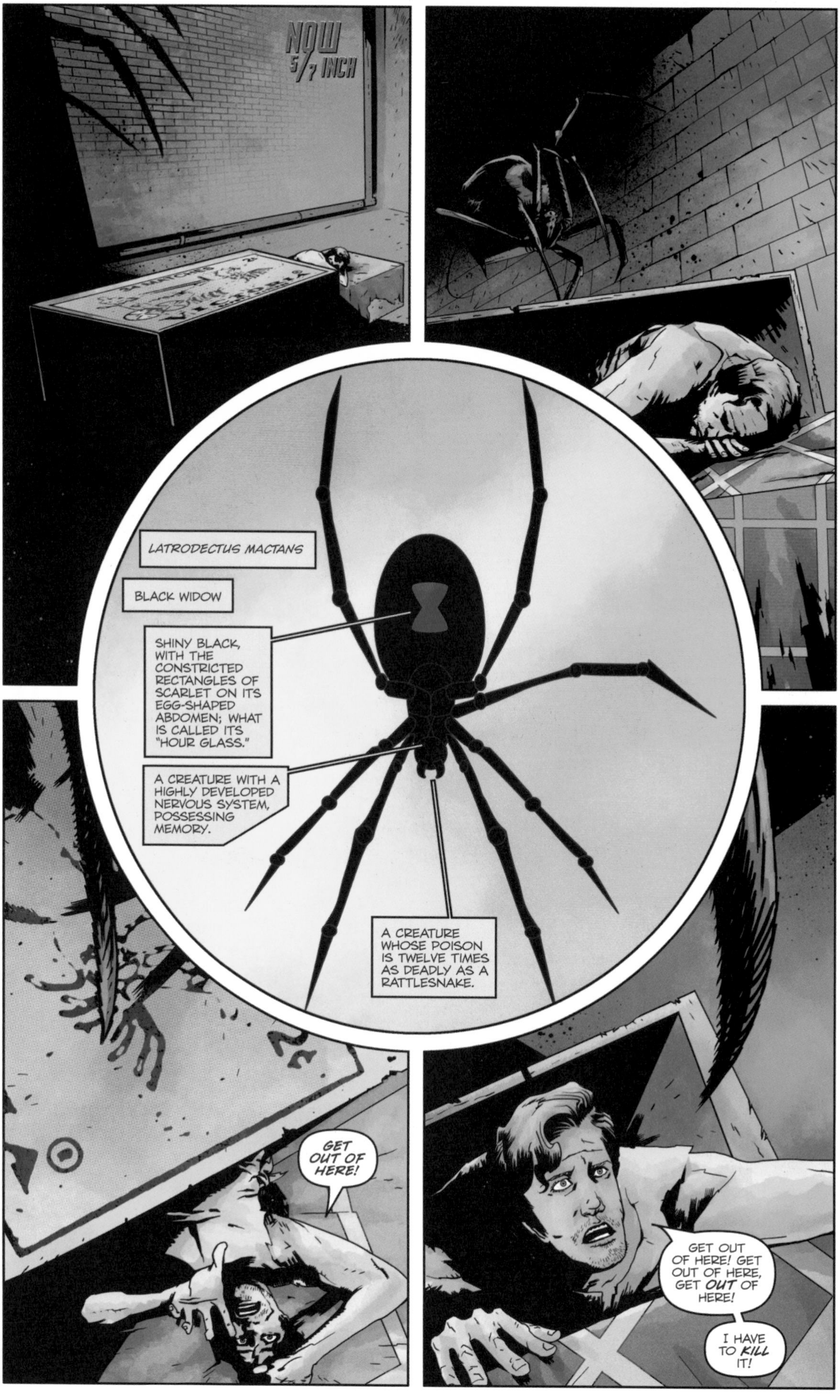
NOW
5/7 INCH
LATRODECTUS MACTANS
BLACK WIDOW
SHINY BLACK, WITH THE CONSTRICTED RECTANGLES OF SCARLET ON ITS EGG-SHAPED ABDOMEN; WHAT IS CALLED ITS "HOUR GLASS."
A CREATURE WITH A HIGHLY DEVELOPED NERVOUS SYSTEM, POSSESSING MEMORY.
A CREATURE WHOSE POISON IS TWELVE TIMES AS DEADLY AS A RATTLESNAKE.
GET OUT OF HERE!
GET OUT OF HERE! GET OUT OF HERE, GET OUT OF HERE!
I HAVE TO KILL IT!

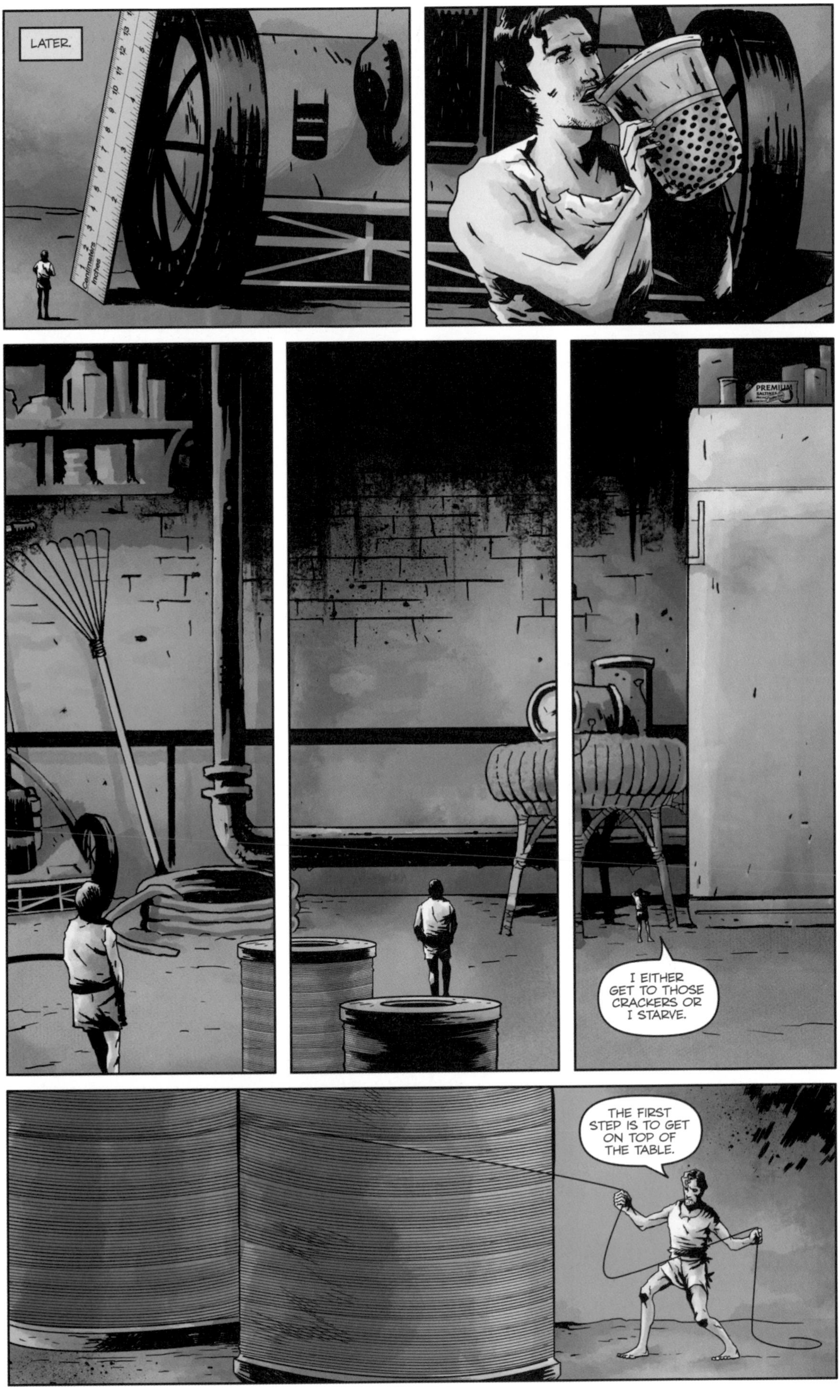
LATER.
Centimeters
Inches
PREMIUM
I EITHER GET TO THOSE CRACKERS OR I STARVE.
THE FIRST STEP IS TO GET ON TOP OF THE TABLE.

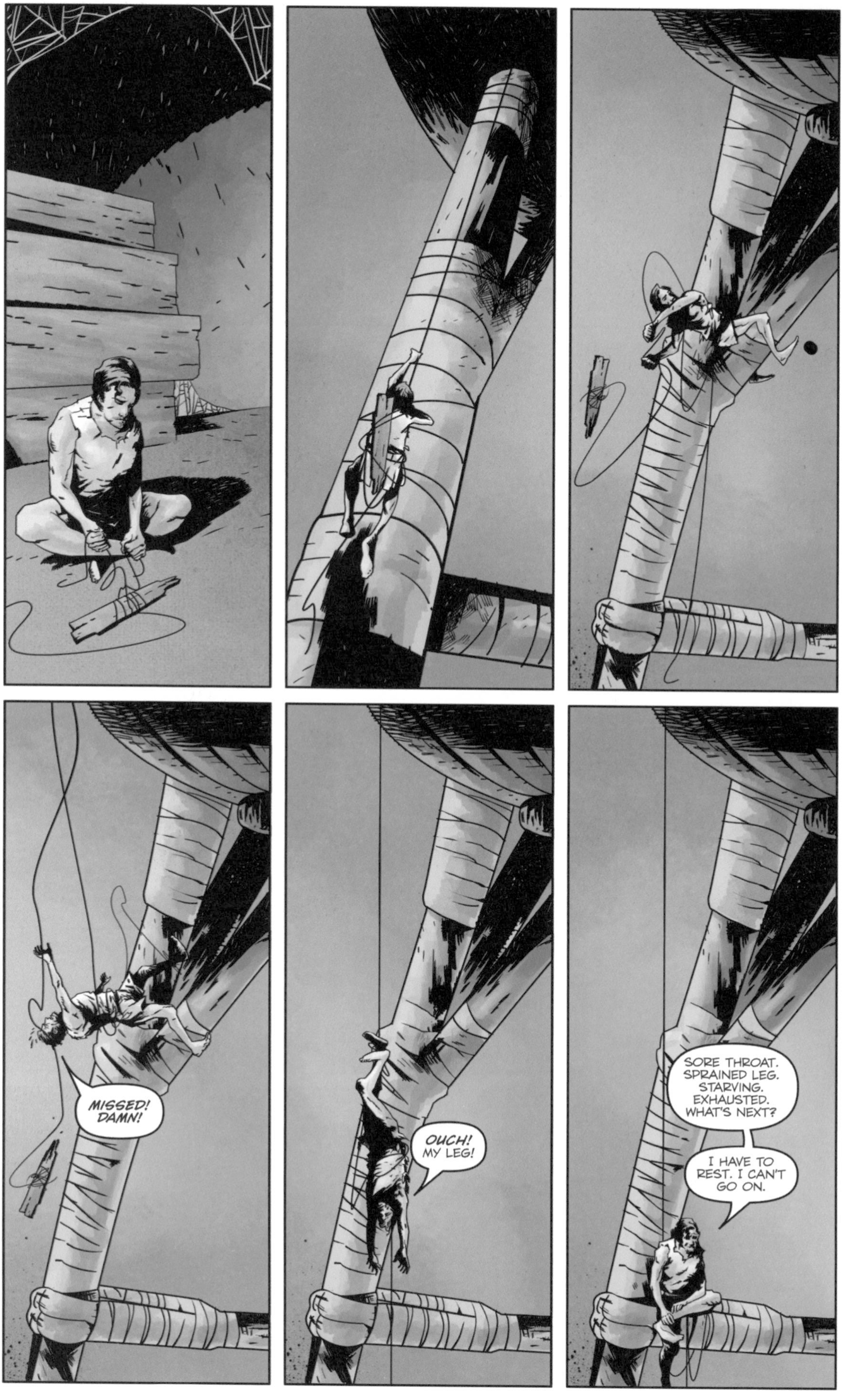
MISSED! DAMN!
OUCH! MY LEG!
SORE THROAT. SPRAINED LEG. STARVING. EXHAUSTED. WHAT'S NEXT?
I HAVE TO REST. I CAN'T GO ON.

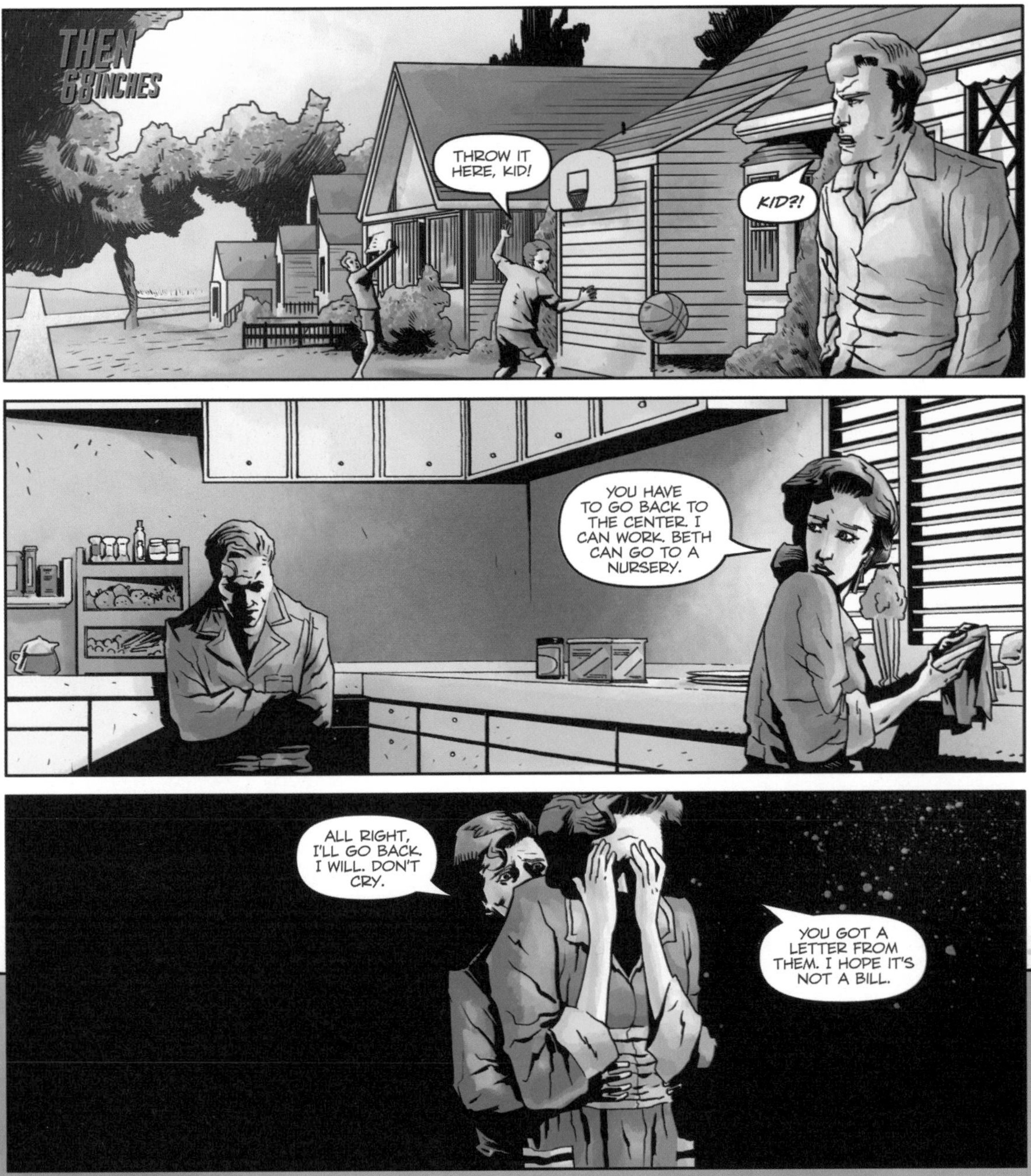
THEN
68 INCHES
THROW IT HERE, KID!
KID?!
YOU HAVE TO GO BACK TO THE CENTER. I CAN WORK. BETH CAN GO TO A NURSERY.
ALL RIGHT, I'LL GO BACK. I WILL. DON'T CRY.
YOU GOT A LETTER FROM THEM. I HOPE IT'S NOT A BILL.

BECAUSE OF THE UNUSUAL NATURE OF YOUR DISORDER, THE INVESTIGATION OF WHICH MIGHT PROVE TO HAVE INESTIMABLE VALUE TO MEDICAL KNOWLEDGE, YOUR MEDICAL CARE WILL BE PROVIDED FREE OF CHARGE.

NOW
5/7 INCH

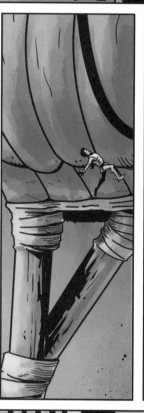

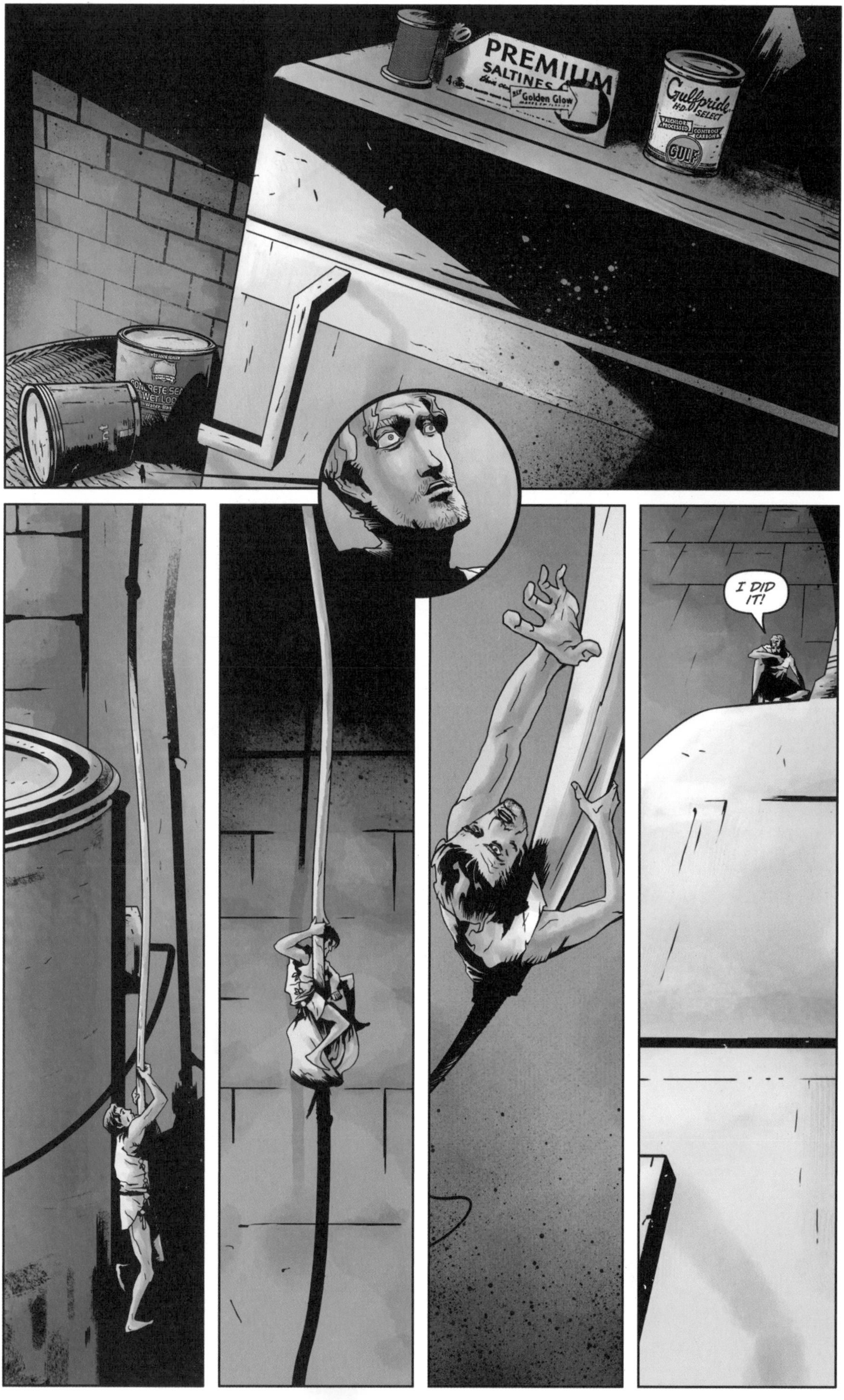
PREMIUM
SALTINES
Golden Glow
Gulfpride
H.D.
SELECT
GULF
I DID IT!

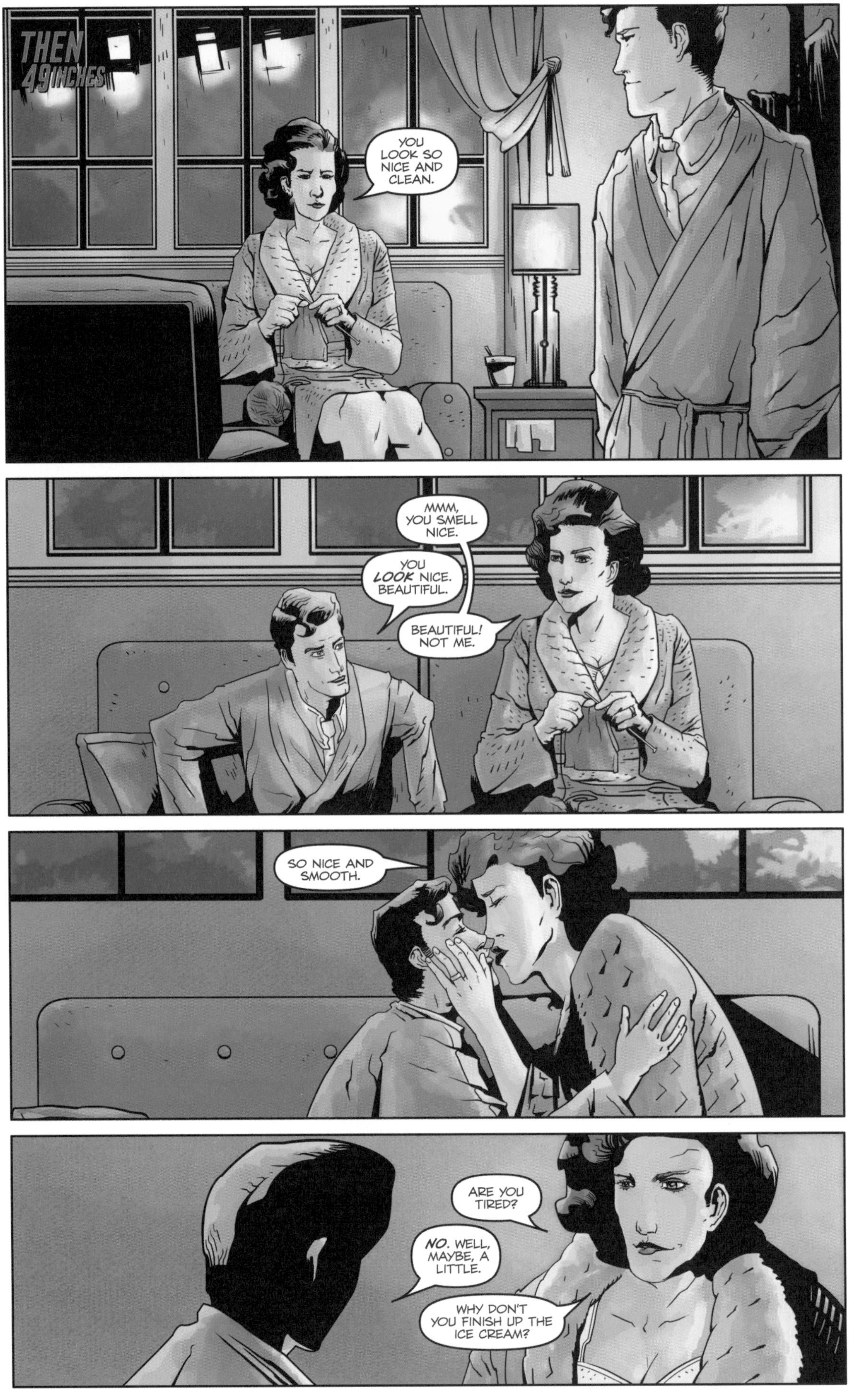
THEN
49 INCHES
YOU LOOK SO NICE AND CLEAN.
MMM, YOU SMELL NICE.
YOU *LOOK* NICE. BEAUTIFUL.
BEAUTIFUL! NOT ME.
SO NICE AND SMOOTH.
ARE YOU TIRED?
NO. WELL, MAYBE, A LITTLE.
WHY DON'T YOU FINISH UP THE ICE CREAM?

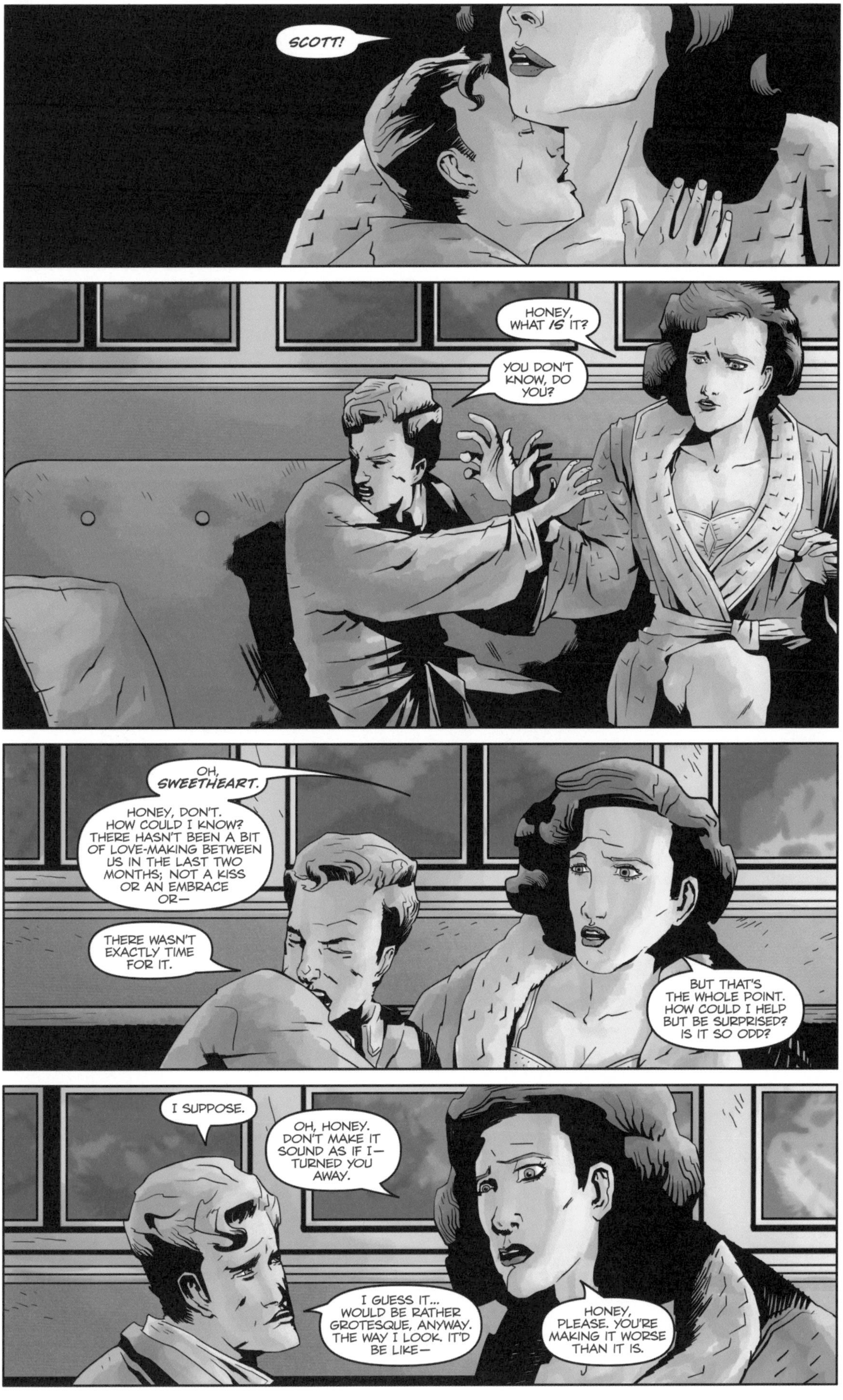
SCOTT!
HONEY, WHAT IS IT?
YOU DON'T KNOW, DO YOU?
OH, SWEETHEART.
HONEY, DON'T. HOW COULD I KNOW? THERE HASN'T BEEN A BIT OF LOVE-MAKING BETWEEN US IN THE LAST TWO MONTHS; NOT A KISS OR AN EMBRACE OR—
THERE WASN'T EXACTLY TIME FOR IT.
BUT THAT'S THE WHOLE POINT. HOW COULD I HELP BUT BE SURPRISED? IS IT SO ODD?
I SUPPOSE.
OH, HONEY. DON'T MAKE IT SOUND AS IF I— TURNED YOU AWAY.
I GUESS IT... WOULD BE RATHER GROTESQUE, ANYWAY. THE WAY I LOOK. IT'D BE LIKE—
HONEY, PLEASE. YOU'RE MAKING IT WORSE THAN IT IS.

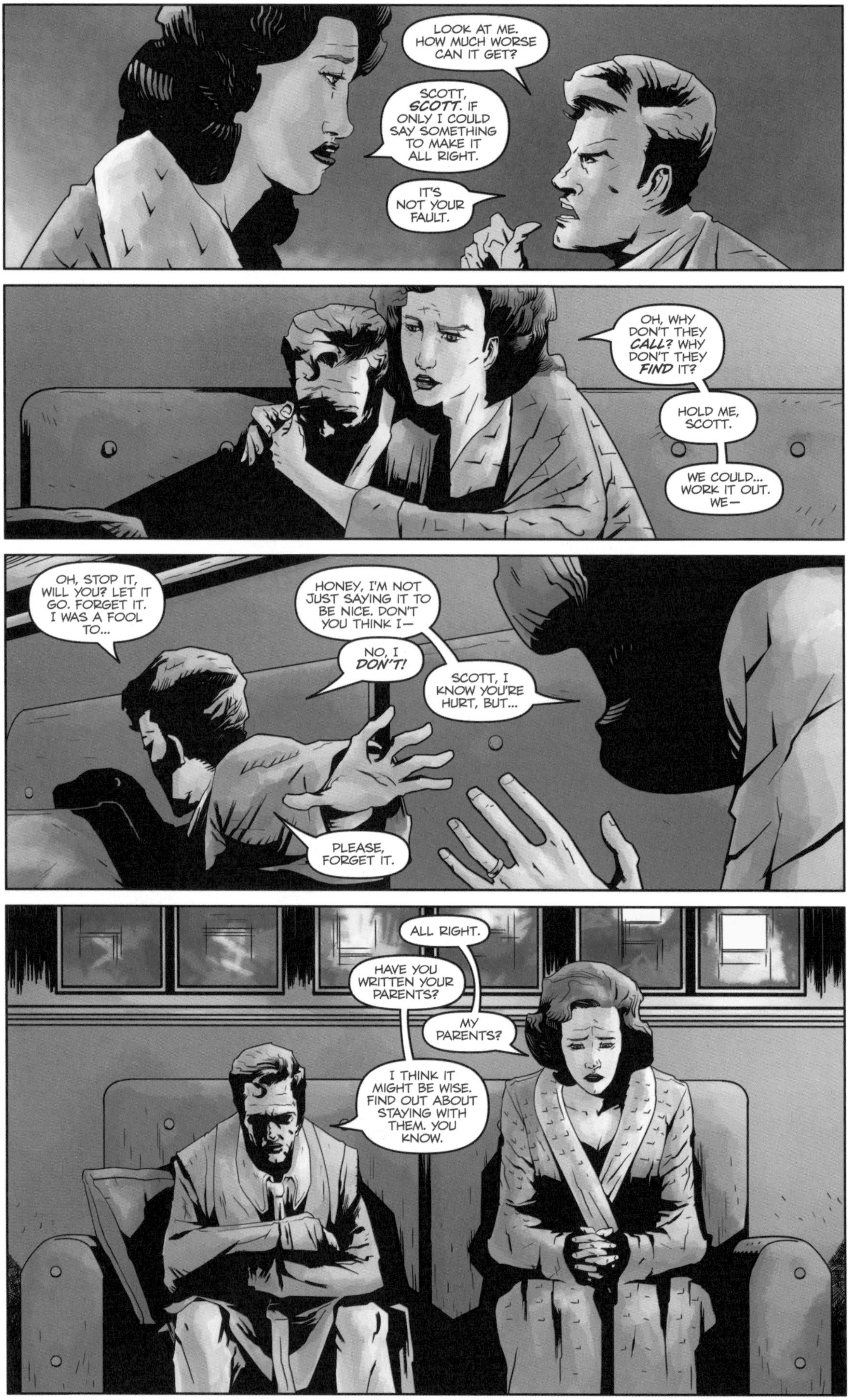
LOOK AT ME. HOW MUCH WORSE CAN IT GET?
SCOTT, SCOTT. IF ONLY I COULD SAY SOMETHING TO MAKE IT ALL RIGHT.
IT'S NOT YOUR FAULT.
OH, WHY DON'T THEY CALL? WHY DON'T THEY FIND IT?
HOLD ME, SCOTT.
WE COULD... WORK IT OUT. WE—
OH, STOP IT, WILL YOU? LET IT GO. FORGET IT. I WAS A FOOL TO...
HONEY, I'M NOT JUST SAYING IT TO BE NICE. DON'T YOU THINK I—
NO, I DON'T!
SCOTT, I KNOW YOU'RE HURT, BUT...
PLEASE, FORGET IT.
ALL RIGHT.
HAVE YOU WRITTEN YOUR PARENTS?
MY PARENTS?
I THINK IT MIGHT BE WISE. FIND OUT ABOUT STAYING WITH THEM. YOU KNOW.

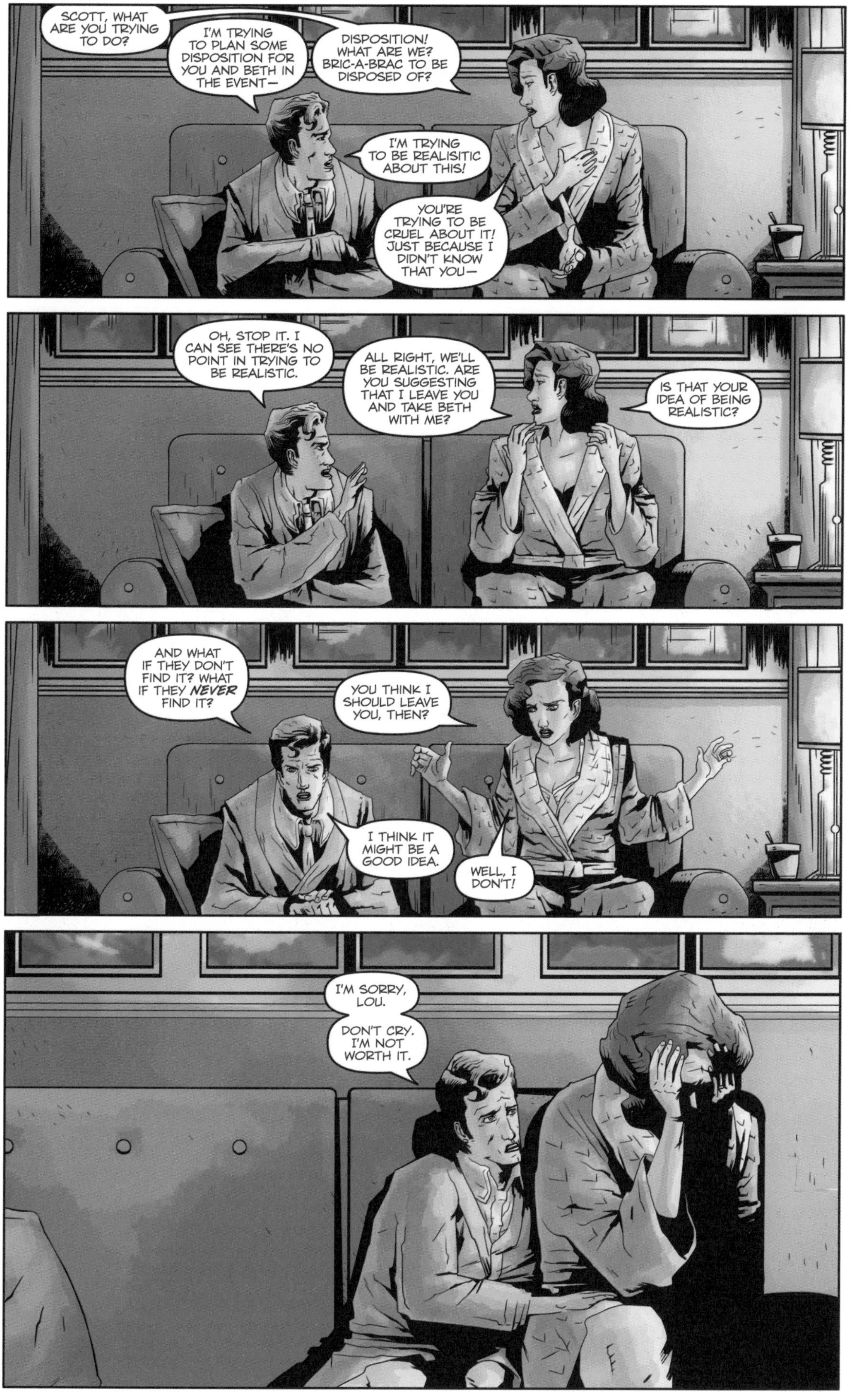
SCOTT, WHAT ARE YOU TRYING TO DO?
I'M TRYING TO PLAN SOME DISPOSITION FOR YOU AND BETH IN THE EVENT—
DISPOSITION! WHAT ARE WE? BRIC-A-BRAC TO BE DISPOSED OF?
I'M TRYING TO BE REALISITIC ABOUT THIS!
YOU'RE TRYING TO BE CRUEL ABOUT IT! JUST BECAUSE I DIDN'T KNOW THAT YOU—
OH, STOP IT. I CAN SEE THERE'S NO POINT IN TRYING TO BE REALISTIC.
ALL RIGHT, WE'LL BE REALISTIC. ARE YOU SUGGESTING THAT I LEAVE YOU AND TAKE BETH WITH ME?
IS THAT YOUR IDEA OF BEING REALISTIC?
AND WHAT IF THEY DON'T FIND IT? WHAT IF THEY *NEVER* FIND IT?
YOU THINK I SHOULD LEAVE YOU, THEN?
I THINK IT MIGHT BE A GOOD IDEA.
WELL, I DON'T!
I'M SORRY, LOU.
DON'T CRY. I'M NOT WORTH IT.

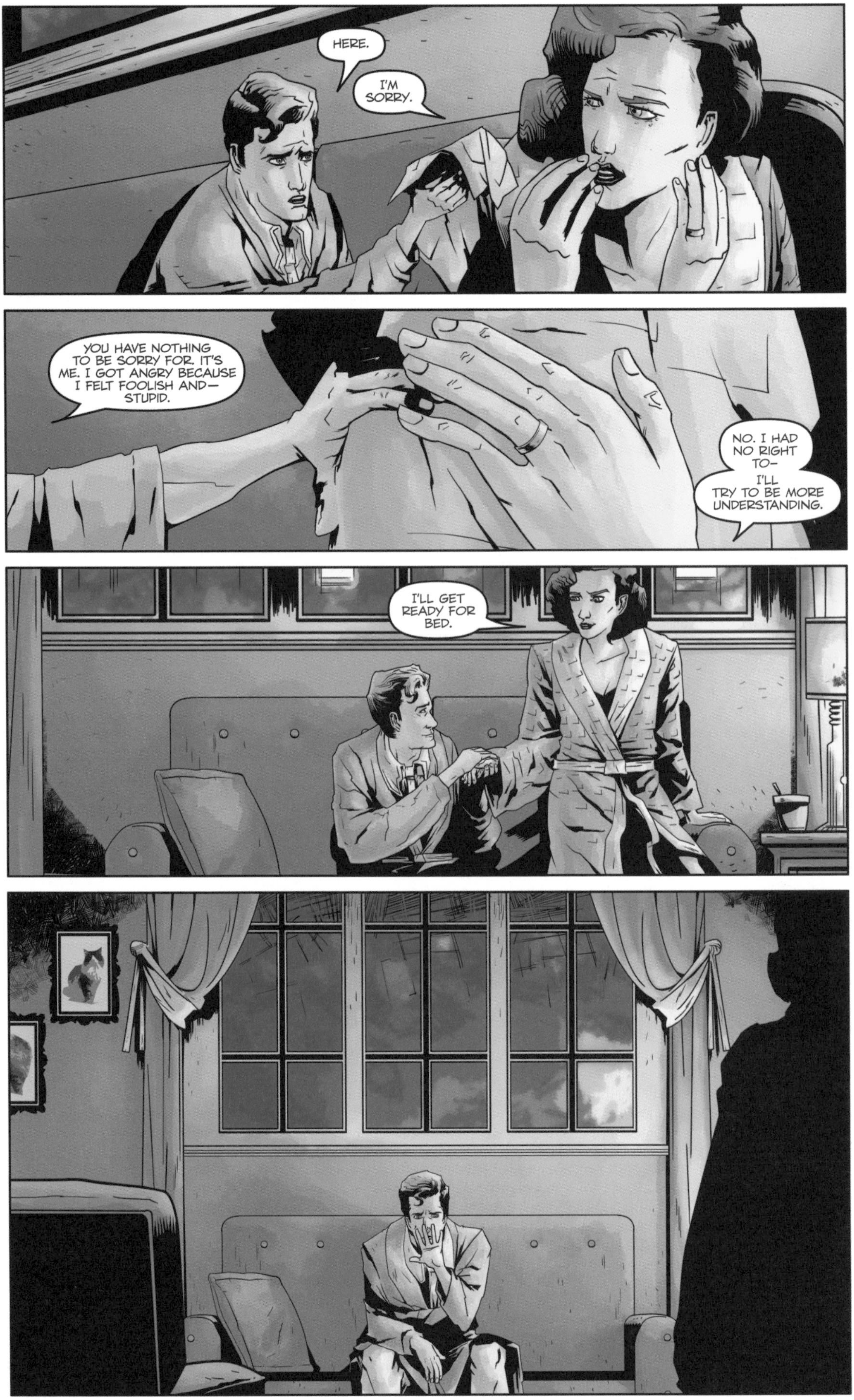
HERE.
I'M SORRY.
YOU HAVE NOTHING TO BE SORRY FOR. IT'S ME. I GOT ANGRY BECAUSE I FELT FOOLISH AND— STUPID.
NO. I HAD NO RIGHT TO—
I'LL TRY TO BE MORE UNDERSTANDING.
I'LL GET READY FOR BED.

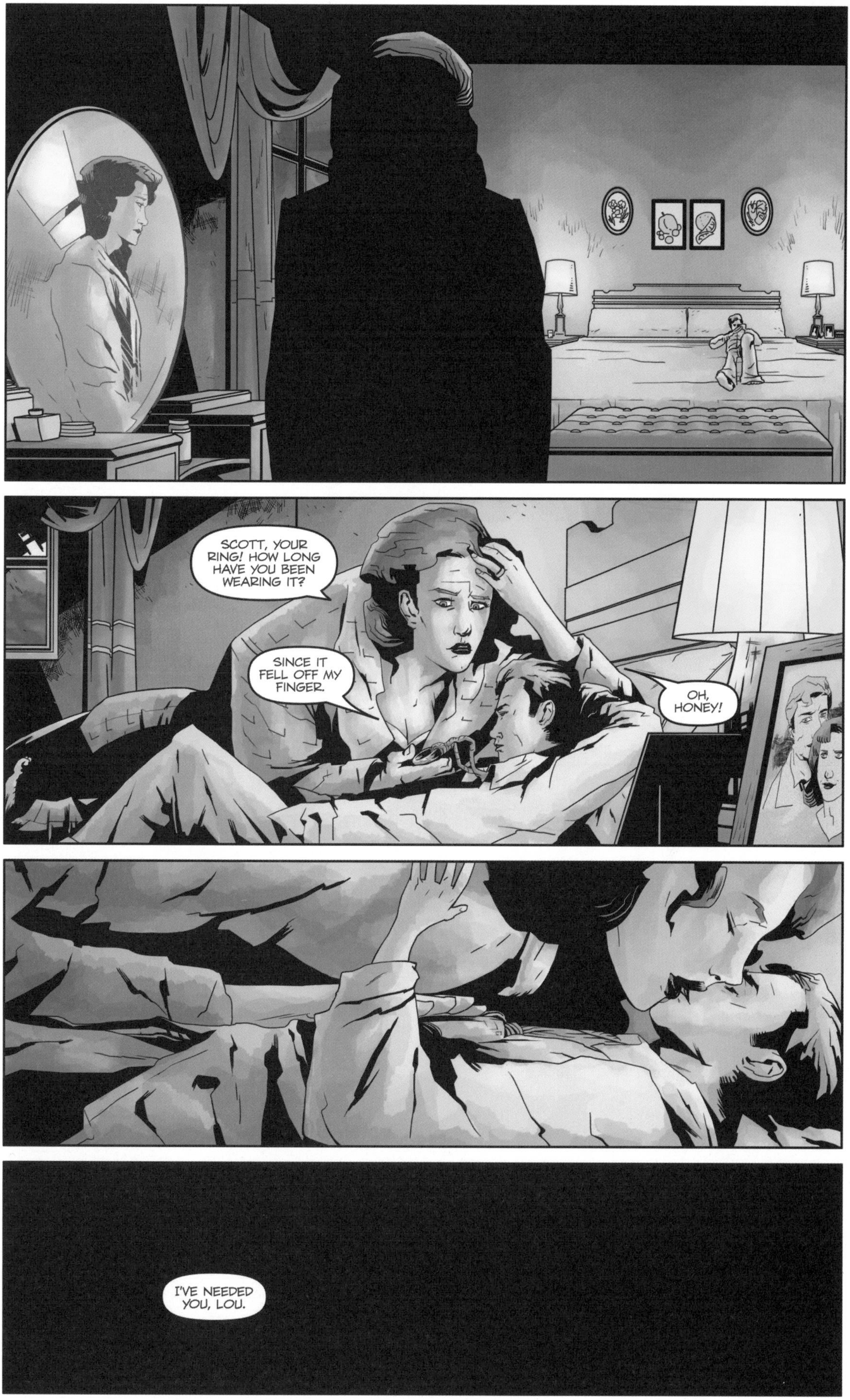
SCOTT, YOUR RING! HOW LONG HAVE YOU BEEN WEARING IT?
SINCE IT FELL OFF MY FINGER.
OH, HONEY!
I'VE NEEDED YOU, LOU.

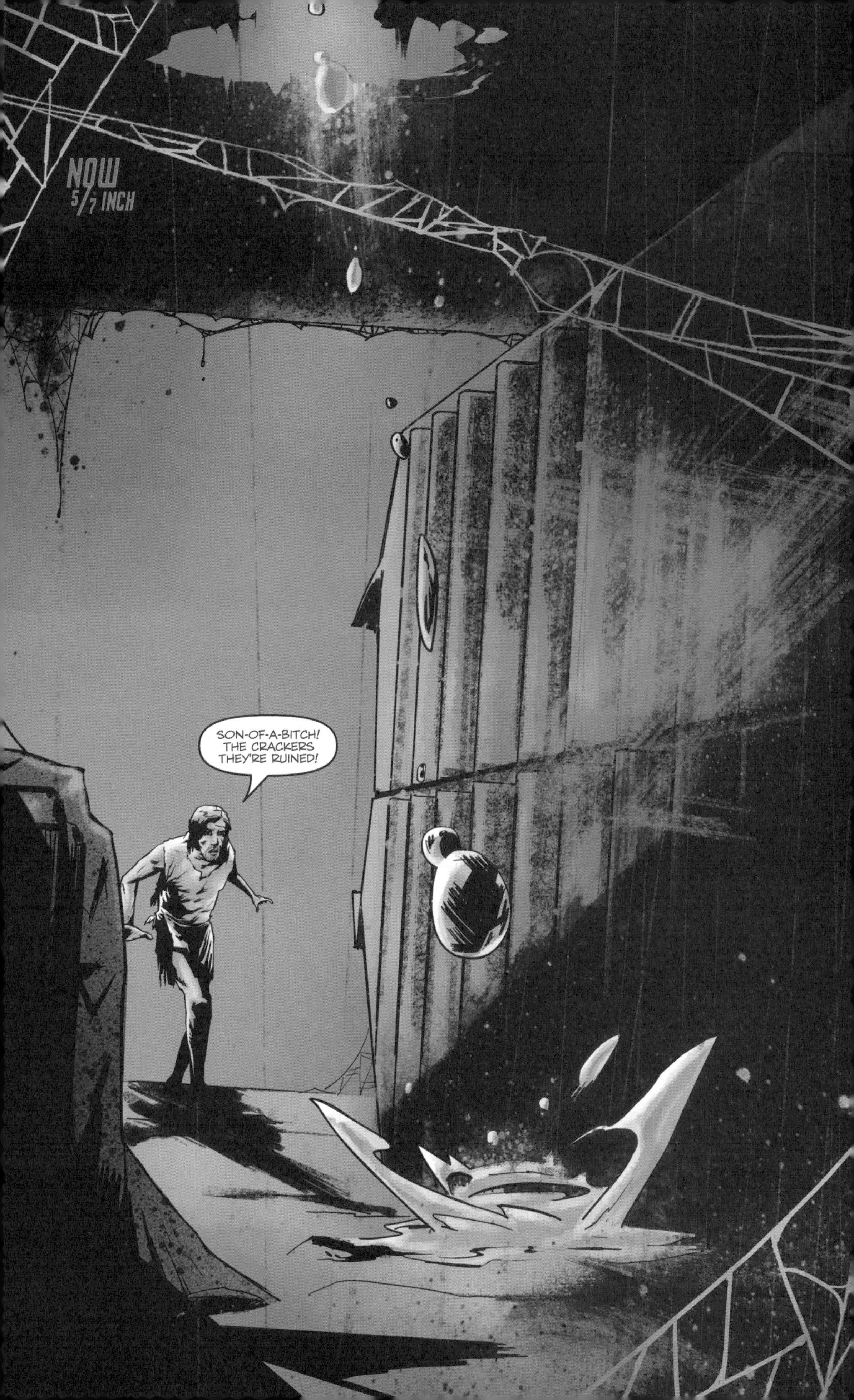
NOW
5/7 INCH
SON-OF-A-BITCH! THE CRACKERS THEY'RE RUINED!

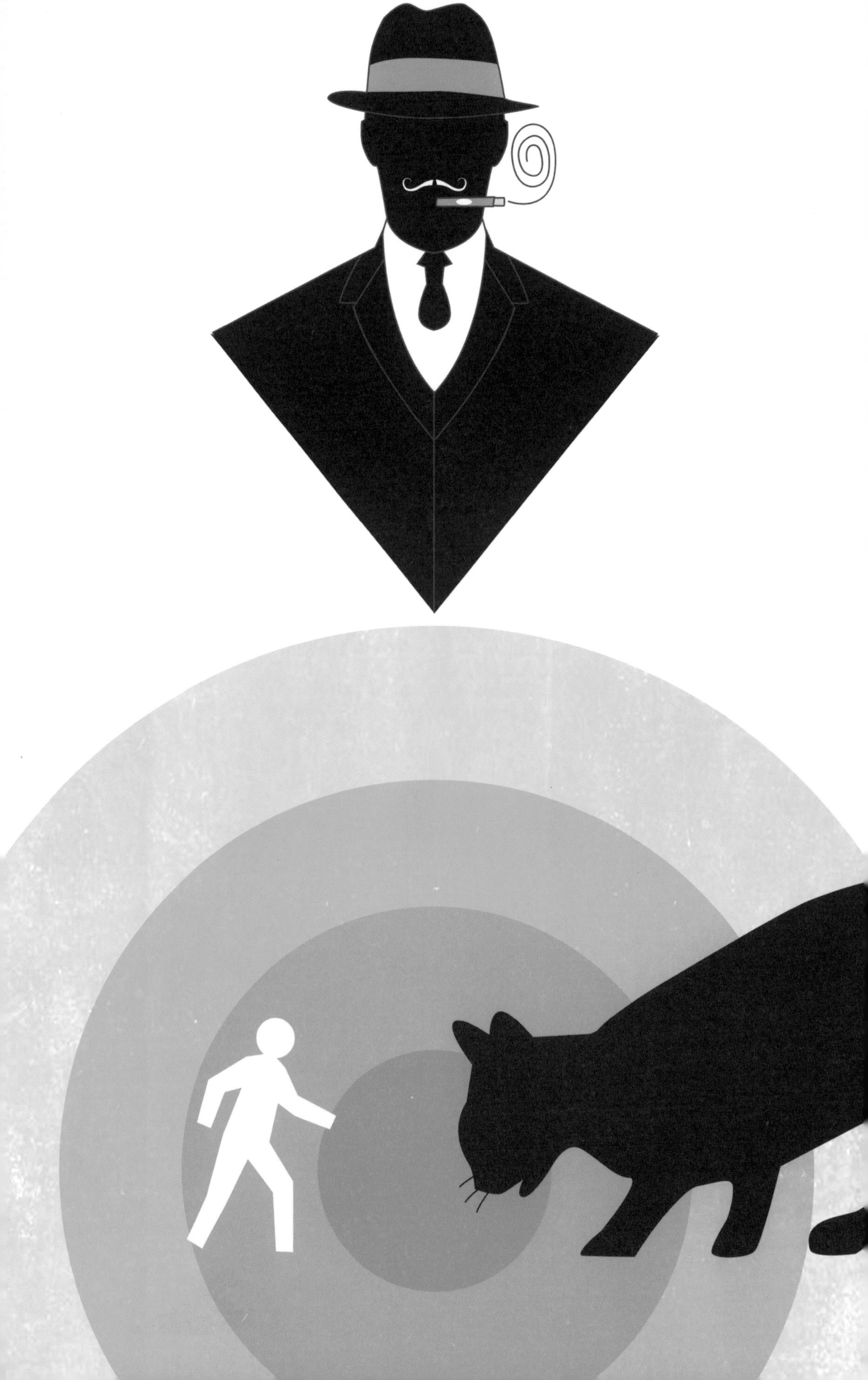

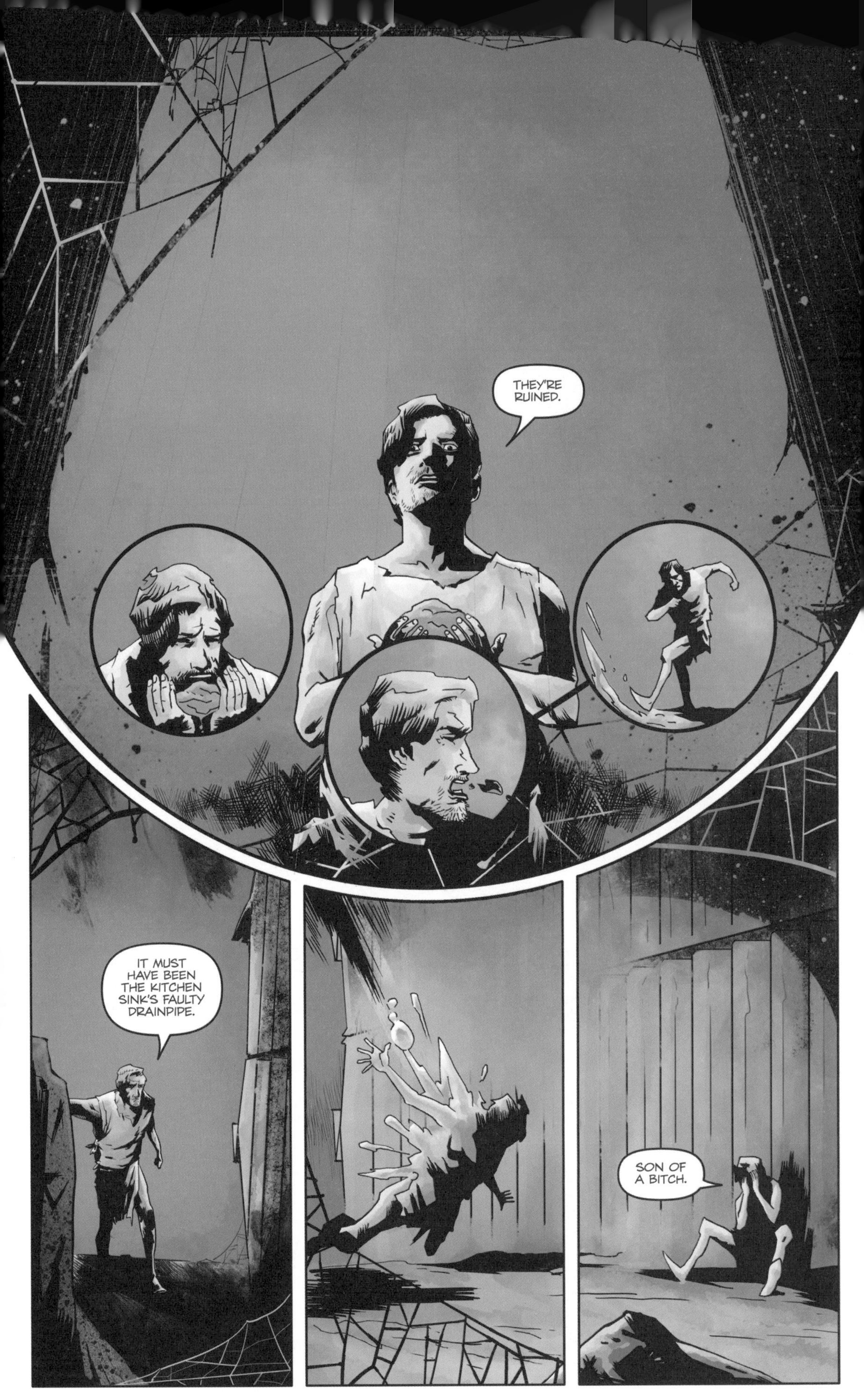
THEY'RE RUINED.
IT MUST HAVE BEEN THE KITCHEN SINK'S FAULTY DRAINPIPE.
SON OF A BITCH.

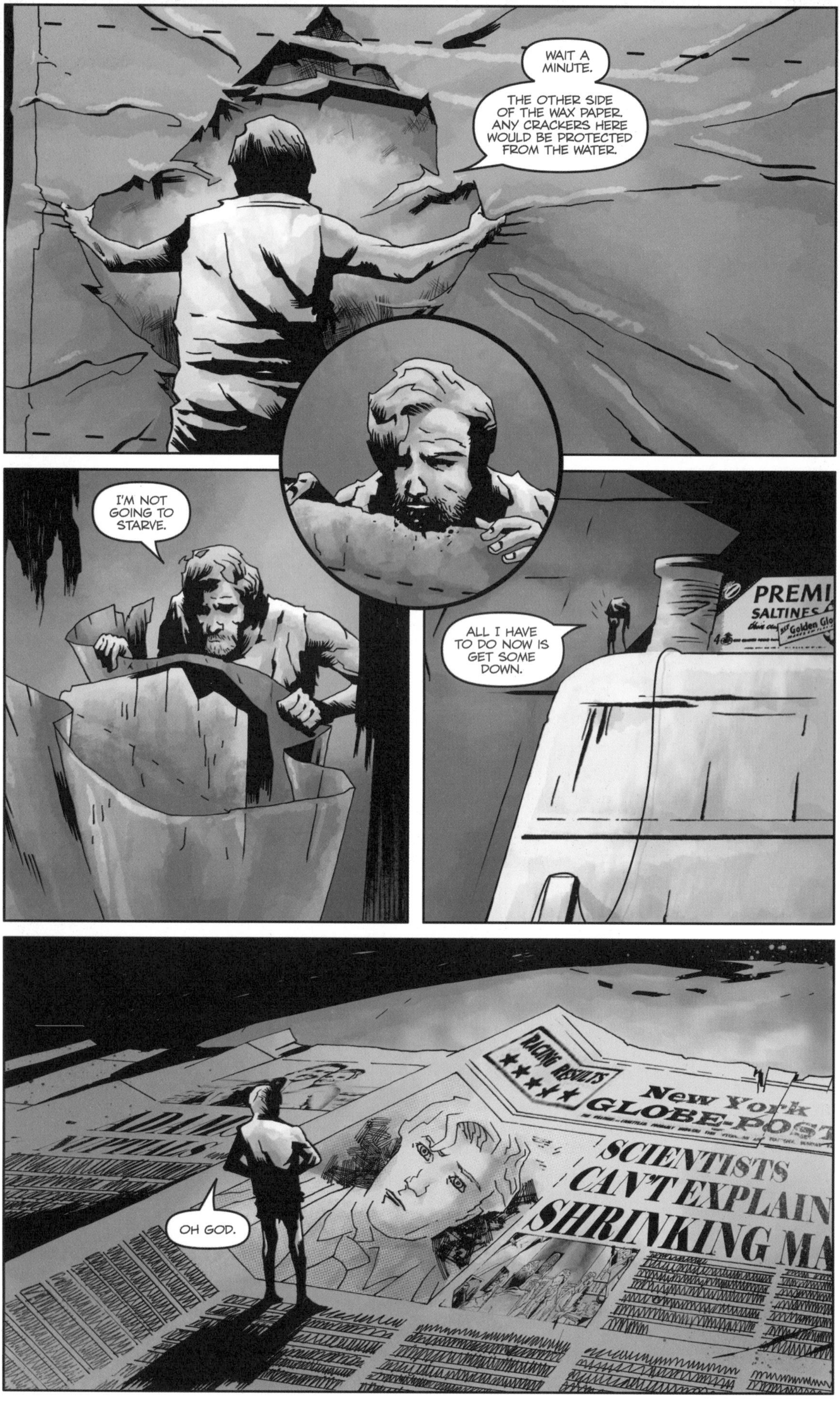
WAIT A MINUTE.
THE OTHER SIDE OF THE WAX PAPER. ANY CRACKERS HERE WOULD BE PROTECTED FROM THE WATER.
I'M NOT GOING TO STARVE.
PREMI
SALTINES
ALL I HAVE TO DO NOW IS GET SOME DOWN.
RACING RESULTS
New York
GLOBE-POST
SCIENTISTS
CAN'T EXPLAIN
SHRINKING MA
OH GOD.

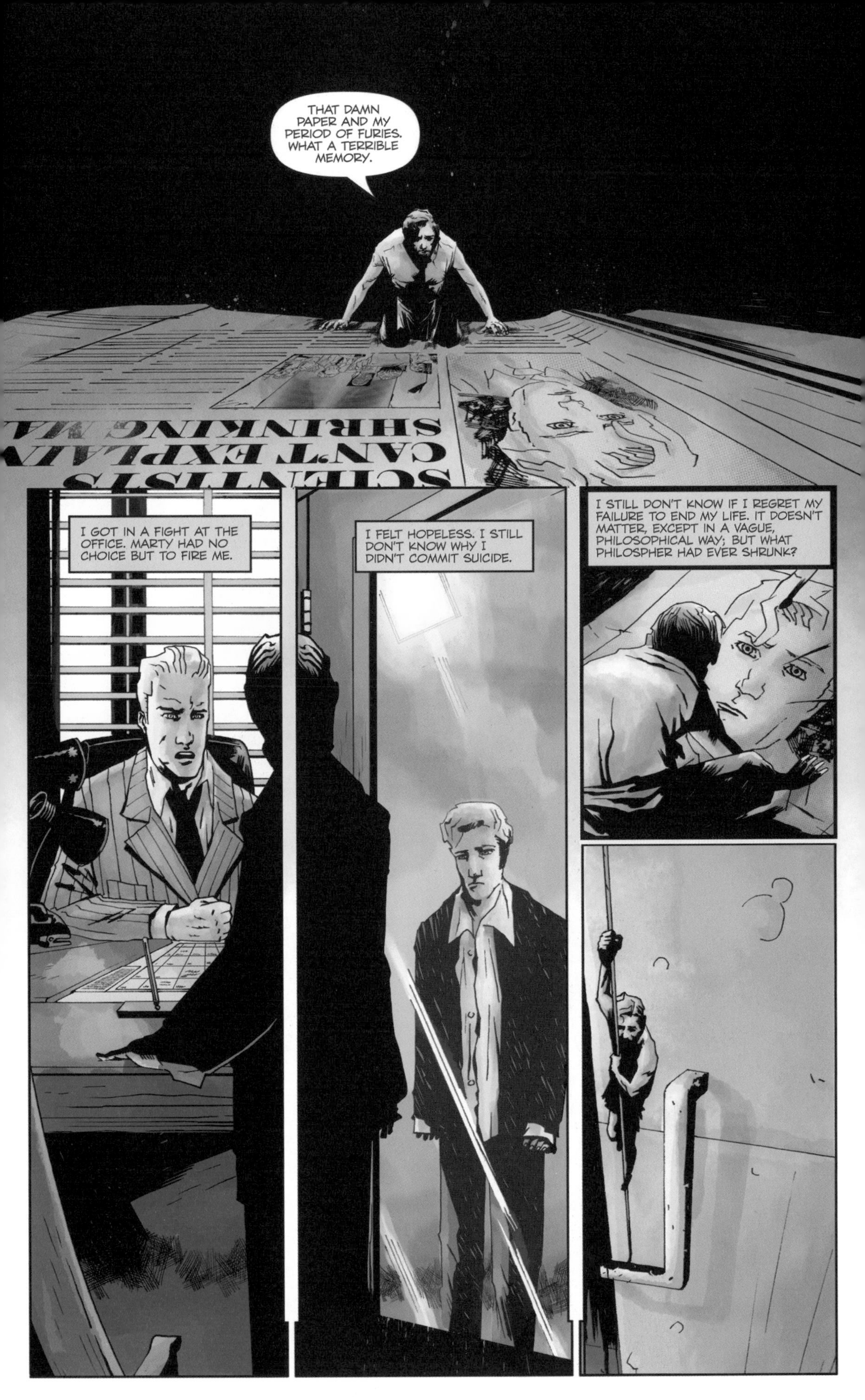
THAT DAMN PAPER AND MY PERIOD OF FURIES. WHAT A TERRIBLE MEMORY.
I GOT IN A FIGHT AT THE OFFICE. MARTY HAD NO CHOICE BUT TO FIRE ME.
I FELT HOPELESS. I STILL DON'T KNOW WHY I DIDN'T COMMIT SUICIDE.
I STILL DON'T KNOW IF I REGRET MY FAILURE TO END MY LIFE. IT DOESN'T MATTER, EXCEPT IN A VAGUE, PHILOSOPHICAL WAY; BUT WHAT PHILOSPHER HAD EVER SHRUNK?

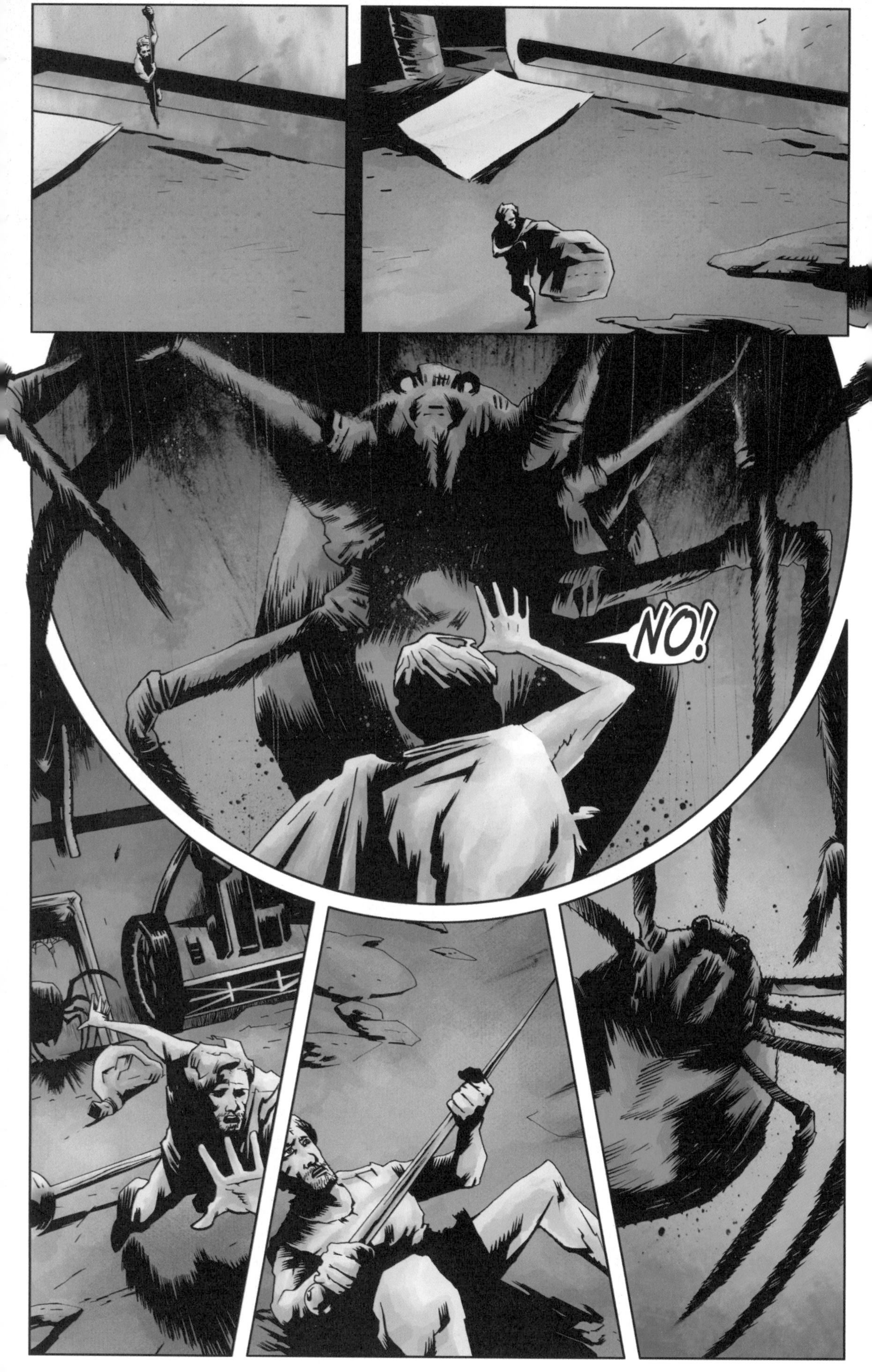
NO!

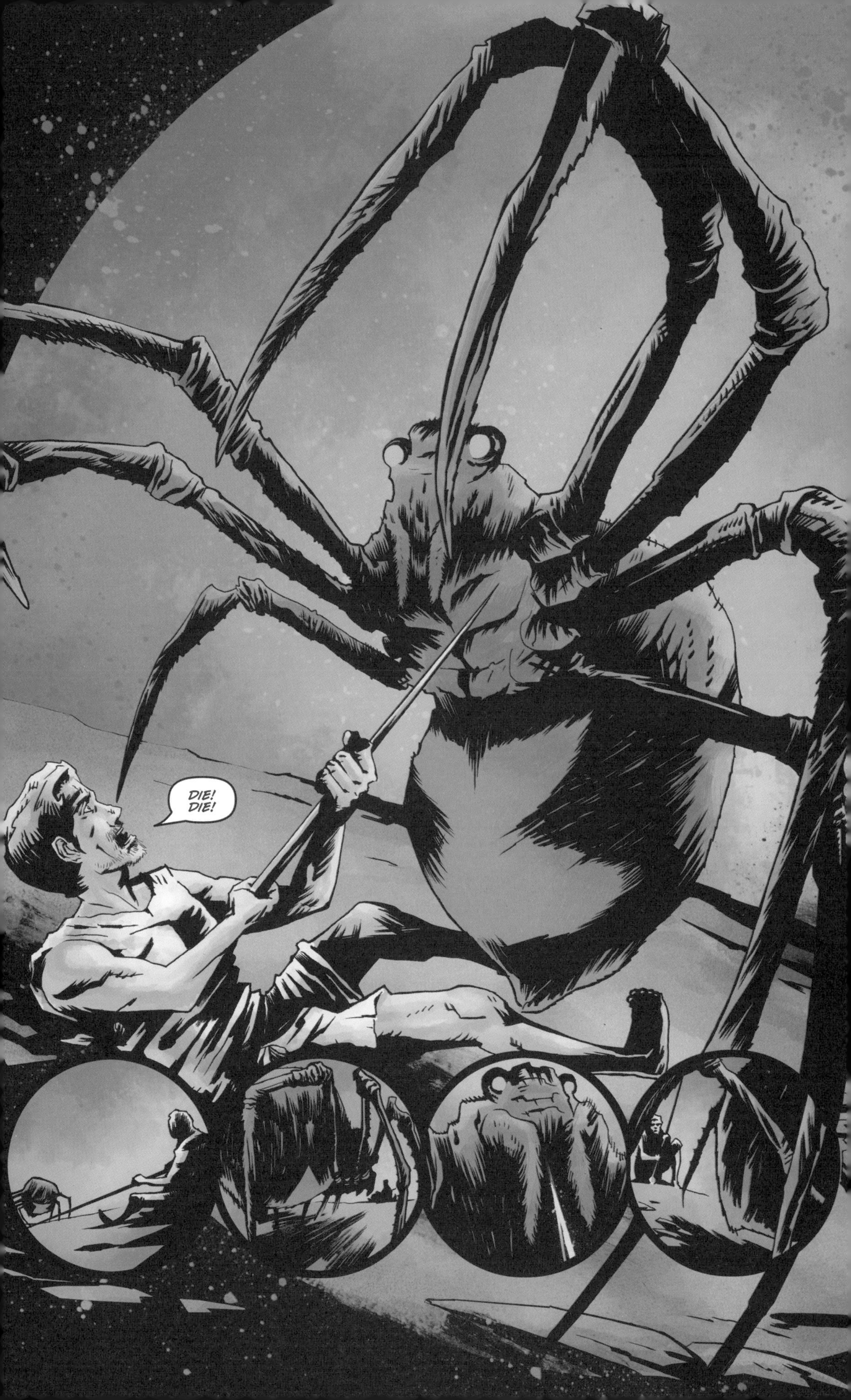
DIE! DIE!

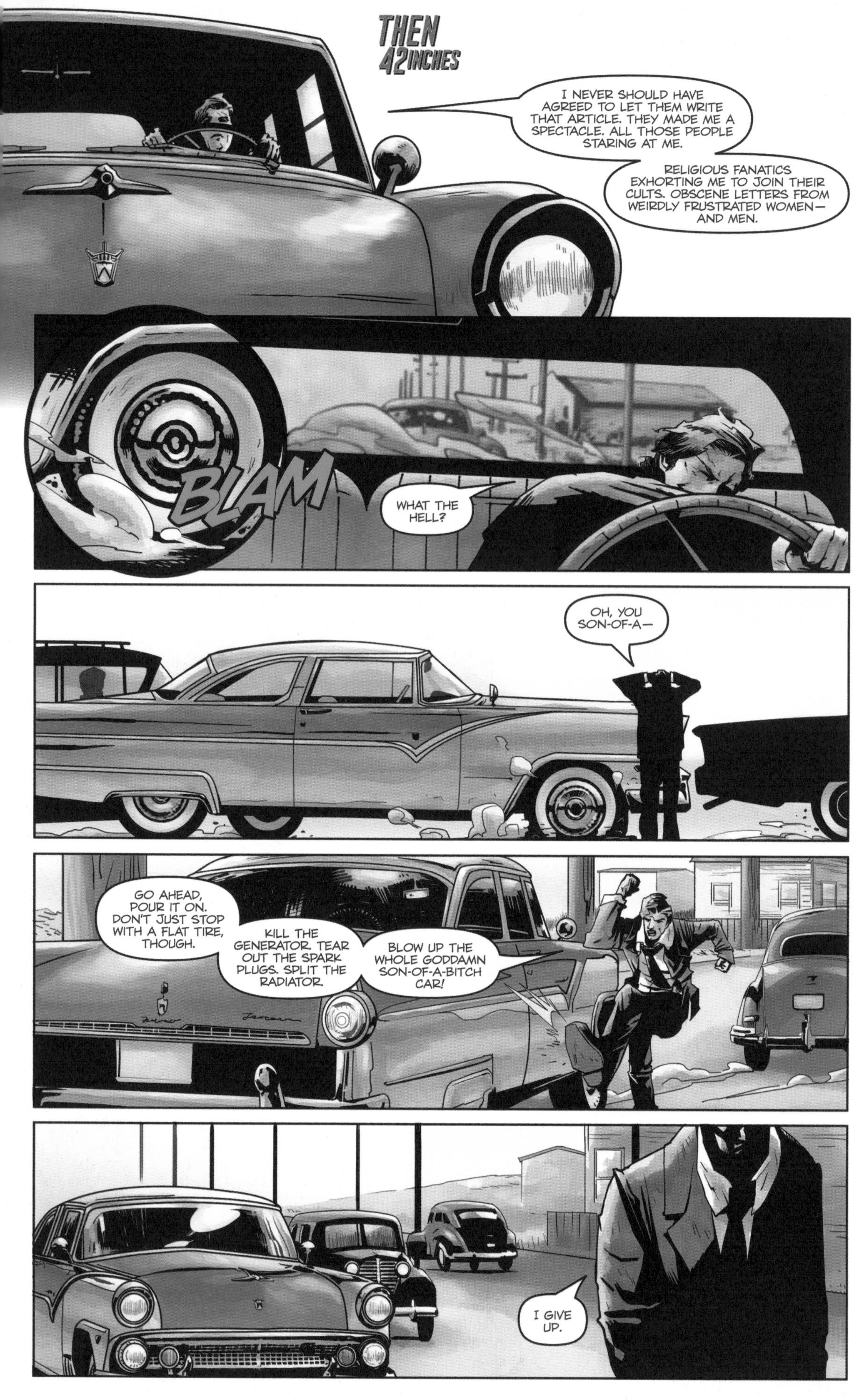
THEN
42 INCHES
I NEVER SHOULD HAVE AGREED TO LET THEM WRITE THAT ARTICLE. THEY MADE ME A SPECTACLE. ALL THOSE PEOPLE STARING AT ME.
RELIGIOUS FANATICS EXHORTING ME TO JOIN THEIR CULTS. OBSCENE LETTERS FROM WEIRDLY FRUSTRATED WOMEN—AND MEN.
BLAM
WHAT THE HELL?
OH, YOU SON-OF-A—
GO AHEAD, POUR IT ON. DON'T JUST STOP WITH A FLAT TIRE, THOUGH.
KILL THE GENERATOR. TEAR OUT THE SPARK PLUGS. SPLIT THE RADIATOR.
BLOW UP THE WHOLE GODDAMN SON-OF-A-BITCH CAR!
I GIVE UP.

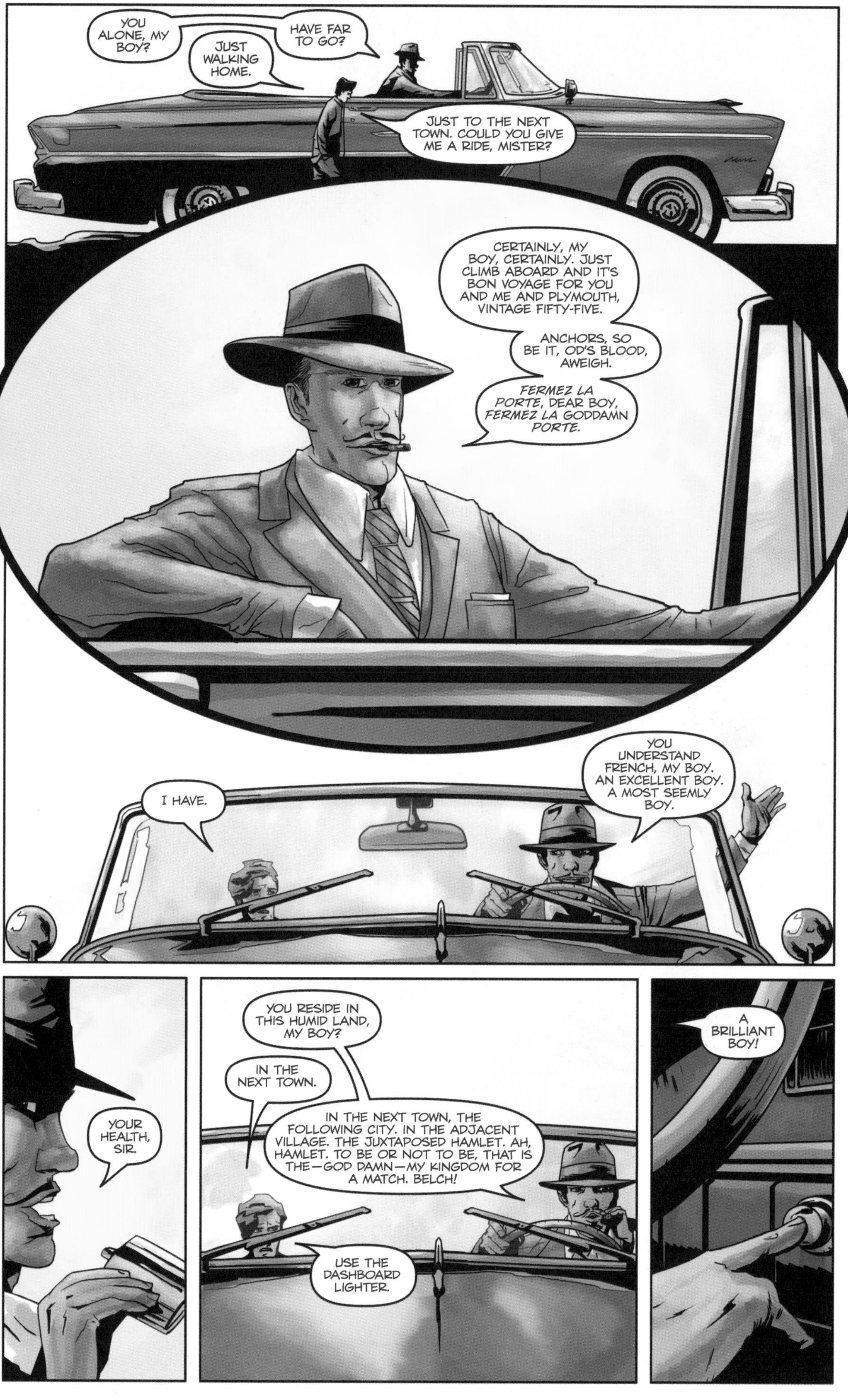
YOU ALONE, MY BOY?
JUST WALKING HOME.
HAVE FAR TO GO?
JUST TO THE NEXT TOWN. COULD YOU GIVE ME A RIDE, MISTER?
CERTAINLY, MY BOY, CERTAINLY. JUST CLIMB ABOARD AND IT'S BON VOYAGE FOR YOU AND ME AND PLYMOUTH, VINTAGE FIFTY-FIVE.
ANCHORS, SO BE IT, OD'S BLOOD, AWEIGH.
FERMEZ LA PORTE, DEAR BOY, *FERMEZ LA* GODDAMN *PORTE*.
YOU UNDERSTAND FRENCH, MY BOY.
I HAVE.
AN EXCELLENT BOY. A MOST SEEMLY BOY.
YOUR HEALTH, SIR.
YOU RESIDE IN THIS HUMID LAND, MY BOY?
IN THE NEXT TOWN.
IN THE NEXT TOWN, THE FOLLOWING CITY. IN THE ADJACENT VILLAGE. THE JUXTAPOSED HAMLET. AH, HAMLET. TO BE OR NOT TO BE, THAT IS THE—GOD DAMN—MY KINGDOM FOR A MATCH. BELCH!
USE THE DASHBOARD LIGHTER.
A BRILLIANT BOY!

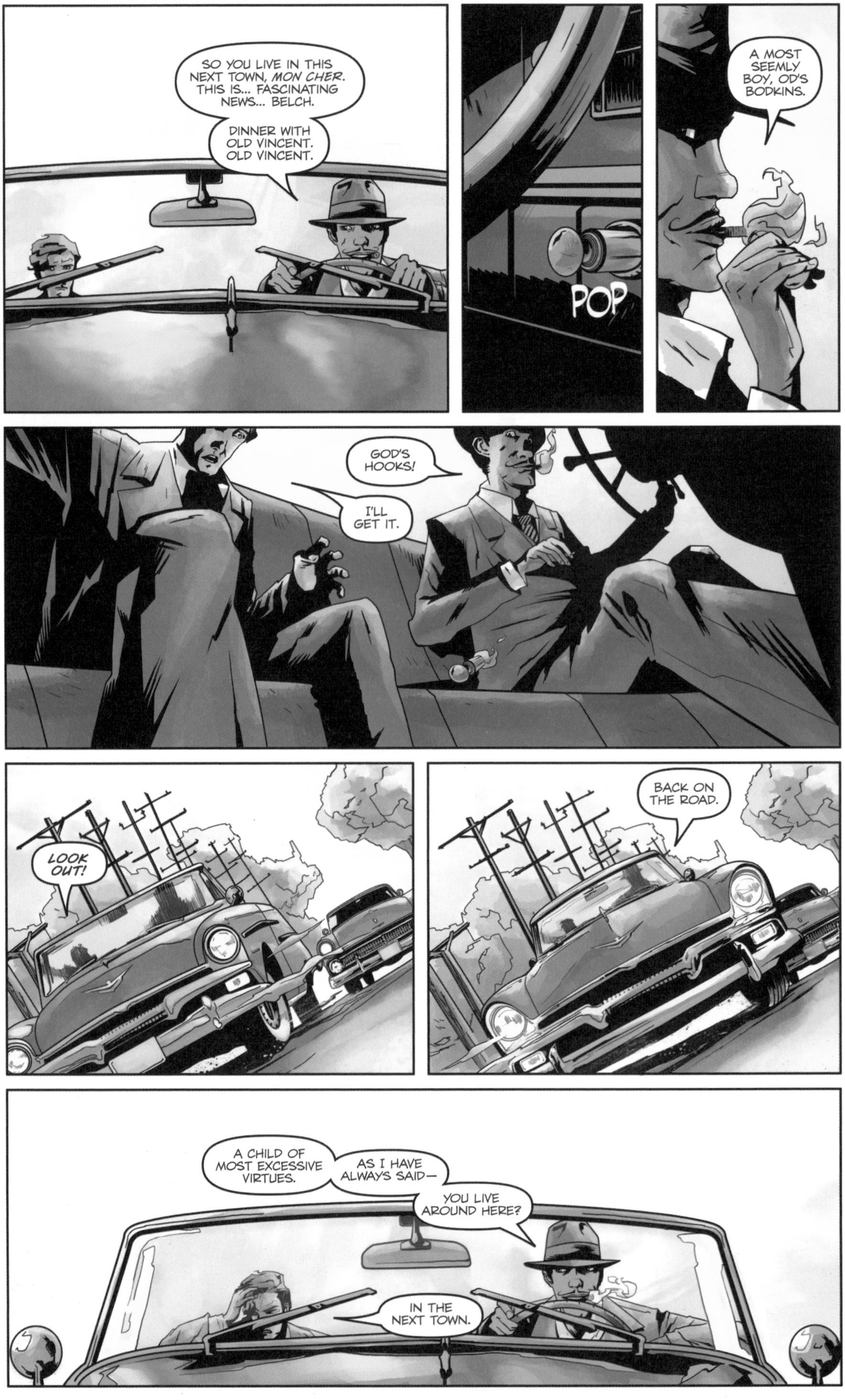
SO YOU LIVE IN THIS NEXT TOWN, *MON CHER*. THIS IS... FASCINATING NEWS... BELCH.
DINNER WITH OLD VINCENT. OLD VINCENT.
POP
A MOST SEEMLY BOY, OD'S BODKINS.
GOD'S HOOKS!
I'LL GET IT.
LOOK OUT!
BACK ON THE ROAD.
A CHILD OF MOST EXCESSIVE VIRTUES.
AS I HAVE ALWAYS SAID—
YOU LIVE AROUND HERE?
IN THE NEXT TOWN.

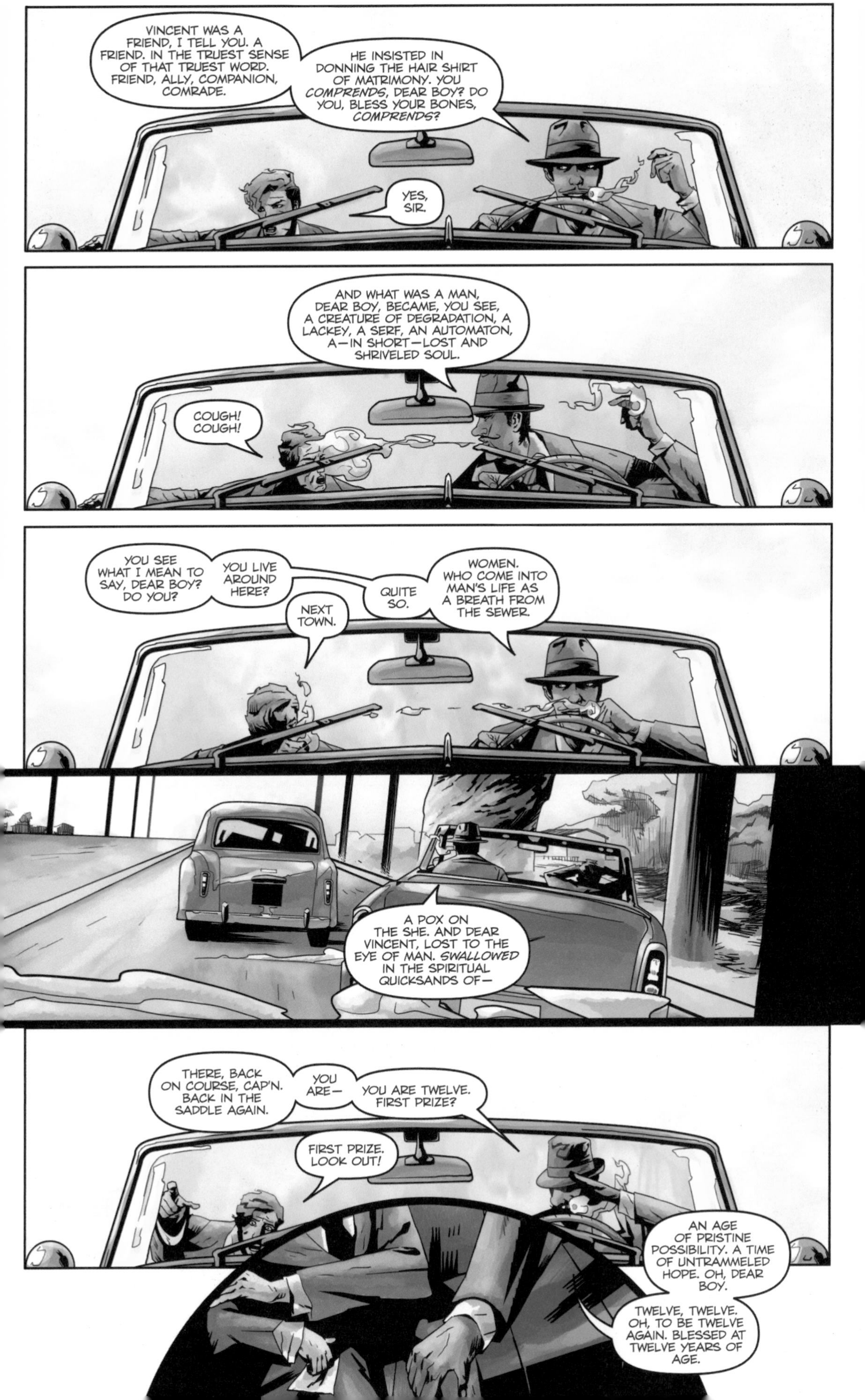
VINCENT WAS A FRIEND, I TELL YOU. A FRIEND. IN THE TRUEST SENSE OF THAT TRUEST WORD. FRIEND, ALLY, COMPANION, COMRADE.
HE INSISTED IN DONNING THE HAIR SHIRT OF MATRIMONY. YOU *COMPRENDS*, DEAR BOY? DO YOU, BLESS YOUR BONES, *COMPRENDS*?
YES, SIR.
AND WHAT WAS A MAN, DEAR BOY, BECAME, YOU SEE, A CREATURE OF DEGRADATION, A LACKEY, A SERF, AN AUTOMATON, A—IN SHORT—LOST AND SHRIVELED SOUL.
COUGH! COUGH!
YOU SEE WHAT I MEAN TO SAY, DEAR BOY? DO YOU?
YOU LIVE AROUND HERE?
NEXT TOWN.
QUITE SO.
WOMEN. WHO COME INTO MAN'S LIFE AS A BREATH FROM THE SEWER.
A POX ON THE SHE. AND DEAR VINCENT, LOST TO THE EYE OF MAN. *SWALLOWED* IN THE SPIRITUAL QUICKSANDS OF—
THERE, BACK ON COURSE, CAP'N. BACK IN THE SADDLE AGAIN.
YOU ARE—
YOU ARE TWELVE. FIRST PRIZE?
FIRST PRIZE. LOOK OUT!
AN AGE OF PRISTINE POSSIBILITY. A TIME OF UNTRAMMELED HOPE. OH, DEAR BOY.
TWELVE, TWELVE. OH, TO BE TWELVE AGAIN. BLESSED AT TWELVE YEARS OF AGE.

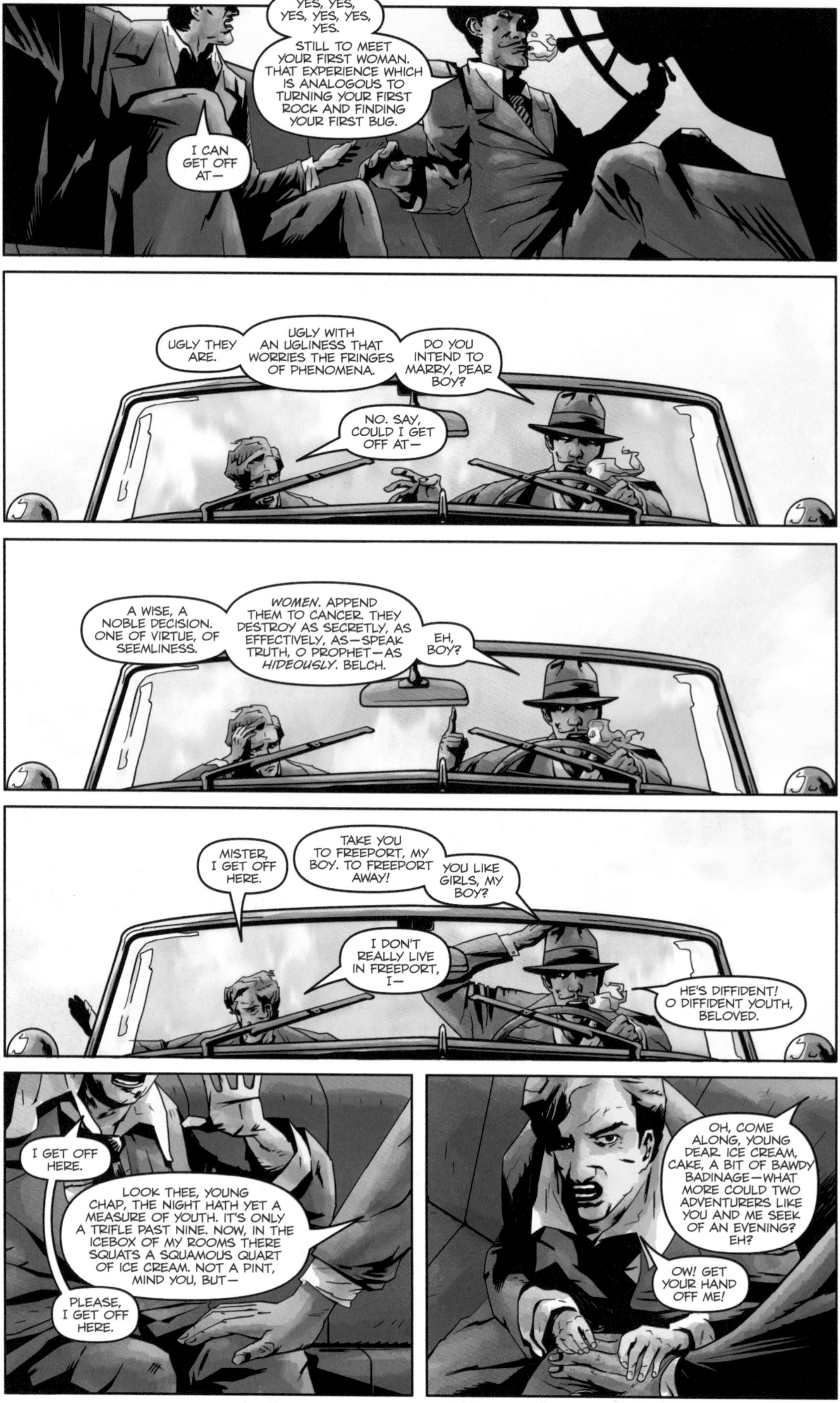
YES, YES, YES, YES, YES, YES.
STILL TO MEET YOUR FIRST WOMAN. THAT EXPERIENCE WHICH IS ANALOGOUS TO TURNING YOUR FIRST ROCK AND FINDING YOUR FIRST BUG.
I CAN GET OFF AT—
UGLY THEY ARE.
UGLY WITH AN UGLINESS THAT WORRIES THE FRINGES OF PHENOMENA.
DO YOU INTEND TO MARRY, DEAR BOY?
NO. SAY, COULD I GET OFF AT—
A WISE, A NOBLE DECISION. ONE OF VIRTUE, OF SEEMLINESS.
WOMEN. APPEND THEM TO CANCER. THEY DESTROY AS SECRETLY, AS EFFECTIVELY, AS—SPEAK TRUTH, O PROPHET—AS *HIDEOUSLY*. BELCH.
EH, BOY?
MISTER, I GET OFF HERE.
TAKE YOU TO FREEPORT, MY BOY. TO FREEPORT AWAY!
YOU LIKE GIRLS, MY BOY?
I DON'T REALLY LIVE IN FREEPORT, I—
HE'S DIFFIDENT! O DIFFIDENT YOUTH, BELOVED.
I GET OFF HERE.
LOOK THEE, YOUNG CHAP, THE NIGHT HATH YET A MEASURE OF YOUTH. IT'S ONLY A TRIFLE PAST NINE. NOW, IN THE ICEBOX OF MY ROOMS THERE SQUATS A SQUAMOUS QUART OF ICE CREAM. NOT A PINT, MIND YOU, BUT—
PLEASE, I GET OFF HERE.
OH, COME ALONG, YOUNG DEAR. ICE CREAM, CAKE, A BIT OF BAWDY BADINAGE—WHAT MORE COULD TWO ADVENTURERS LIKE YOU AND ME SEEK OF AN EVENING? EH?
OW! GET YOUR HAND OFF ME!

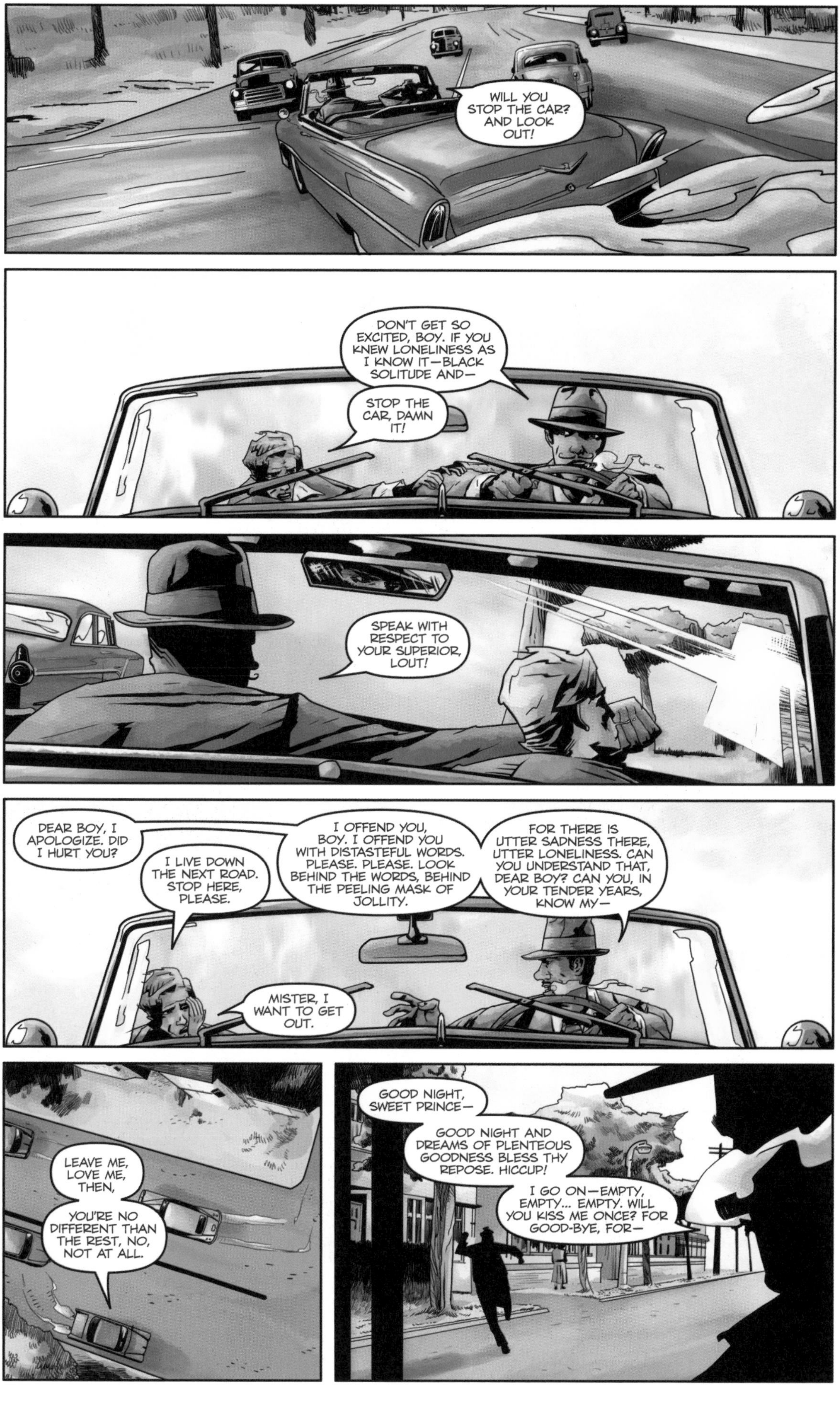
WILL YOU STOP THE CAR? AND LOOK OUT!
DON'T GET SO EXCITED, BOY. IF YOU KNEW LONELINESS AS I KNOW IT—BLACK SOLITUDE AND—
STOP THE CAR, DAMN IT!
SPEAK WITH RESPECT TO YOUR SUPERIOR, LOUT!
DEAR BOY, I APOLOGIZE. DID I HURT YOU?
I LIVE DOWN THE NEXT ROAD. STOP HERE, PLEASE.
I OFFEND YOU, BOY. I OFFEND YOU WITH DISTASTEFUL WORDS. PLEASE. PLEASE. LOOK BEHIND THE WORDS, BEHIND THE PEELING MASK OF JOLLITY.
FOR THERE IS UTTER SADNESS THERE, UTTER LONELINESS. CAN YOU UNDERSTAND THAT, DEAR BOY? CAN YOU, IN YOUR TENDER YEARS, KNOW MY—
MISTER, I WANT TO GET OUT.
LEAVE ME, LOVE ME, THEN,
YOU'RE NO DIFFERENT THAN THE REST, NO, NOT AT ALL.
GOOD NIGHT, SWEET PRINCE—
GOOD NIGHT AND DREAMS OF PLENTEOUS GOODNESS BLESS THY REPOSE. HICCUP!
I GO ON—EMPTY, EMPTY... EMPTY. WILL YOU KISS ME ONCE? FOR GOOD-BYE, FOR—

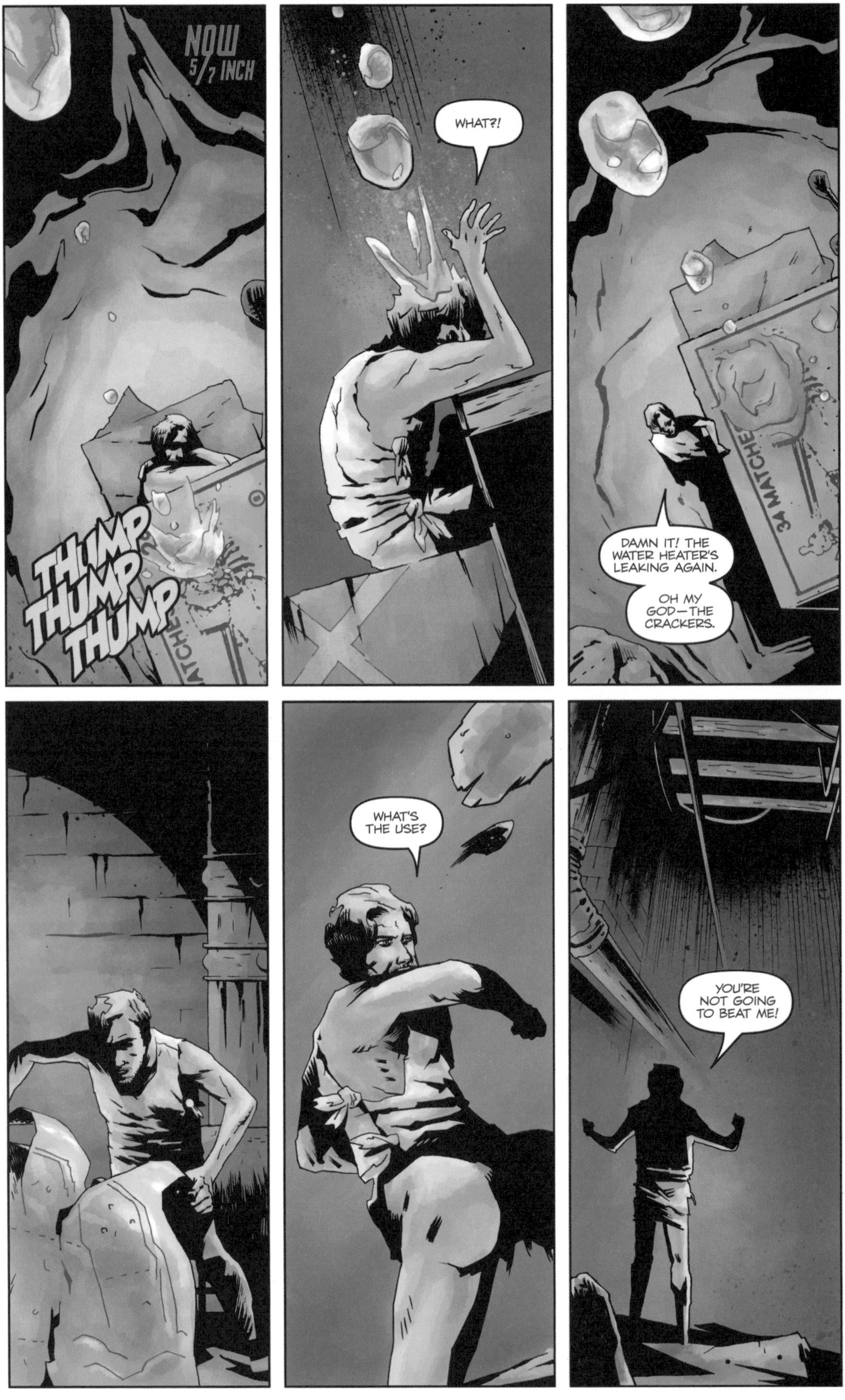
NOW
5/7 INCH
THUMP THUMP THUMP
MATCHES
WHAT?!
34 MATCHES
DAMN IT! THE WATER HEATER'S LEAKING AGAIN.
OH MY GOD—THE CRACKERS.
WHAT'S THE USE?
YOU'RE NOT GOING TO BEAT ME!

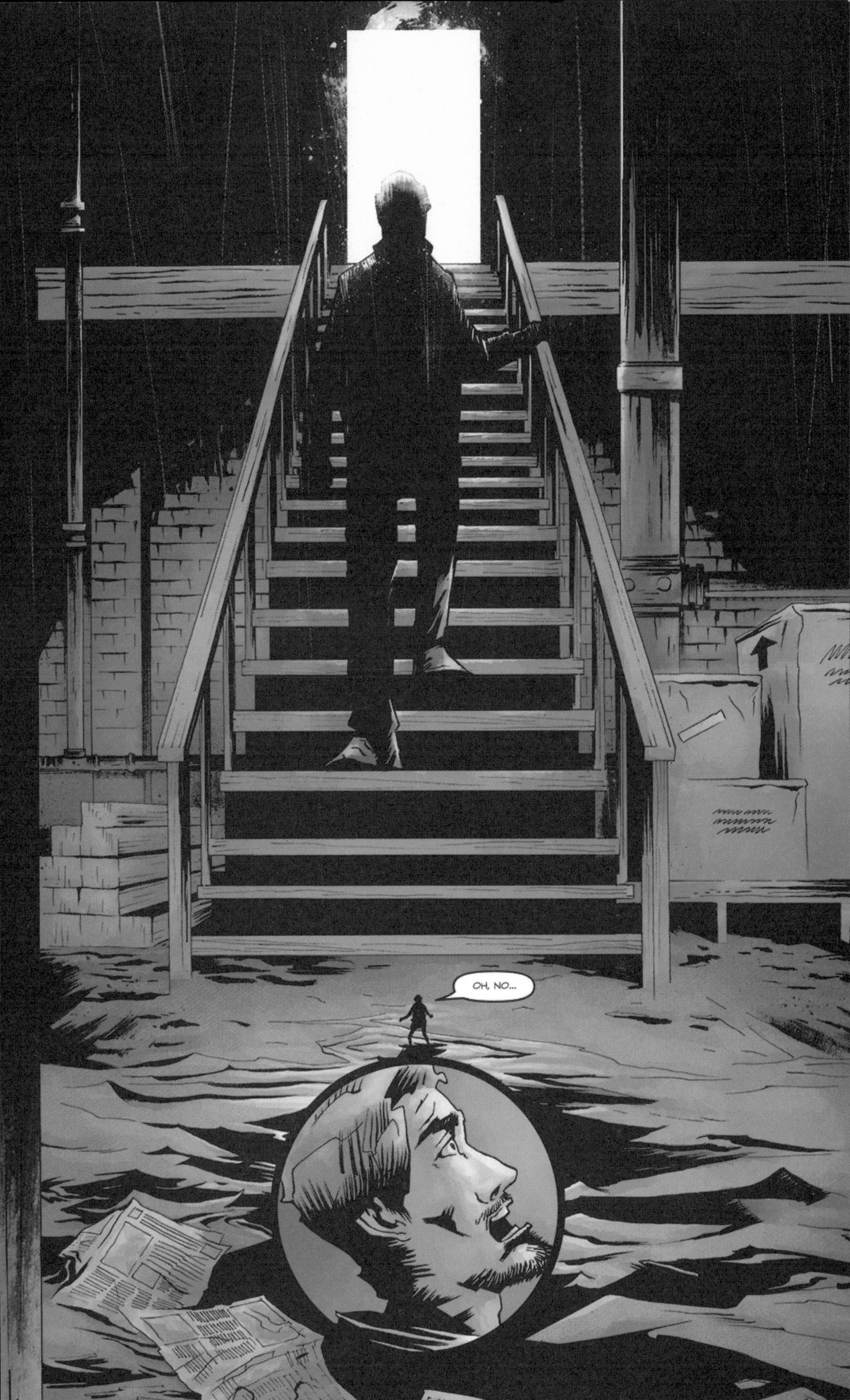
OH, NO...

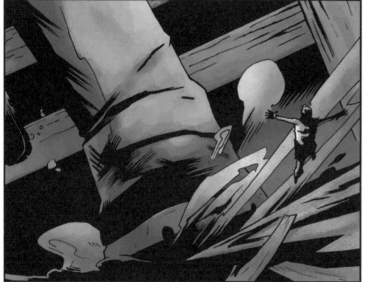

THAT'S WHAT LOU LOOKS LIKE NOW. I CAN ONLY SEE HER AS MONSTROUSLY TALL, FINGERS AS THICK AS REDWOOD TREES, BREASTS LIKE PLIANT, HILL-PEAKED PYRAMIDS.

I HAVE TO KEEP TRYING. THE DOOR'S OPEN. I CAN FINALLY GET OUT OF THIS DAMNED BASEMENT.

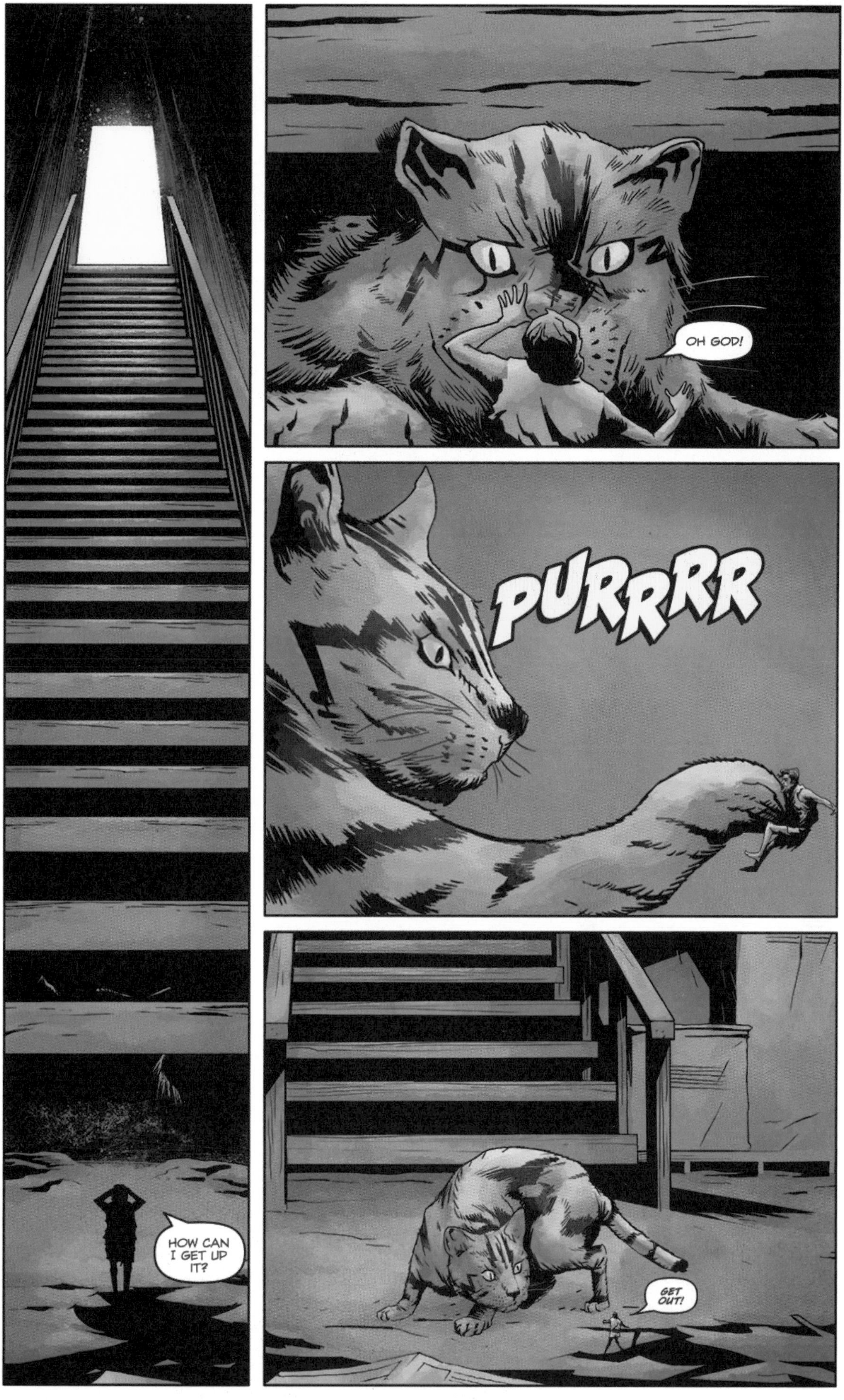
HOW CAN I GET UP IT?
OH GOD!
PURRRR
GET OUT!

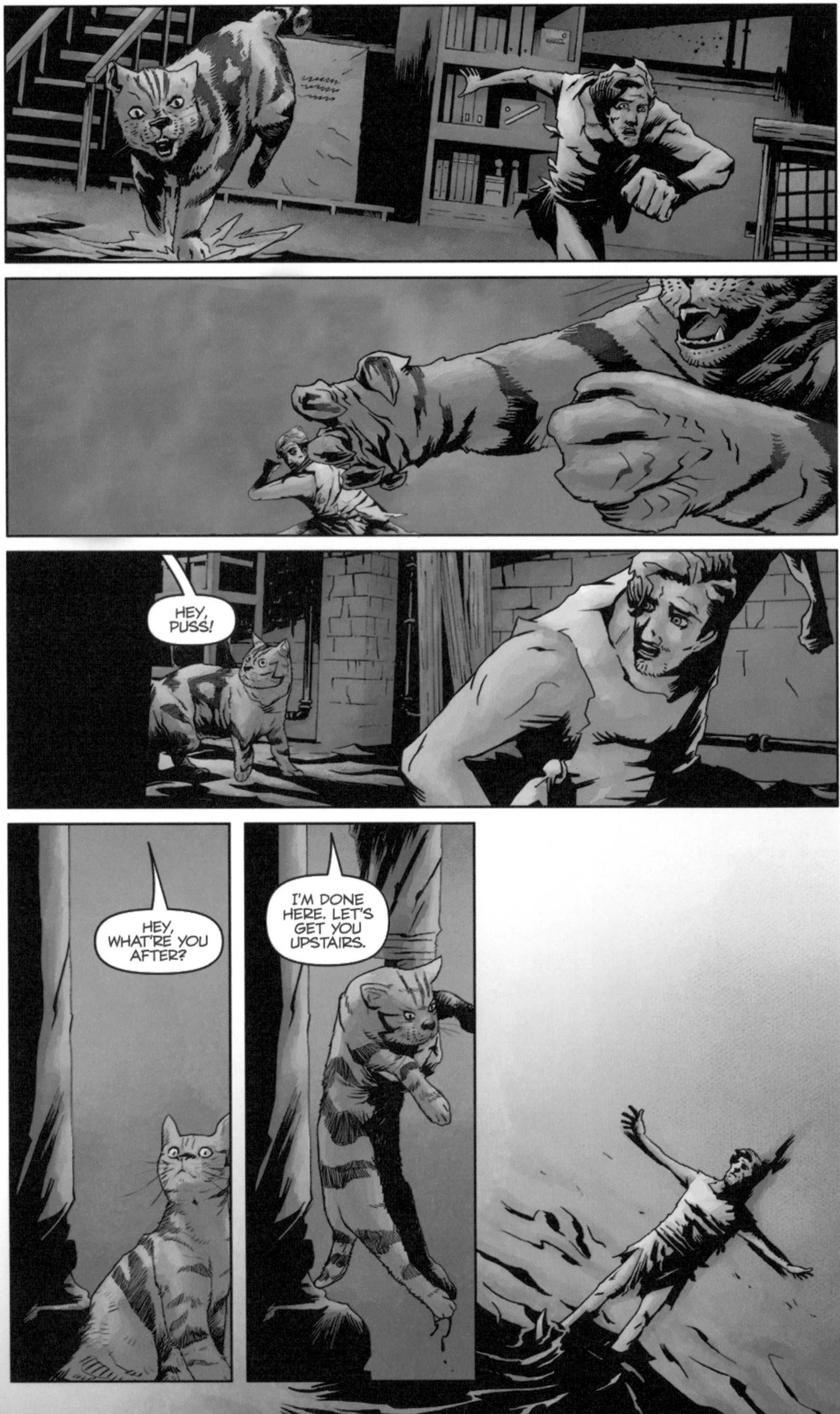
HEY, PUSS!
HEY, WHAT'RE YOU AFTER?
I'M DONE HERE. LET'S GET YOU UPSTAIRS.

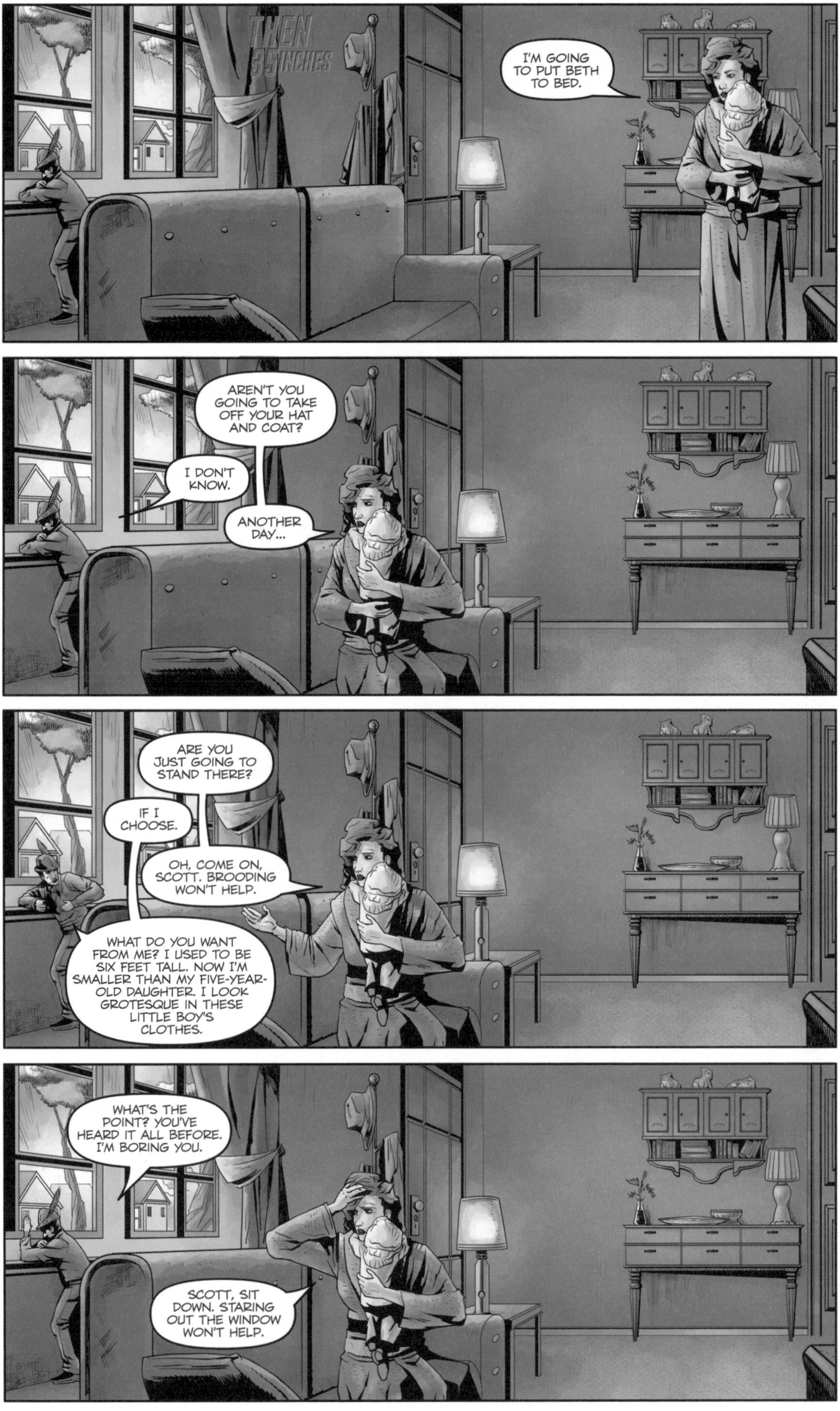
THEN 35 INCHES
I'M GOING TO PUT BETH TO BED.
AREN'T YOU GOING TO TAKE OFF YOUR HAT AND COAT?
I DON'T KNOW.
ANOTHER DAY...
ARE YOU JUST GOING TO STAND THERE?
IF I CHOOSE.
OH, COME ON, SCOTT. BROODING WON'T HELP.
WHAT DO YOU WANT FROM ME? I USED TO BE SIX FEET TALL. NOW I'M SMALLER THAN MY FIVE-YEAR-OLD DAUGHTER. I LOOK GROTESQUE IN THESE LITTLE BOY'S CLOTHES.
WHAT'S THE POINT? YOU'VE HEARD IT ALL BEFORE. I'M BORING YOU.
SCOTT, SIT DOWN. STARING OUT THE WINDOW WON'T HELP.

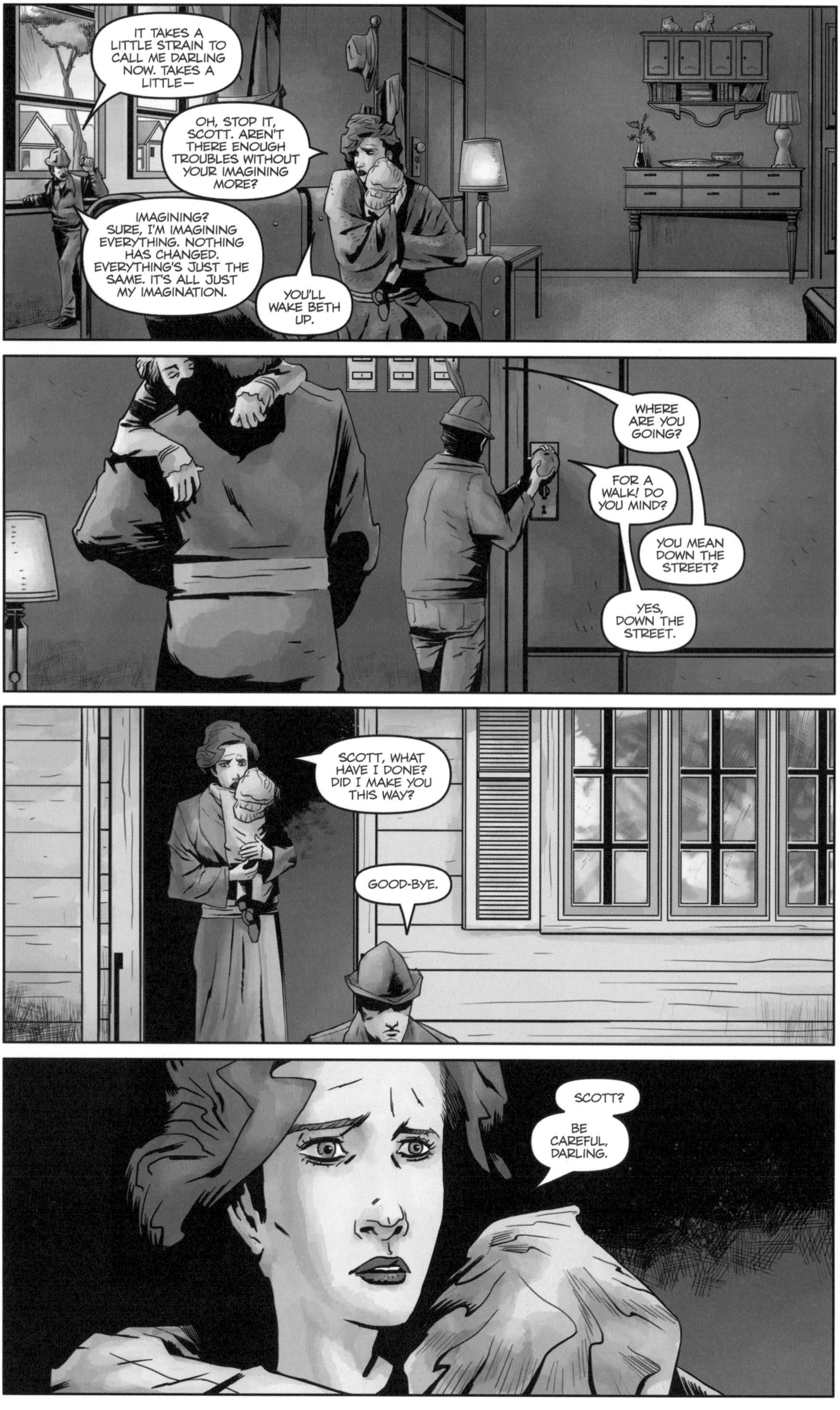
IT TAKES A LITTLE STRAIN TO CALL ME DARLING NOW. TAKES A LITTLE—
OH, STOP IT, SCOTT. AREN'T THERE ENOUGH TROUBLES WITHOUT YOUR IMAGINING MORE?
IMAGINING? SURE, I'M IMAGINING EVERYTHING. NOTHING HAS CHANGED. EVERYTHING'S JUST THE SAME. IT'S ALL JUST MY IMAGINATION.
YOU'LL WAKE BETH UP.
WHERE ARE YOU GOING?
FOR A WALK! DO YOU MIND?
YOU MEAN DOWN THE STREET?
YES, DOWN THE STREET.
SCOTT, WHAT HAVE I DONE? DID I MAKE YOU THIS WAY?
GOOD-BYE.
SCOTT?
BE CAREFUL, DARLING.

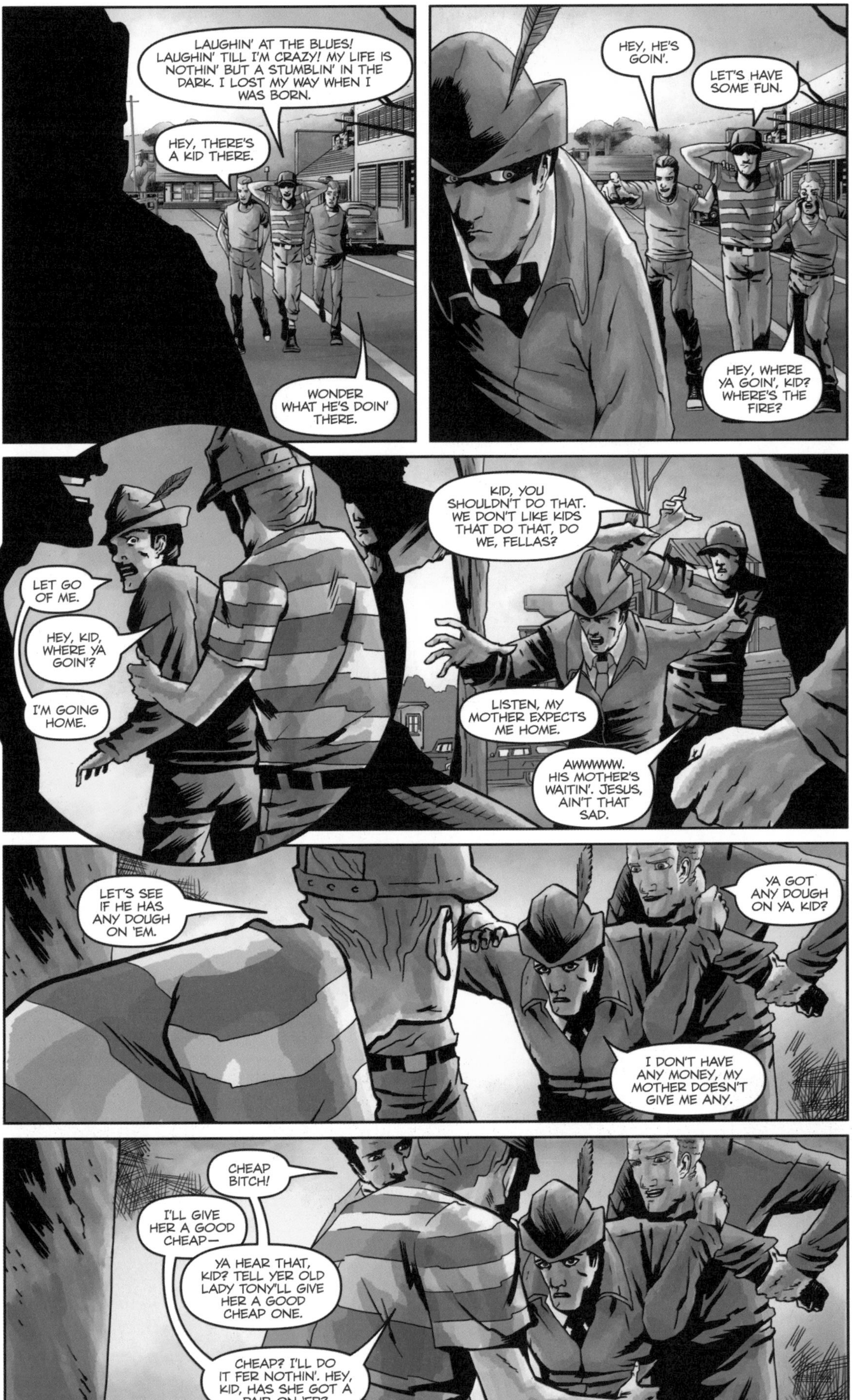
LAUGHIN' AT THE BLUES! LAUGHIN' TILL I'M CRAZY! MY LIFE IS NOTHIN' BUT A STUMBLIN' IN THE DARK. I LOST MY WAY WHEN I WAS BORN.
HEY, THERE'S A KID THERE.
WONDER WHAT HE'S DOIN' THERE.
HEY, HE'S GOIN'.
LET'S HAVE SOME FUN.
HEY, WHERE YA GOIN', KID? WHERE'S THE FIRE?
LET GO OF ME.
HEY, KID, WHERE YA GOIN'?
I'M GOING HOME.
KID, YOU SHOULDN'T DO THAT. WE DON'T LIKE KIDS THAT DO THAT, DO WE, FELLAS?
LISTEN, MY MOTHER EXPECTS ME HOME.
AWWWWW. HIS MOTHER'S WAITIN'. JESUS, AIN'T THAT SAD.
LET'S SEE IF HE HAS ANY DOUGH ON 'EM.
YA GOT ANY DOUGH ON YA, KID?
I DON'T HAVE ANY MONEY, MY MOTHER DOESN'T GIVE ME ANY.
CHEAP BITCH!
I'LL GIVE HER A GOOD CHEAP—
YA HEAR THAT, KID? TELL YER OLD LADY TONY'LL GIVE HER A GOOD CHEAP ONE.
CHEAP? I'LL DO IT FER NOTHIN'. HEY, KID, HAS SHE GOT A PAIR ON 'ER?

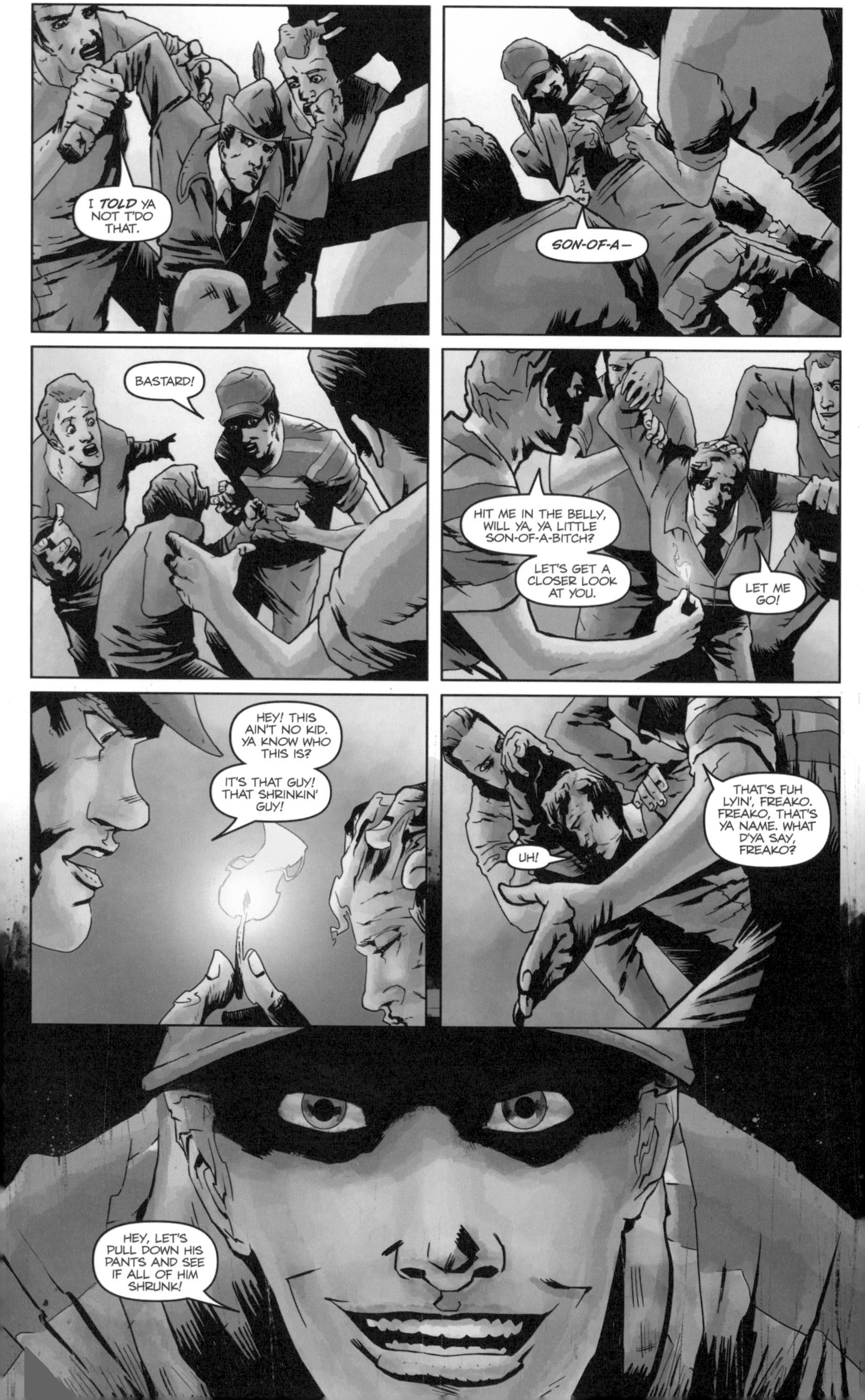
I TOLD YA NOT T'DO THAT.
SON-OF-A—
BASTARD!
HIT ME IN THE BELLY, WILL YA, YA LITTLE SON-OF-A-BITCH?
LET'S GET A CLOSER LOOK AT YOU.
LET ME GO!
HEY! THIS AIN'T NO KID. YA KNOW WHO THIS IS?
IT'S THAT GUY! THAT SHRINKIN' GUY!
THAT'S FUH LYIN', FREAKO. FREAKO, THAT'S YA NAME. WHAT D'YA SAY, FREAKO?
UH!
HEY, LET'S PULL DOWN HIS PANTS AND SEE IF ALL OF HIM SHRUNK!

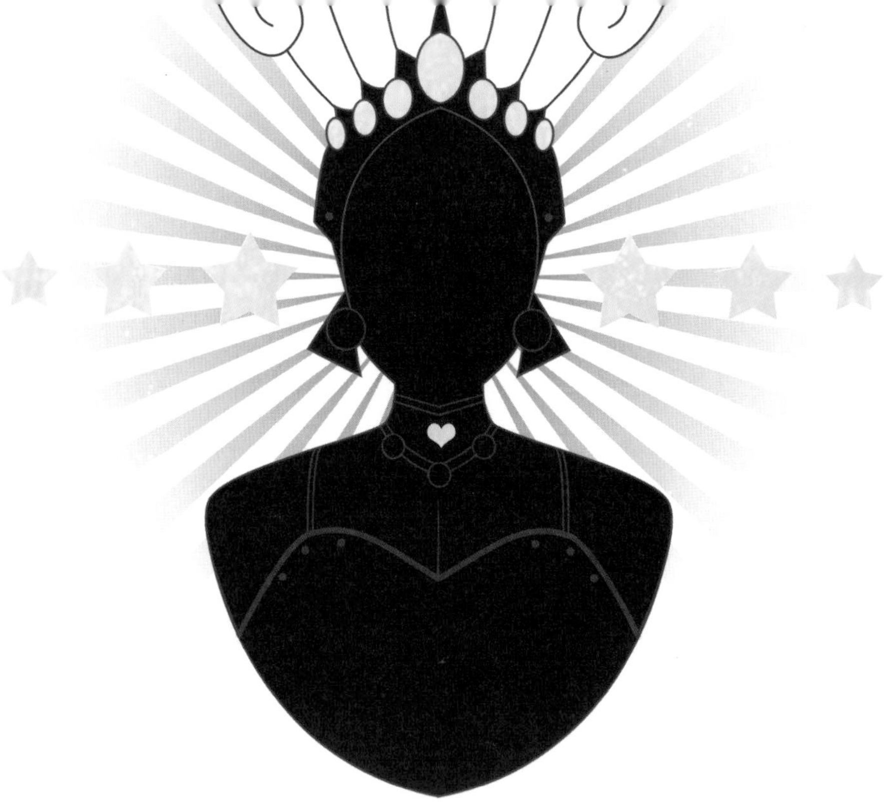

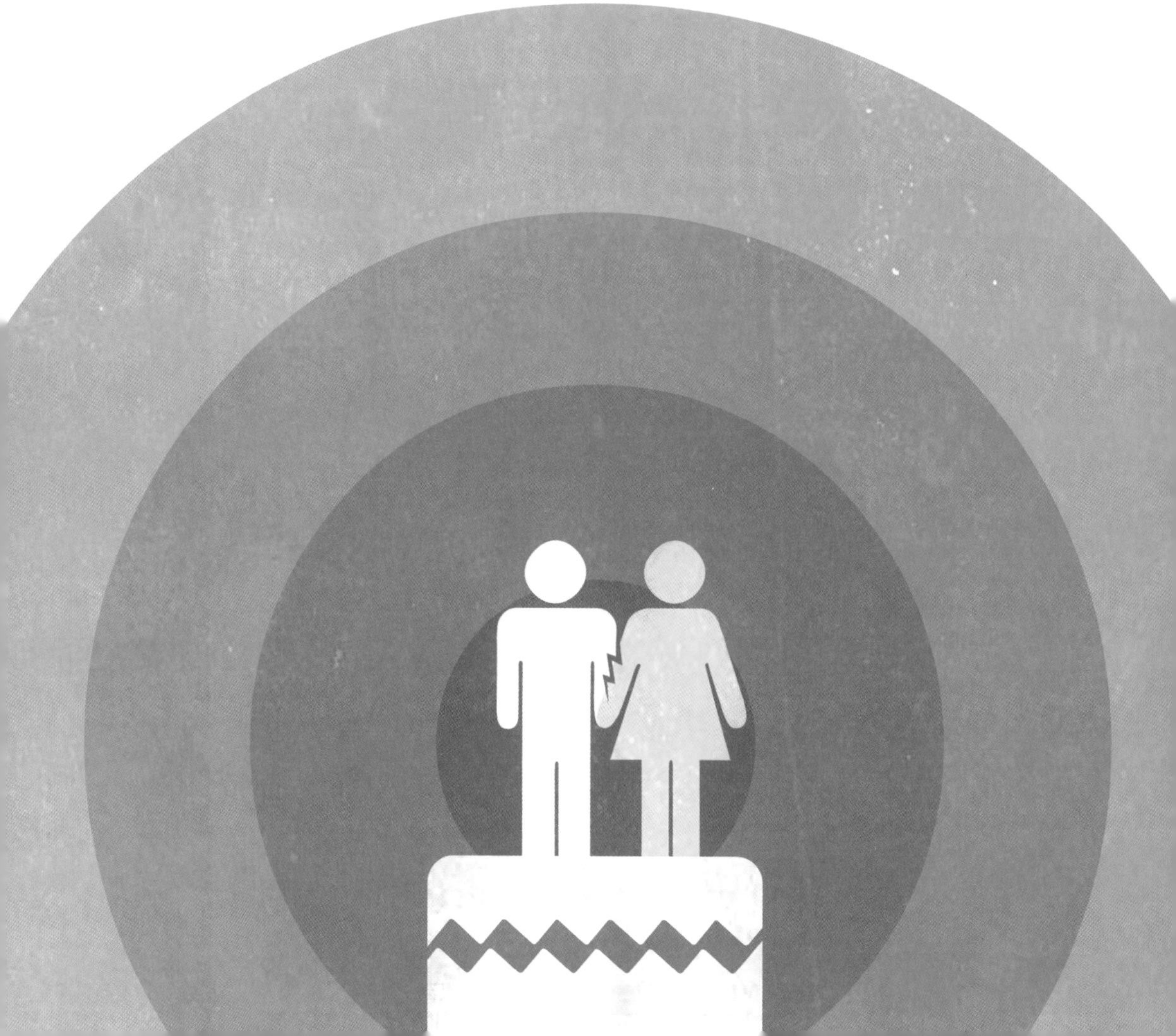

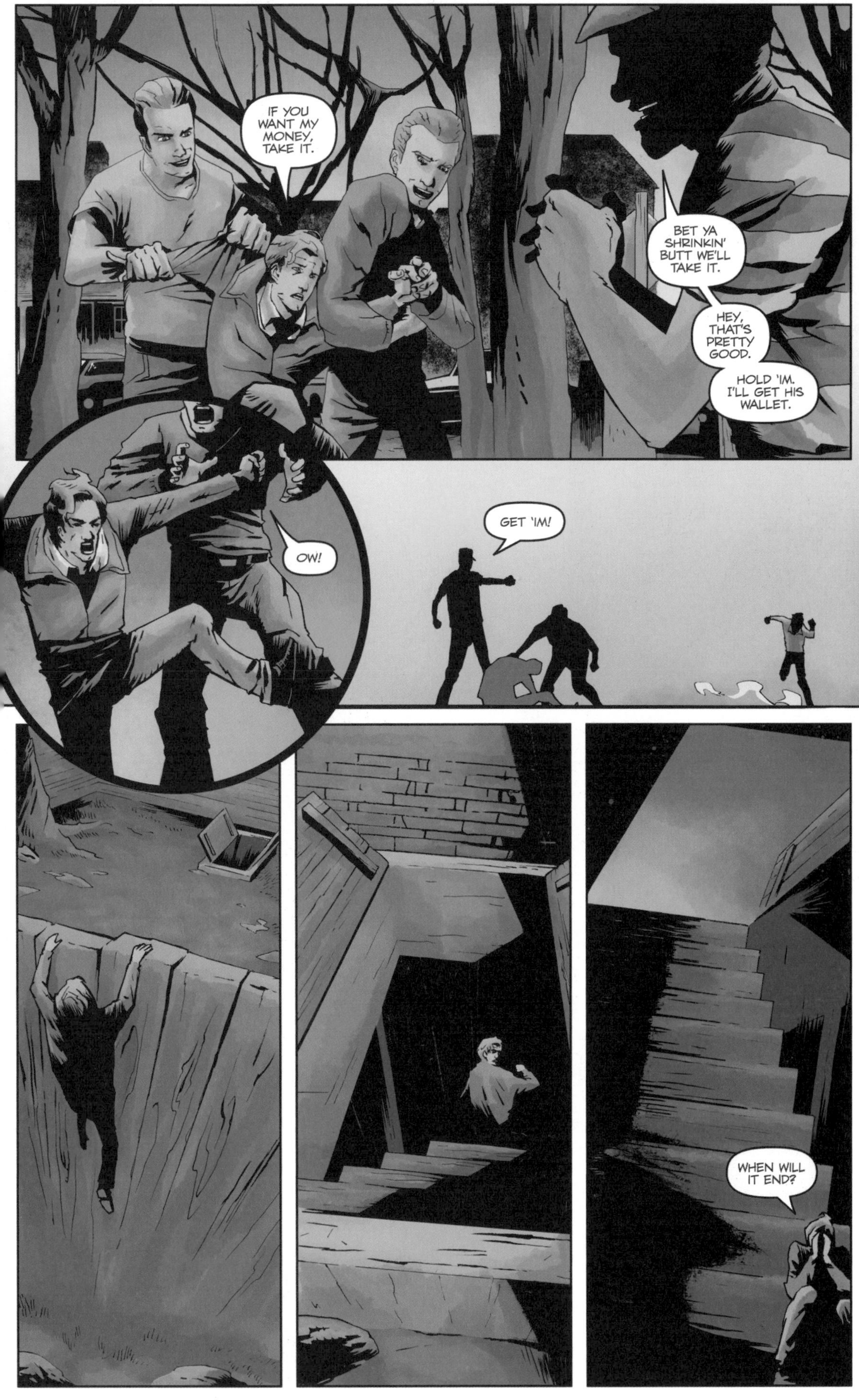
IF YOU WANT MY MONEY, TAKE IT.
BET YA SHRINKIN' BUTT WE'LL TAKE IT.
HEY, THAT'S PRETTY GOOD.
HOLD 'IM. I'LL GET HIS WALLET.
OW!
GET 'IM!
WHEN WILL IT END?

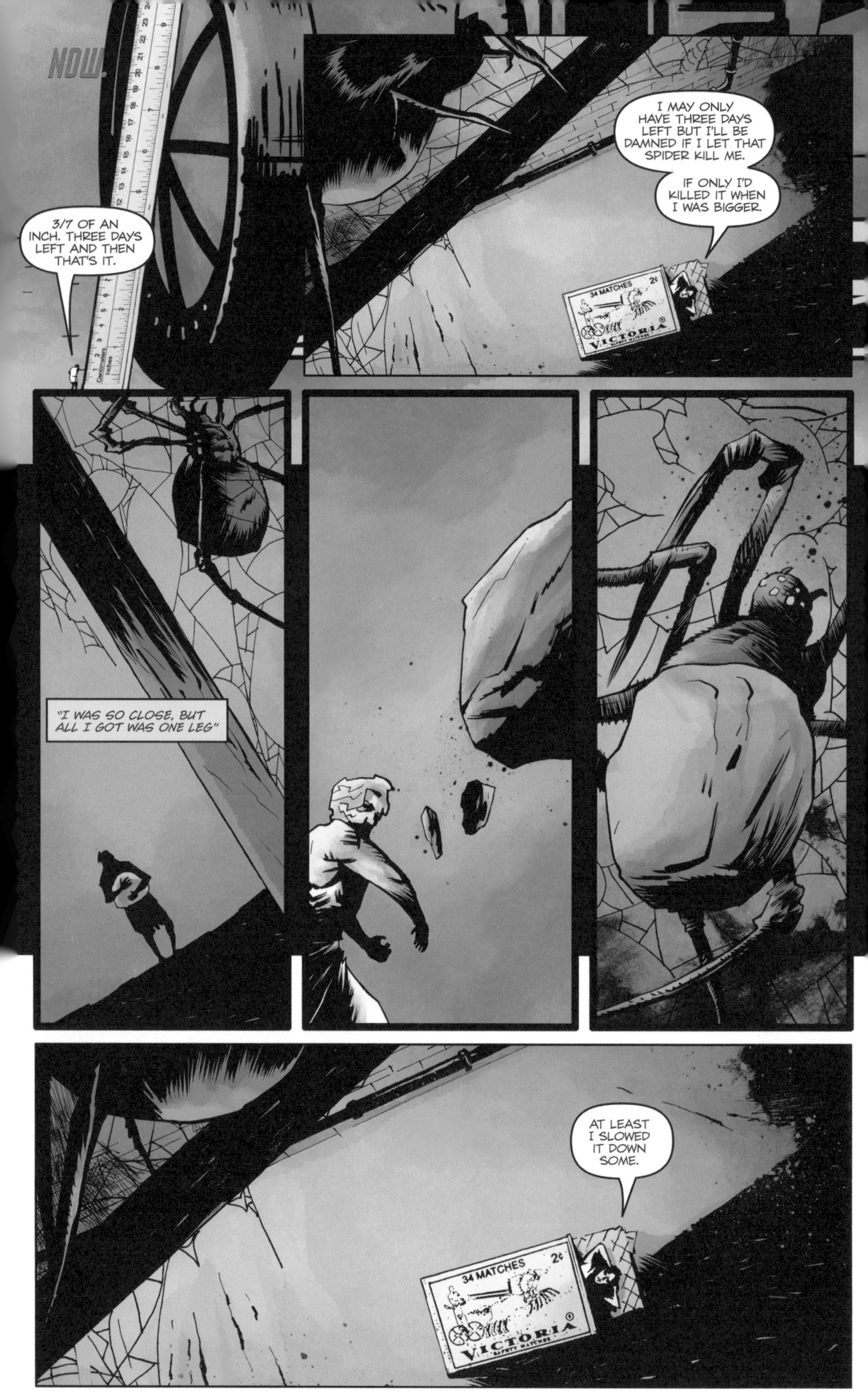
NOW:
3/7 OF AN INCH. THREE DAYS LEFT AND THEN THAT'S IT.
I MAY ONLY HAVE THREE DAYS LEFT BUT I'LL BE DAMNED IF I LET THAT SPIDER KILL ME.
IF ONLY I'D KILLED IT WHEN I WAS BIGGER.
34 MATCHES 2¢
VICTORIA
SAFETY MATCHES
"I WAS SO CLOSE, BUT ALL I GOT WAS ONE LEG"
AT LEAST I SLOWED IT DOWN SOME.
34 MATCHES 2¢
VICTORIA
SAFETY MATCHES

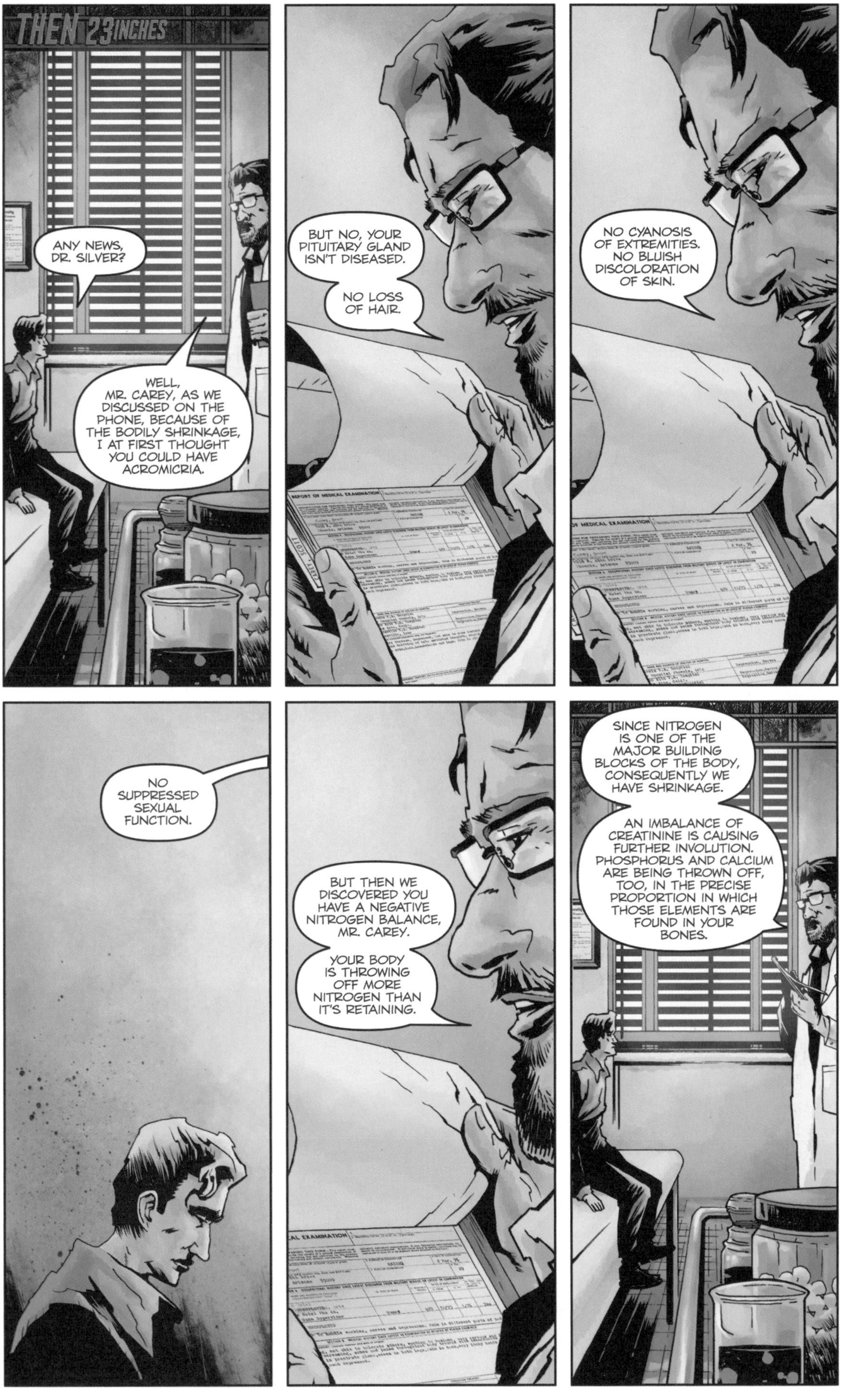
THEN 23 INCHES
ANY NEWS, DR. SILVER?
WELL, MR. CAREY, AS WE DISCUSSED ON THE PHONE, BECAUSE OF THE BODILY SHRINKAGE, I AT FIRST THOUGHT YOU COULD HAVE ACROMICRIA.
BUT NO, YOUR PITUITARY GLAND ISN'T DISEASED.
NO LOSS OF HAIR.
REPORT OF MEDICAL EXAMINATION
NO CYANOSIS OF EXTREMITIES. NO BLUISH DISCOLORATION OF SKIN.
NO SUPPRESSED SEXUAL FUNCTION.
BUT THEN WE DISCOVERED YOU HAVE A NEGATIVE NITROGEN BALANCE, MR. CAREY.
YOUR BODY IS THROWING OFF MORE NITROGEN THAN IT'S RETAINING.
SINCE NITROGEN IS ONE OF THE MAJOR BUILDING BLOCKS OF THE BODY, CONSEQUENTLY WE HAVE SHRINKAGE.
AN IMBALANCE OF CREATININE IS CAUSING FURTHER INVOLUTION. PHOSPHORUS AND CALCIUM ARE BEING THROWN OFF, TOO, IN THE PRECISE PROPORTION IN WHICH THOSE ELEMENTS ARE FOUND IN YOUR BONES.

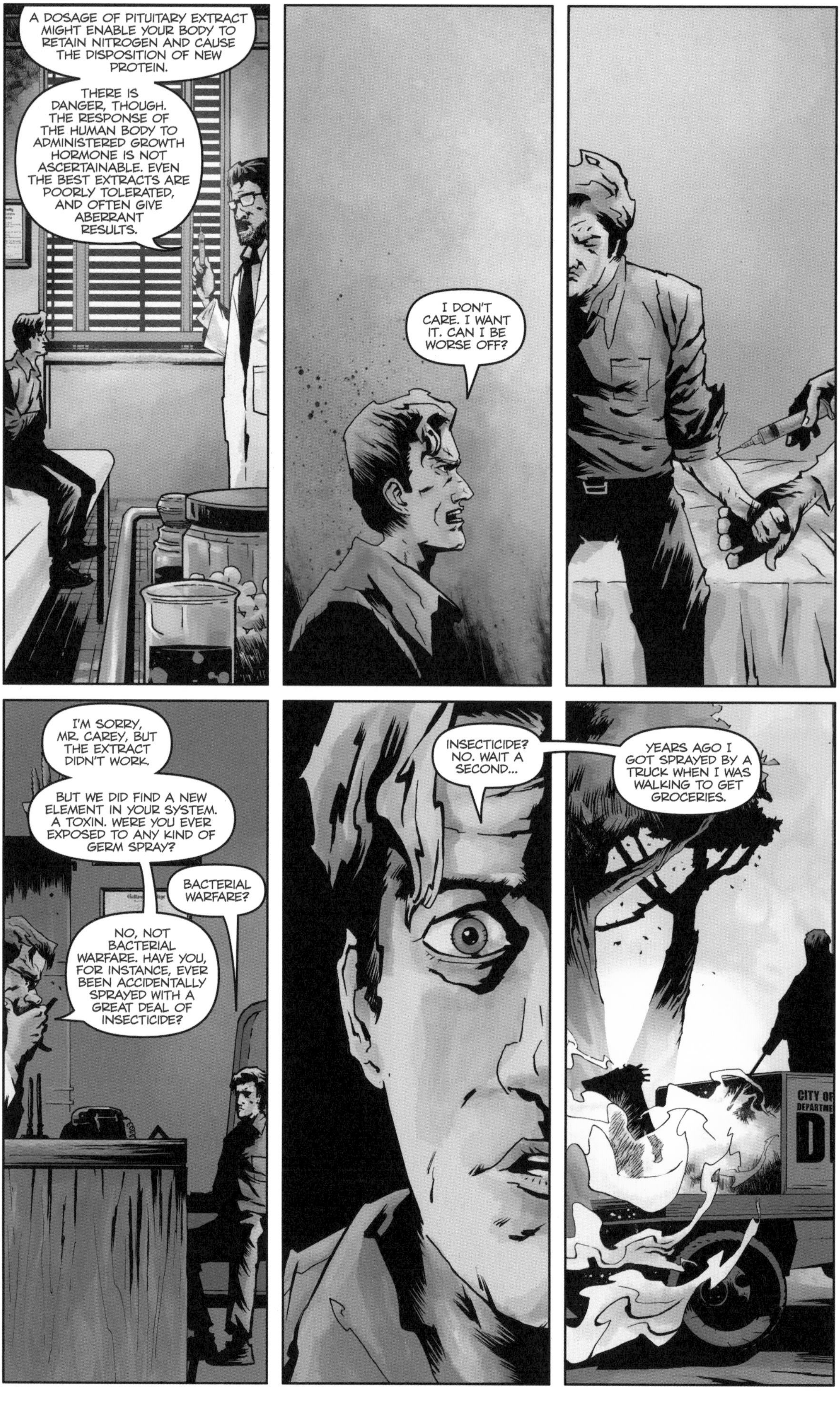
A DOSAGE OF PITUITARY EXTRACT MIGHT ENABLE YOUR BODY TO RETAIN NITROGEN AND CAUSE THE DISPOSITION OF NEW PROTEIN.
THERE IS DANGER, THOUGH. THE RESPONSE OF THE HUMAN BODY TO ADMINISTERED GROWTH HORMONE IS NOT ASCERTAINABLE. EVEN THE BEST EXTRACTS ARE POORLY TOLERATED, AND OFTEN GIVE ABERRANT RESULTS.
I DON'T CARE. I WANT IT. CAN I BE WORSE OFF?
I'M SORRY, MR. CAREY, BUT THE EXTRACT DIDN'T WORK.
BUT WE DID FIND A NEW ELEMENT IN YOUR SYSTEM. A TOXIN. WERE YOU EVER EXPOSED TO ANY KIND OF GERM SPRAY?
BACTERIAL WARFARE?
NO, NOT BACTERIAL WARFARE. HAVE YOU, FOR INSTANCE, EVER BEEN ACCIDENTALLY SPRAYED WITH A GREAT DEAL OF INSECTICIDE?
INSECTICIDE? NO. WAIT A SECOND...
YEARS AGO I GOT SPRAYED BY A TRUCK WHEN I WAS WALKING TO GET GROCERIES.
CITY OF

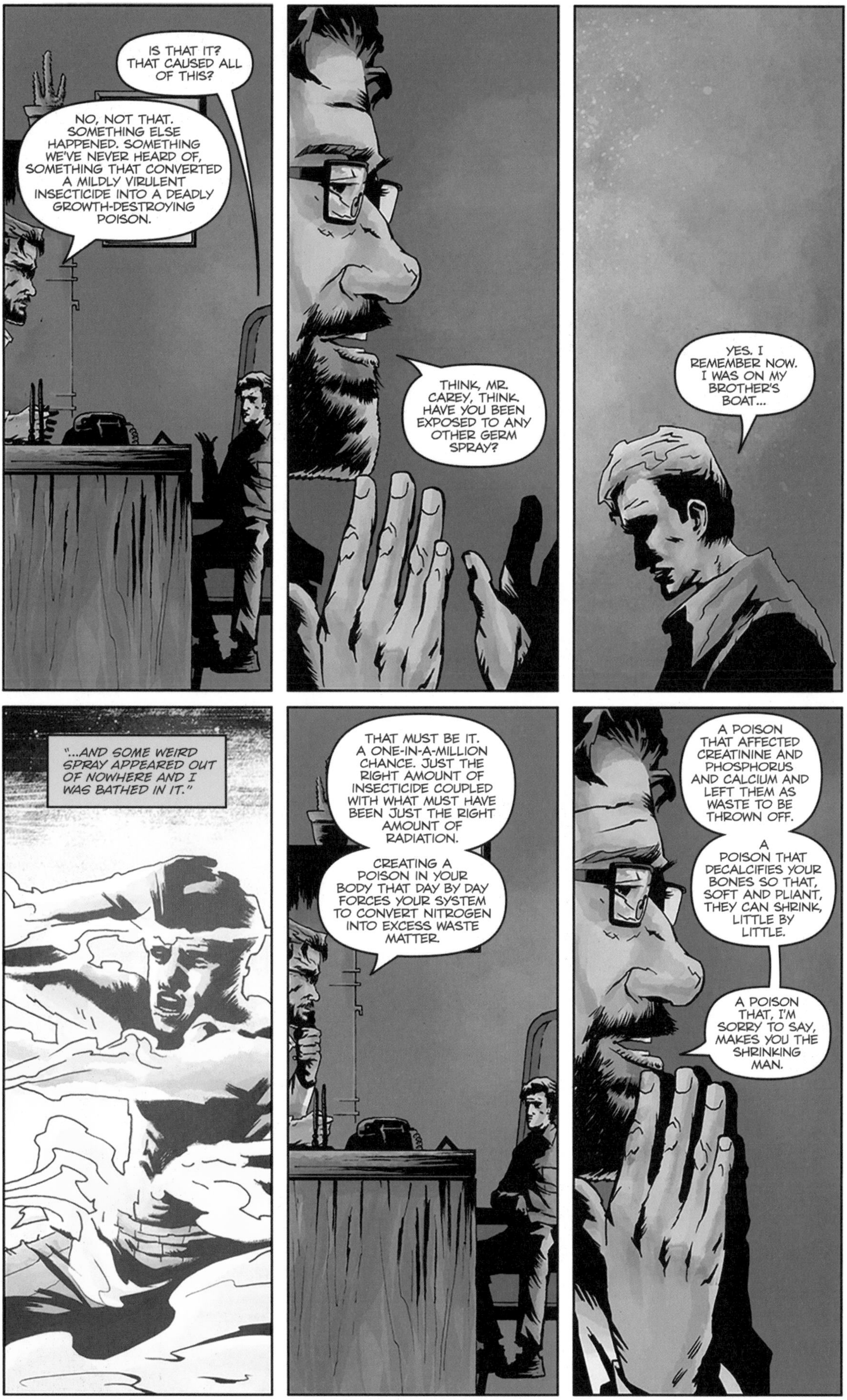
IS THAT IT? THAT CAUSED ALL OF THIS?
NO, NOT THAT. SOMETHING ELSE HAPPENED. SOMETHING WE'VE NEVER HEARD OF, SOMETHING THAT CONVERTED A MILDLY VIRULENT INSECTICIDE INTO A DEADLY GROWTH-DESTROYING POISON.
THINK, MR. CAREY, THINK. HAVE YOU BEEN EXPOSED TO ANY OTHER GERM SPRAY?
YES. I REMEMBER NOW. I WAS ON MY BROTHER'S BOAT...
"...AND SOME WEIRD SPRAY APPEARED OUT OF NOWHERE AND I WAS BATHED IN IT."
THAT MUST BE IT. A ONE-IN-A-MILLION CHANCE. JUST THE RIGHT AMOUNT OF INSECTICIDE COUPLED WITH WHAT MUST HAVE BEEN JUST THE RIGHT AMOUNT OF RADIATION.
CREATING A POISON IN YOUR BODY THAT DAY BY DAY FORCES YOUR SYSTEM TO CONVERT NITROGEN INTO EXCESS WASTE MATTER.
A POISON THAT AFFECTED CREATININE AND PHOSPHORUS AND CALCIUM AND LEFT THEM AS WASTE TO BE THROWN OFF.
A POISON THAT DECALCIFIES YOUR BONES SO THAT, SOFT AND PLIANT, THEY CAN SHRINK, LITTLE BY LITTLE.
A POISON THAT, I'M SORRY TO SAY, MAKES YOU THE SHRINKING MAN.

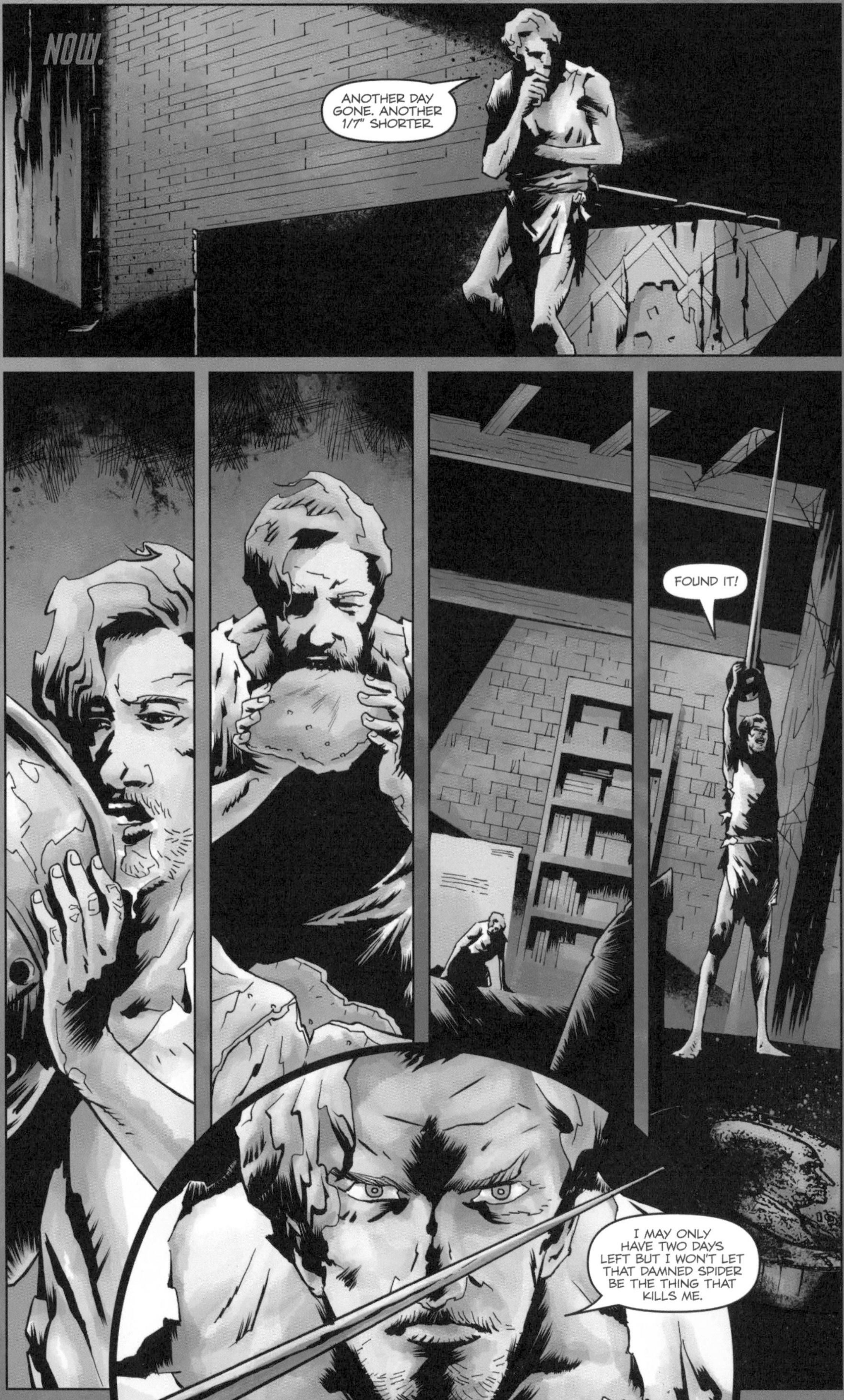
NOW.
ANOTHER DAY GONE. ANOTHER 1/7" SHORTER.
FOUND IT!
I MAY ONLY HAVE TWO DAYS LEFT BUT I WON'T LET THAT DAMNED SPIDER BE THE THING THAT KILLS ME.

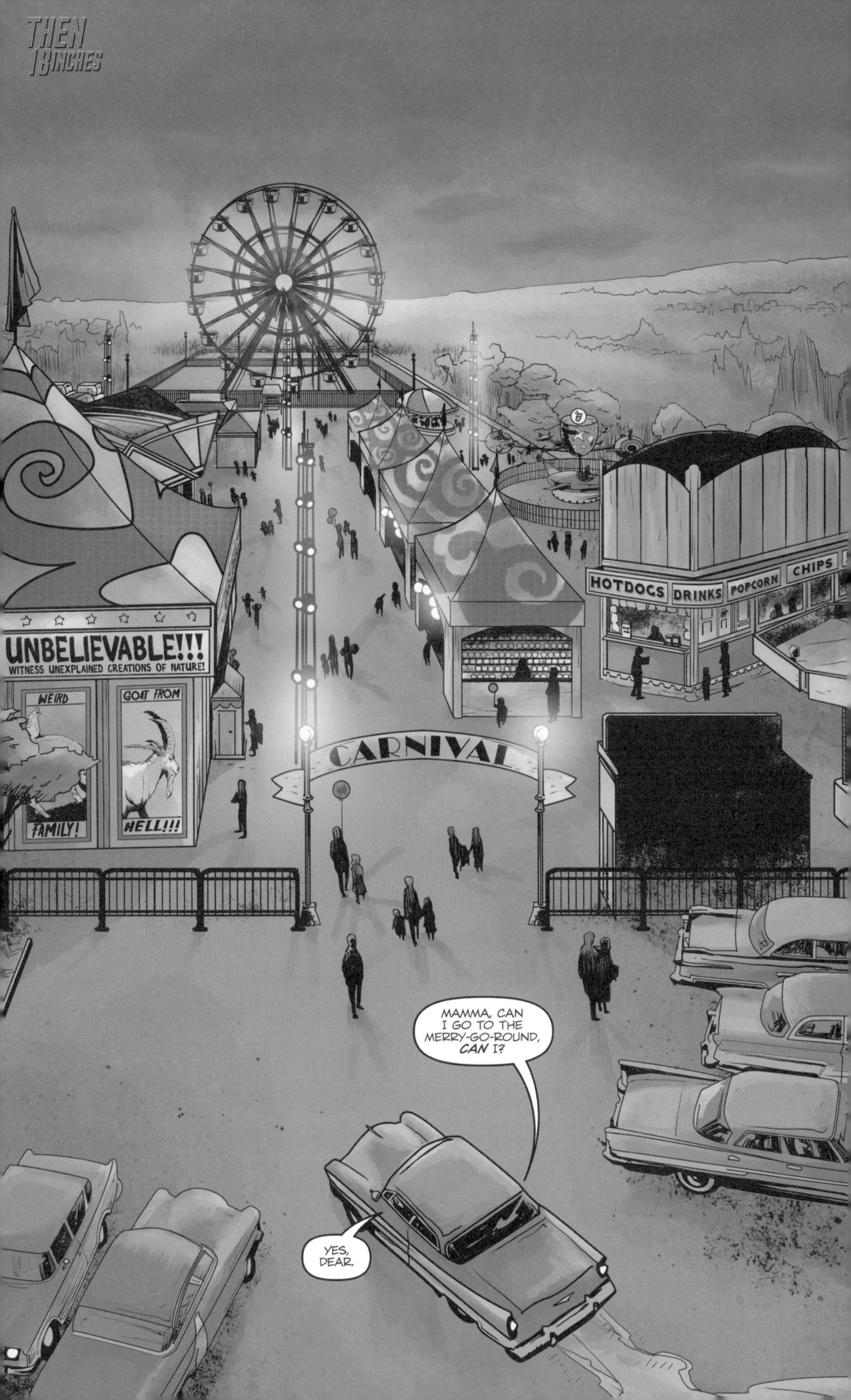
THEN
18 INCHES
UNBELIEVABLE!!!
WITNESS UNEXPLAINED CREATIONS OF NATURE!
WEIRD
FAMILY!
GOAT FROM
HELL!!!
CARNIVAL
HOTDOGS
DRINKS
POPCORN
CHIPS
MAMMA, CAN I GO TO THE MERRY-GO-ROUND, CAN I?
YES, DEAR.

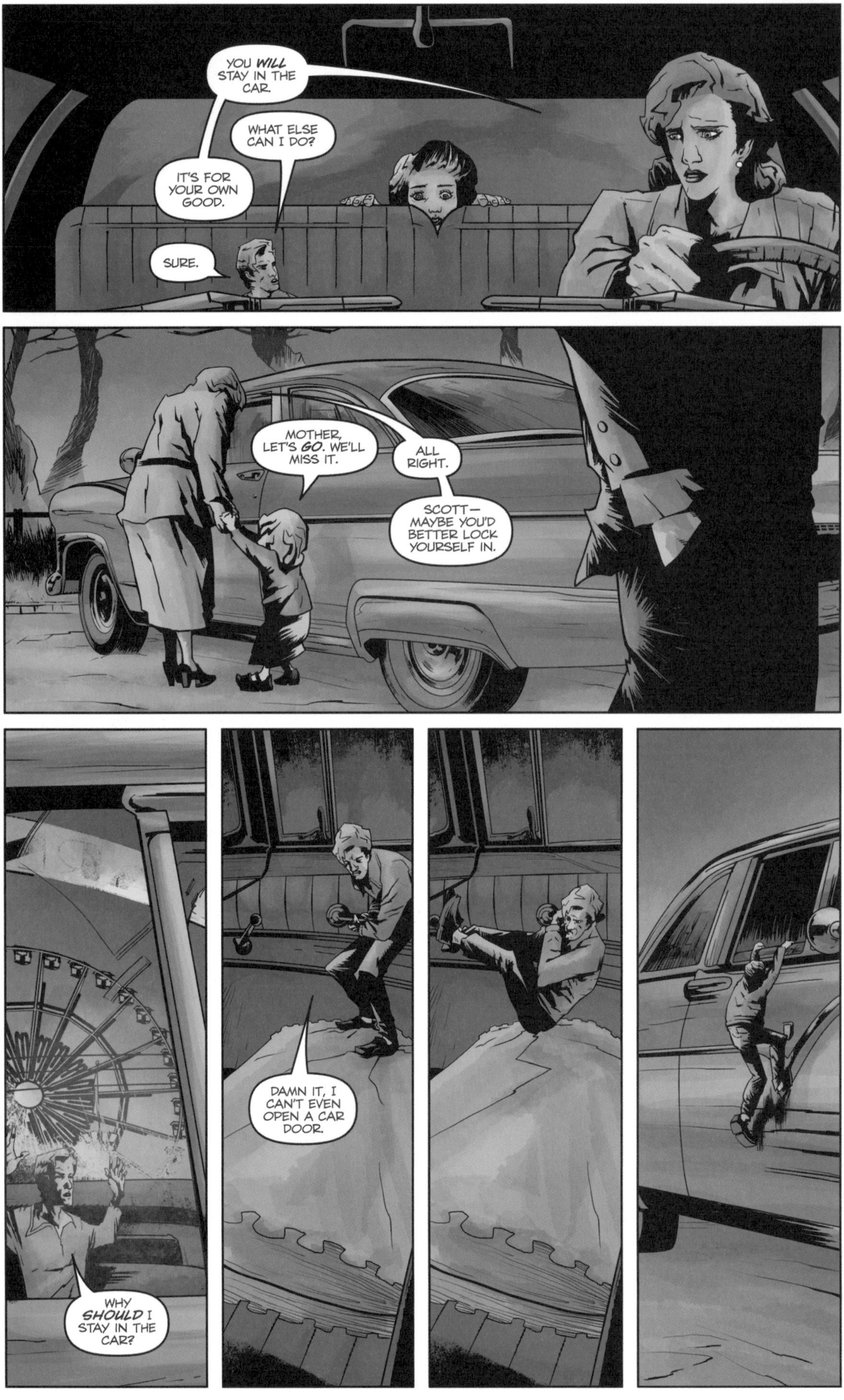
YOU WILL STAY IN THE CAR.
WHAT ELSE CAN I DO?
IT'S FOR YOUR OWN GOOD.
SURE.
MOTHER, LET'S GO. WE'LL MISS IT.
ALL RIGHT.
SCOTT— MAYBE YOU'D BETTER LOCK YOURSELF IN.
WHY SHOULD I STAY IN THE CAR?
DAMN IT, I CAN'T EVEN OPEN A CAR DOOR.

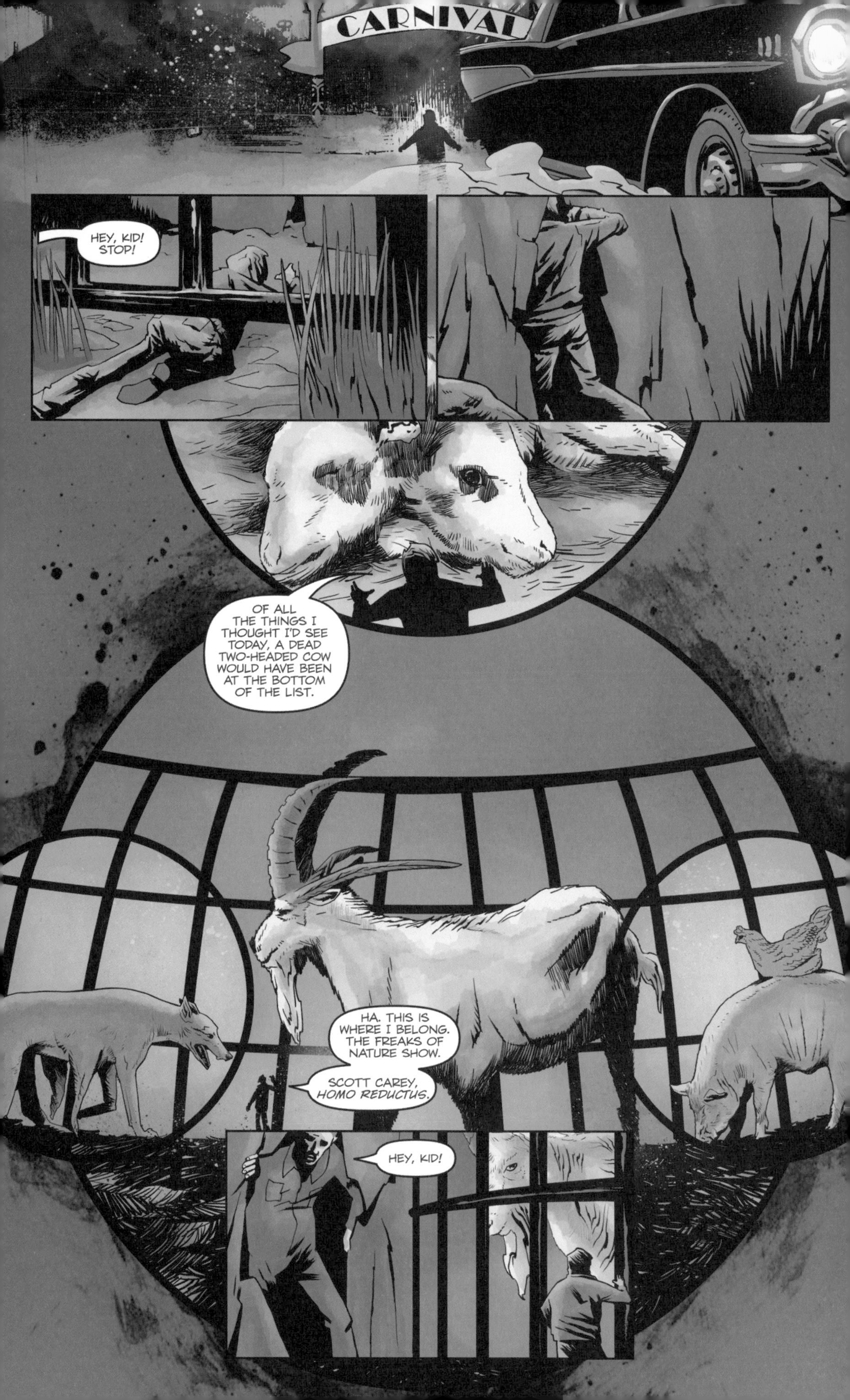
CARNIVAL
HEY, KID! STOP!
OF ALL THE THINGS I THOUGHT I'D SEE TODAY, A DEAD TWO-HEADED COW WOULD HAVE BEEN AT THE BOTTOM OF THE LIST.
HA. THIS IS WHERE I BELONG. THE FREAKS OF NATURE SHOW.
SCOTT CAREY, *HOMO REDUCTUS.*
HEY, KID!

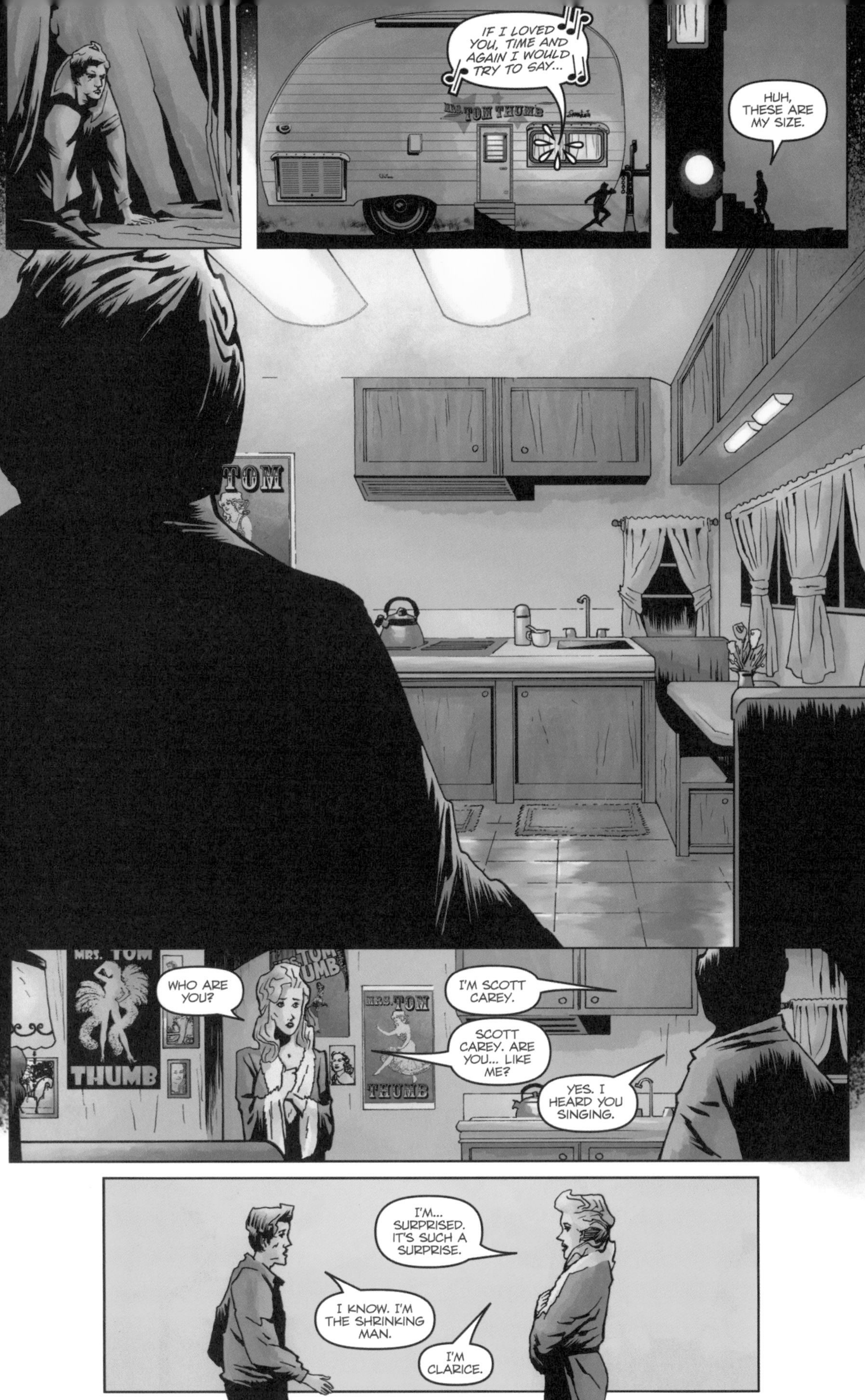
IF I LOVED YOU, TIME AND AGAIN I WOULD TRY TO SAY...
HUH, THESE ARE MY SIZE.
WHO ARE YOU?
I'M SCOTT CAREY.
SCOTT CAREY. ARE YOU... LIKE ME?
YES. I HEARD YOU SINGING.
I'M... SURPRISED. IT'S SUCH A SURPRISE.
I KNOW. I'M THE SHRINKING MAN.
I'M CLARICE.

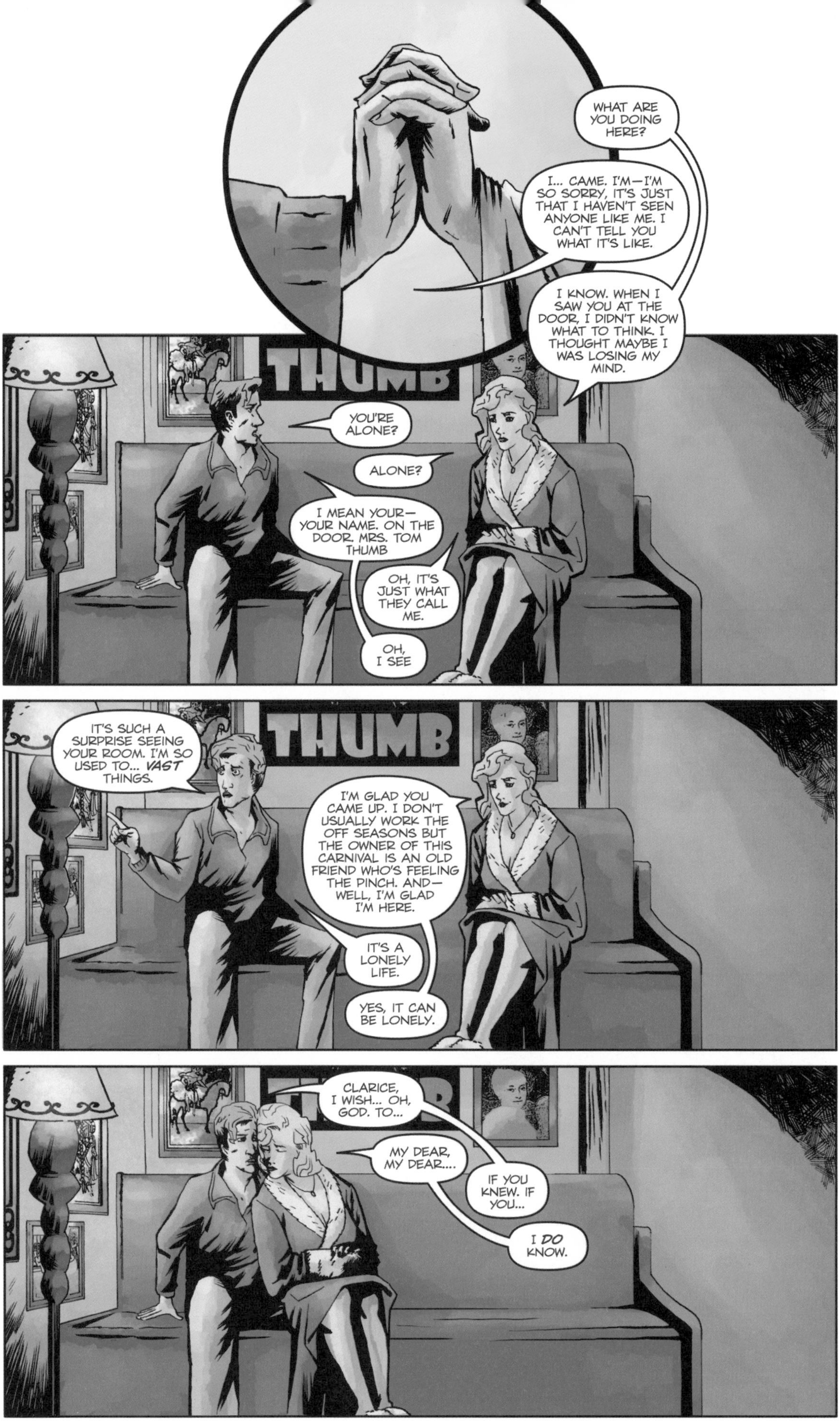
THUMB
WHAT ARE YOU DOING HERE?
I... CAME. I'M—I'M SO SORRY, IT'S JUST THAT I HAVEN'T SEEN ANYONE LIKE ME. I CAN'T TELL YOU WHAT IT'S LIKE.
I KNOW. WHEN I SAW YOU AT THE DOOR, I DIDN'T KNOW WHAT TO THINK. I THOUGHT MAYBE I WAS LOSING MY MIND.
YOU'RE ALONE?
ALONE?
I MEAN YOUR— YOUR NAME. ON THE DOOR. MRS. TOM THUMB
OH, IT'S JUST WHAT THEY CALL ME.
OH, I SEE
THUMB
IT'S SUCH A SURPRISE SEEING YOUR ROOM. I'M SO USED TO... *VAST* THINGS.
I'M GLAD YOU CAME UP. I DON'T USUALLY WORK THE OFF SEASONS BUT THE OWNER OF THIS CARNIVAL IS AN OLD FRIEND WHO'S FEELING THE PINCH. AND— WELL, I'M GLAD I'M HERE.
IT'S A LONELY LIFE.
YES, IT CAN BE LONELY.
CLARICE, I WISH... OH, GOD. TO...
MY DEAR, MY DEAR....
IF YOU KNEW. IF YOU...
I *DO* KNOW.

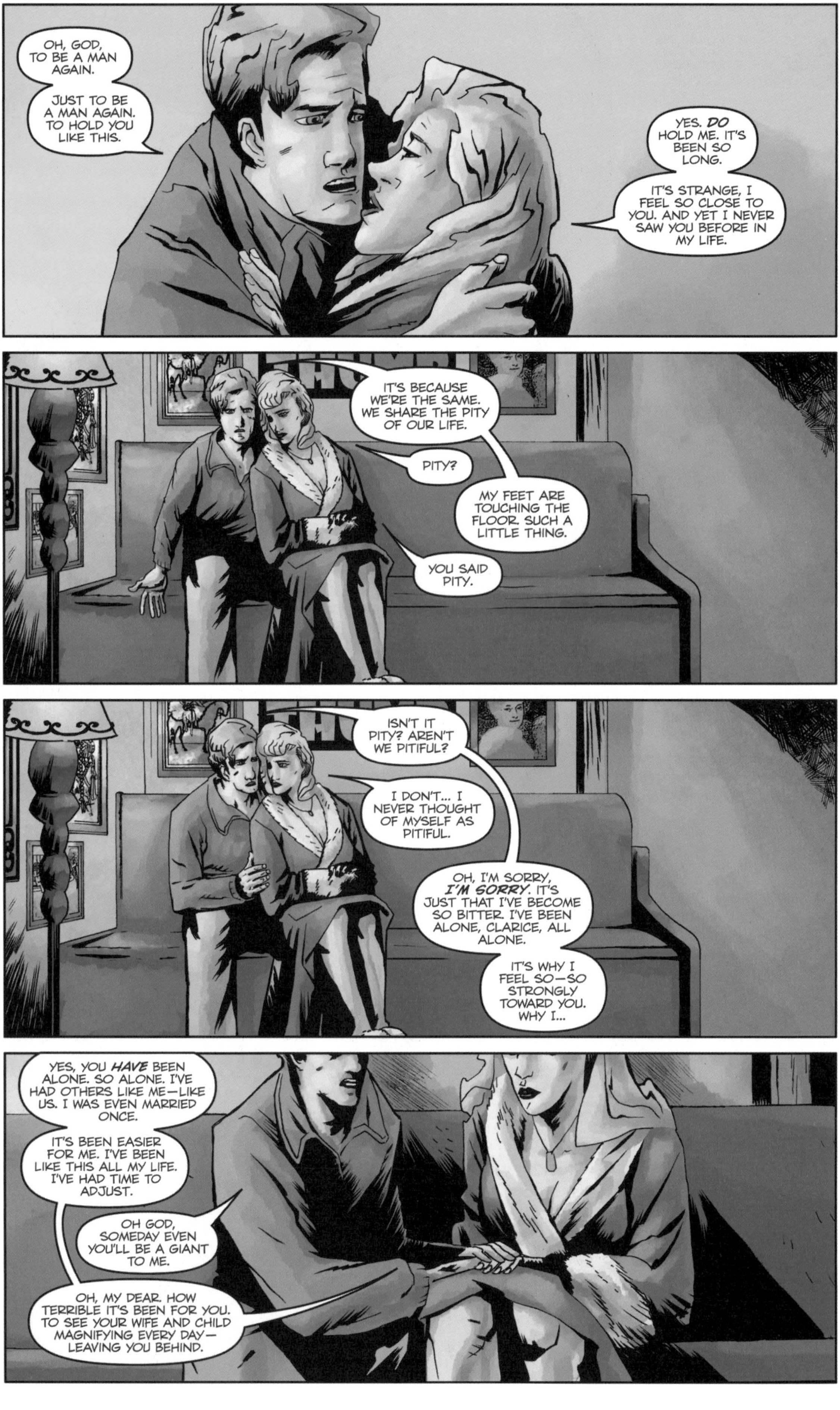
OH, GOD, TO BE A MAN AGAIN.
JUST TO BE A MAN AGAIN. TO HOLD YOU LIKE THIS.
YES. *DO* HOLD ME. IT'S BEEN SO LONG.
IT'S STRANGE, I FEEL SO CLOSE TO YOU. AND YET I NEVER SAW YOU BEFORE IN MY LIFE.
IT'S BECAUSE WE'RE THE SAME. WE SHARE THE PITY OF OUR LIFE.
PITY?
MY FEET ARE TOUCHING THE FLOOR. SUCH A LITTLE THING.
YOU SAID PITY.
ISN'T IT PITY? AREN'T WE PITIFUL?
I DON'T... I NEVER THOUGHT OF MYSELF AS PITIFUL.
OH, I'M SORRY, *I'M SORRY*. IT'S JUST THAT I'VE BECOME SO BITTER. I'VE BEEN ALONE, CLARICE, ALL ALONE.
IT'S WHY I FEEL SO—SO STRONGLY TOWARD YOU. WHY I...
YES, YOU *HAVE* BEEN ALONE. SO ALONE. I'VE HAD OTHERS LIKE ME—LIKE US. I WAS EVEN MARRIED ONCE.
IT'S BEEN EASIER FOR ME. I'VE BEEN LIKE THIS ALL MY LIFE. I'VE HAD TIME TO ADJUST.
OH GOD, SOMEDAY EVEN YOU'LL BE A GIANT TO ME.
OH, MY DEAR. HOW TERRIBLE IT'S BEEN FOR YOU. TO SEE YOUR WIFE AND CHILD MAGNIFYING EVERY DAY—LEAVING YOU BEHIND.

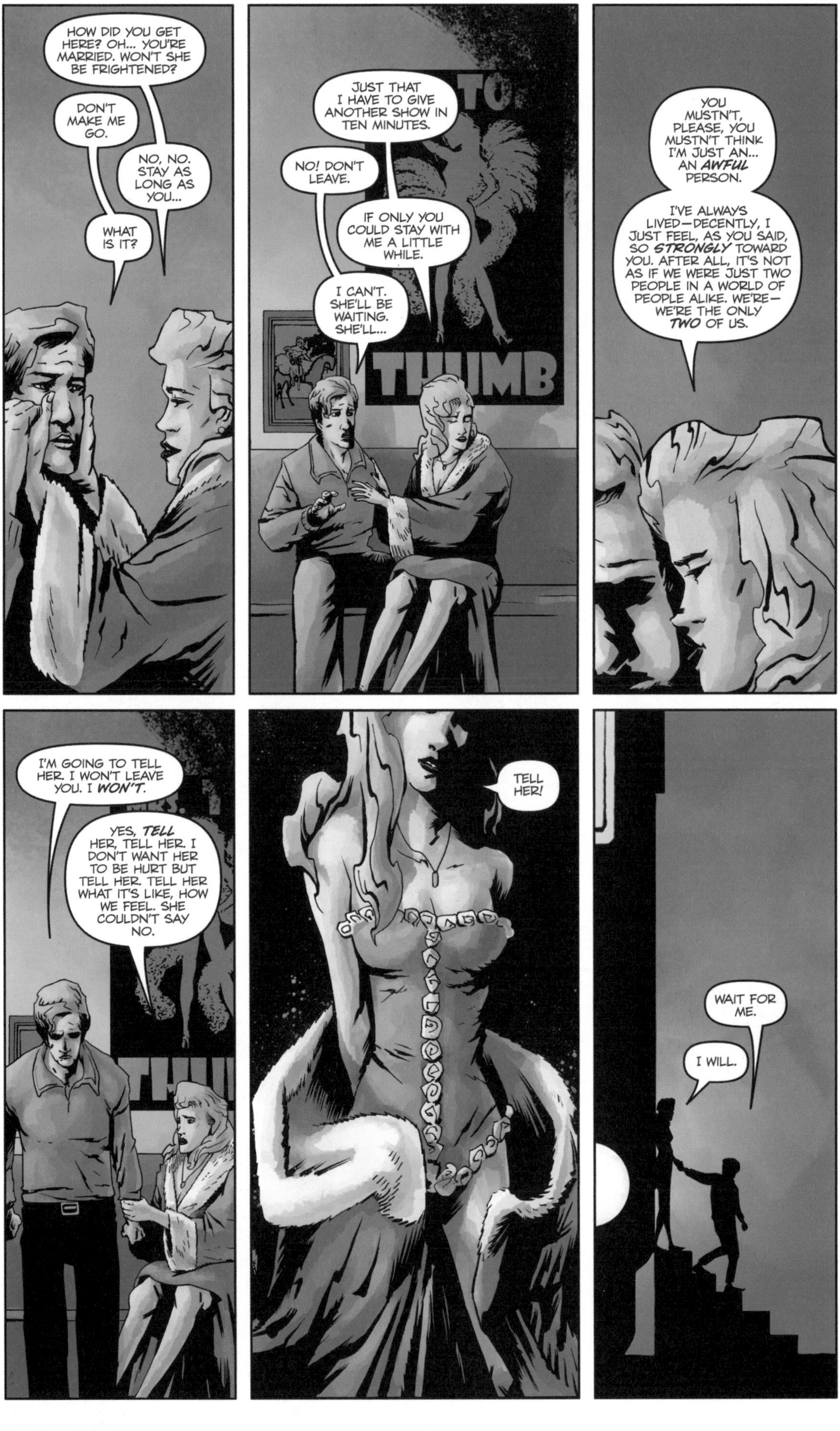
HOW DID YOU GET HERE? OH... YOU'RE MARRIED. WON'T SHE BE FRIGHTENED?
DON'T MAKE ME GO.
NO, NO. STAY AS LONG AS YOU...
WHAT IS IT?
JUST THAT I HAVE TO GIVE ANOTHER SHOW IN TEN MINUTES.
NO! DON'T LEAVE.
IF ONLY YOU COULD STAY WITH ME A LITTLE WHILE.
I CAN'T. SHE'LL BE WAITING. SHE'LL...
THUMB
YOU MUSTN'T, PLEASE, YOU MUSTN'T THINK I'M JUST AN... AN AWFUL PERSON.
I'VE ALWAYS LIVED—DECENTLY, I JUST FEEL, AS YOU SAID, SO STRONGLY TOWARD YOU. AFTER ALL, IT'S NOT AS IF WE WERE JUST TWO PEOPLE IN A WORLD OF PEOPLE ALIKE. WE'RE—WE'RE THE ONLY TWO OF US.
I'M GOING TO TELL HER. I WON'T LEAVE YOU. I WON'T.
YES, TELL HER, TELL HER. I DON'T WANT HER TO BE HURT BUT TELL HER. TELL HER WHAT IT'S LIKE, HOW WE FEEL. SHE COULDN'T SAY NO.
TELL HER!
WAIT FOR ME.
I WILL.

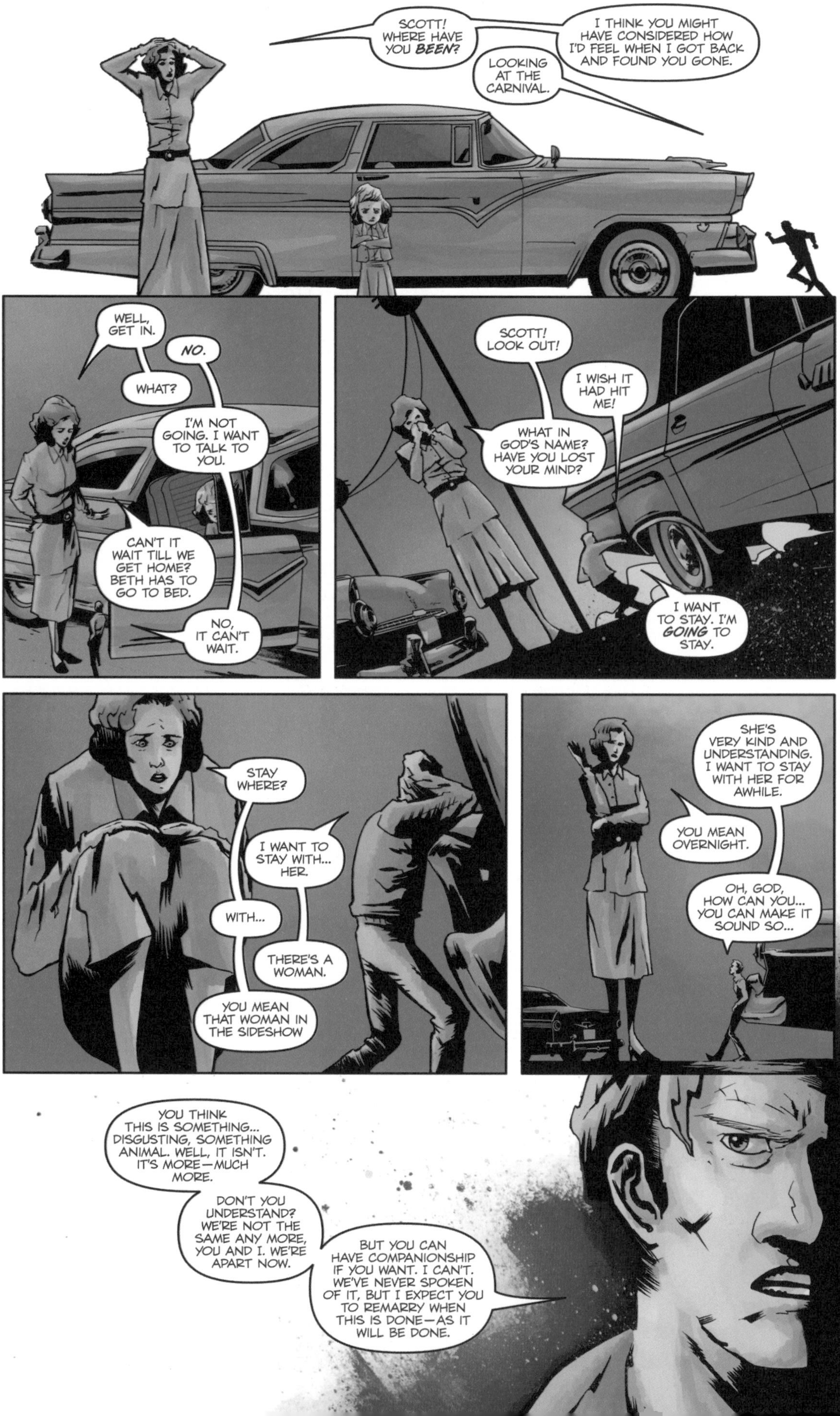
SCOTT! WHERE HAVE YOU BEEN?
LOOKING AT THE CARNIVAL.
I THINK YOU MIGHT HAVE CONSIDERED HOW I'D FEEL WHEN I GOT BACK AND FOUND YOU GONE.
WELL, GET IN.
NO.
WHAT?
I'M NOT GOING. I WANT TO TALK TO YOU.
CAN'T IT WAIT TILL WE GET HOME? BETH HAS TO GO TO BED.
NO, IT CAN'T WAIT.
SCOTT! LOOK OUT!
I WISH IT HAD HIT ME!
WHAT IN GOD'S NAME? HAVE YOU LOST YOUR MIND?
I WANT TO STAY. I'M GOING TO STAY.
STAY WHERE?
I WANT TO STAY WITH... HER.
WITH...
THERE'S A WOMAN.
YOU MEAN THAT WOMAN IN THE SIDESHOW
SHE'S VERY KIND AND UNDERSTANDING. I WANT TO STAY WITH HER FOR AWHILE.
YOU MEAN OVERNIGHT.
OH, GOD, HOW CAN YOU... YOU CAN MAKE IT SOUND SO...
YOU THINK THIS IS SOMETHING... DISGUSTING, SOMETHING ANIMAL. WELL, IT ISN'T. IT'S MORE—MUCH MORE.
DON'T YOU UNDERSTAND? WE'RE NOT THE SAME ANY MORE, YOU AND I. WE'RE APART NOW.
BUT YOU CAN HAVE COMPANIONSHIP IF YOU WANT. I CAN'T. WE'VE NEVER SPOKEN OF IT, BUT I EXPECT YOU TO REMARRY WHEN THIS IS DONE—AS IT WILL BE DONE.

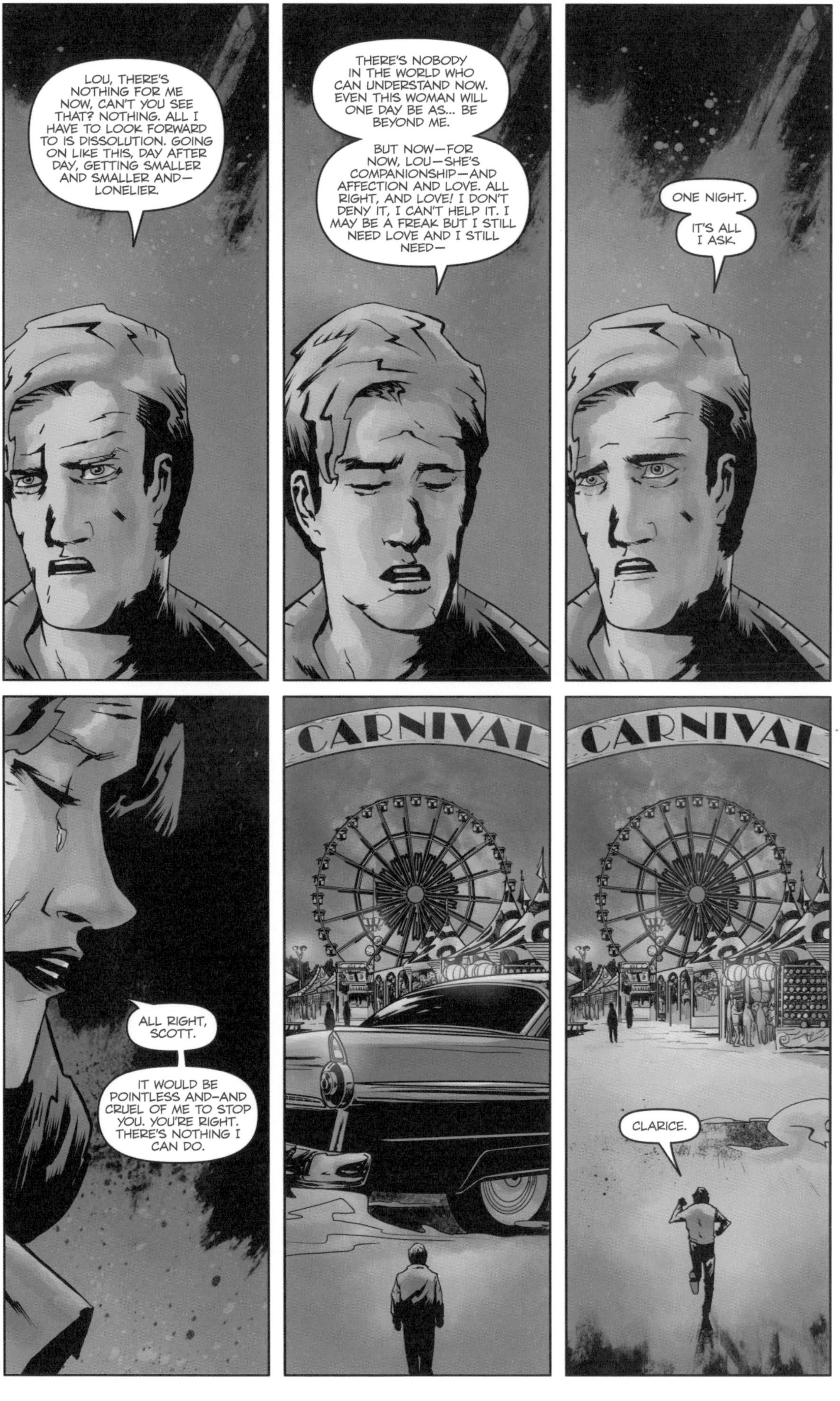
LOU, THERE'S NOTHING FOR ME NOW, CAN'T YOU SEE THAT? NOTHING. ALL I HAVE TO LOOK FORWARD TO IS DISSOLUTION. GOING ON LIKE THIS, DAY AFTER DAY, GETTING SMALLER AND SMALLER AND— LONELIER.
THERE'S NOBODY IN THE WORLD WHO CAN UNDERSTAND NOW. EVEN THIS WOMAN WILL ONE DAY BE AS... BE BEYOND ME.
BUT NOW—FOR NOW, LOU—SHE'S COMPANIONSHIP—AND AFFECTION AND LOVE. ALL RIGHT, AND LOVE! I DON'T DENY IT, I CAN'T HELP IT. I MAY BE A FREAK BUT I STILL NEED LOVE AND I STILL NEED—
ONE NIGHT.
IT'S ALL I ASK.
ALL RIGHT, SCOTT.
IT WOULD BE POINTLESS AND–AND CRUEL OF ME TO STOP YOU. YOU'RE RIGHT. THERE'S NOTHING I CAN DO.
CARNIVAL
CARNIVAL
CLARICE.

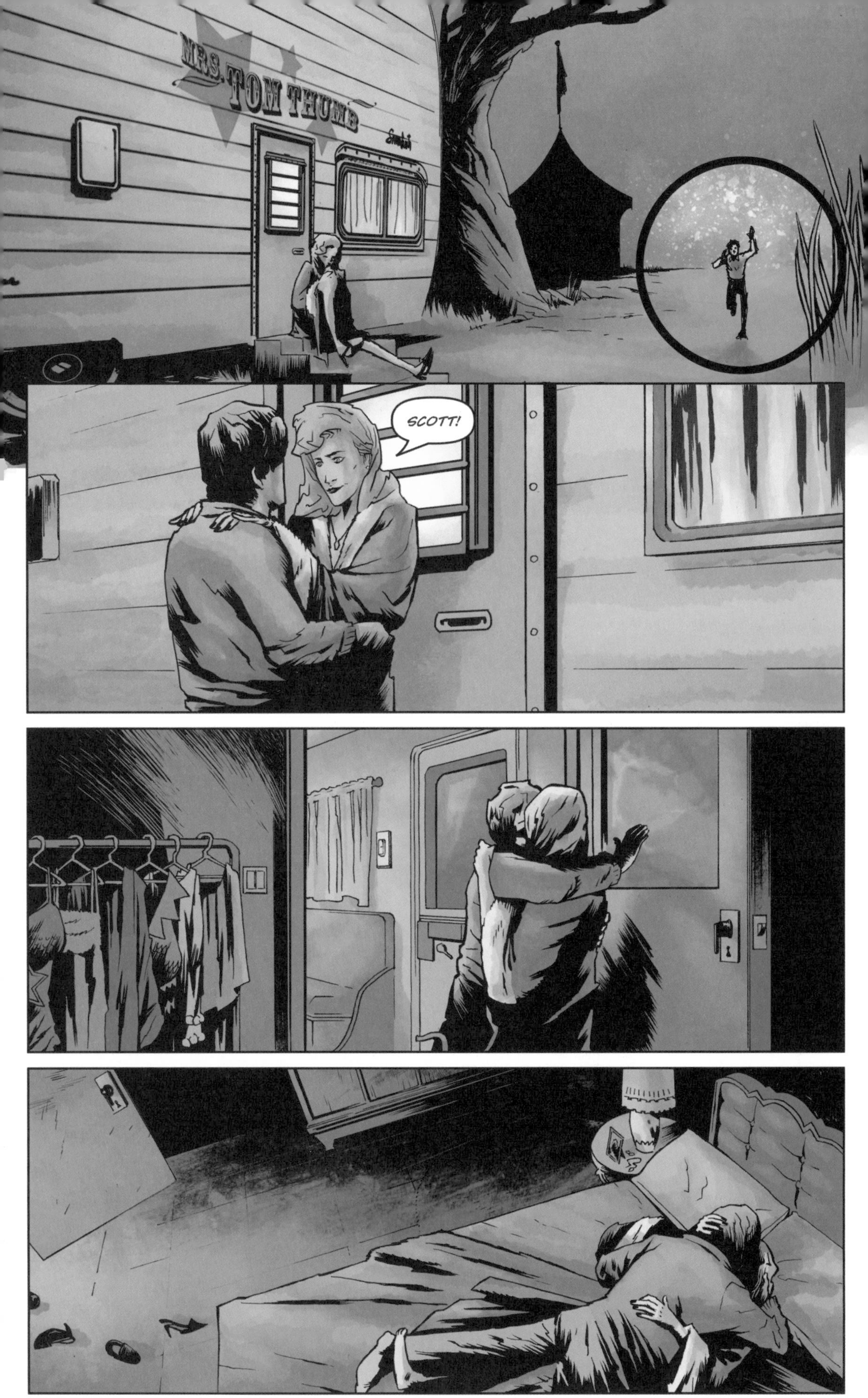
MRS. TOM THUMB
SCOTT!

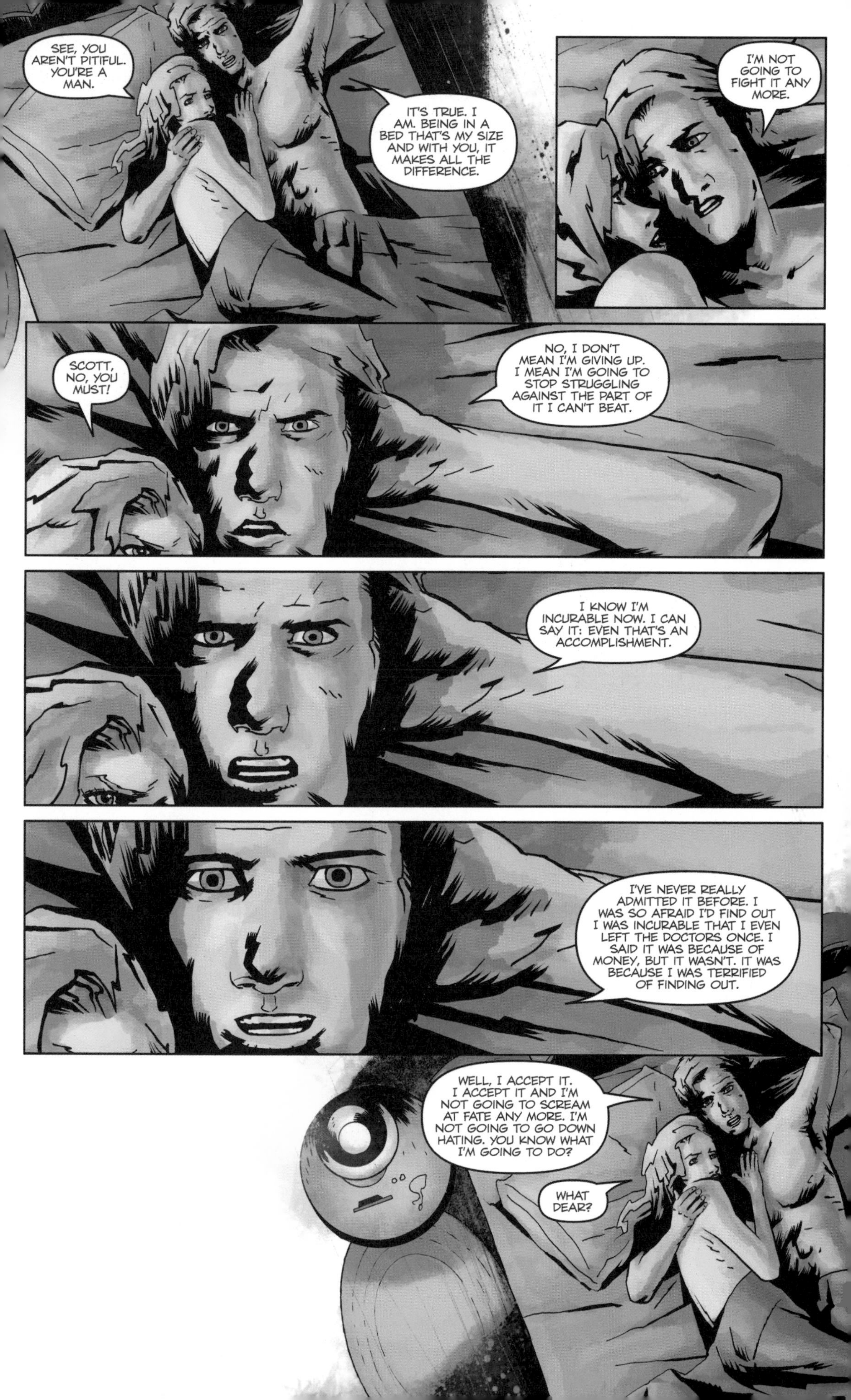
SEE, YOU AREN'T PITIFUL. YOU'RE A MAN.
IT'S TRUE. I AM. BEING IN A BED THAT'S MY SIZE AND WITH YOU, IT MAKES ALL THE DIFFERENCE.
I'M NOT GOING TO FIGHT IT ANY MORE.
SCOTT, NO, YOU MUST!
NO, I DON'T MEAN I'M GIVING UP. I MEAN I'M GOING TO STOP STRUGGLING AGAINST THE PART OF IT I CAN'T BEAT.
I KNOW I'M INCURABLE NOW. I CAN SAY IT: EVEN THAT'S AN ACCOMPLISHMENT.
I'VE NEVER REALLY ADMITTED IT BEFORE. I WAS SO AFRAID I'D FIND OUT I WAS INCURABLE THAT I EVEN LEFT THE DOCTORS ONCE. I SAID IT WAS BECAUSE OF MONEY, BUT IT WASN'T. IT WAS BECAUSE I WAS TERRIFIED OF FINDING OUT.
WELL, I ACCEPT IT. I ACCEPT IT AND I'M NOT GOING TO SCREAM AT FATE ANY MORE. I'M NOT GOING TO GO DOWN HATING. YOU KNOW WHAT I'M GOING TO DO?
WHAT DEAR?

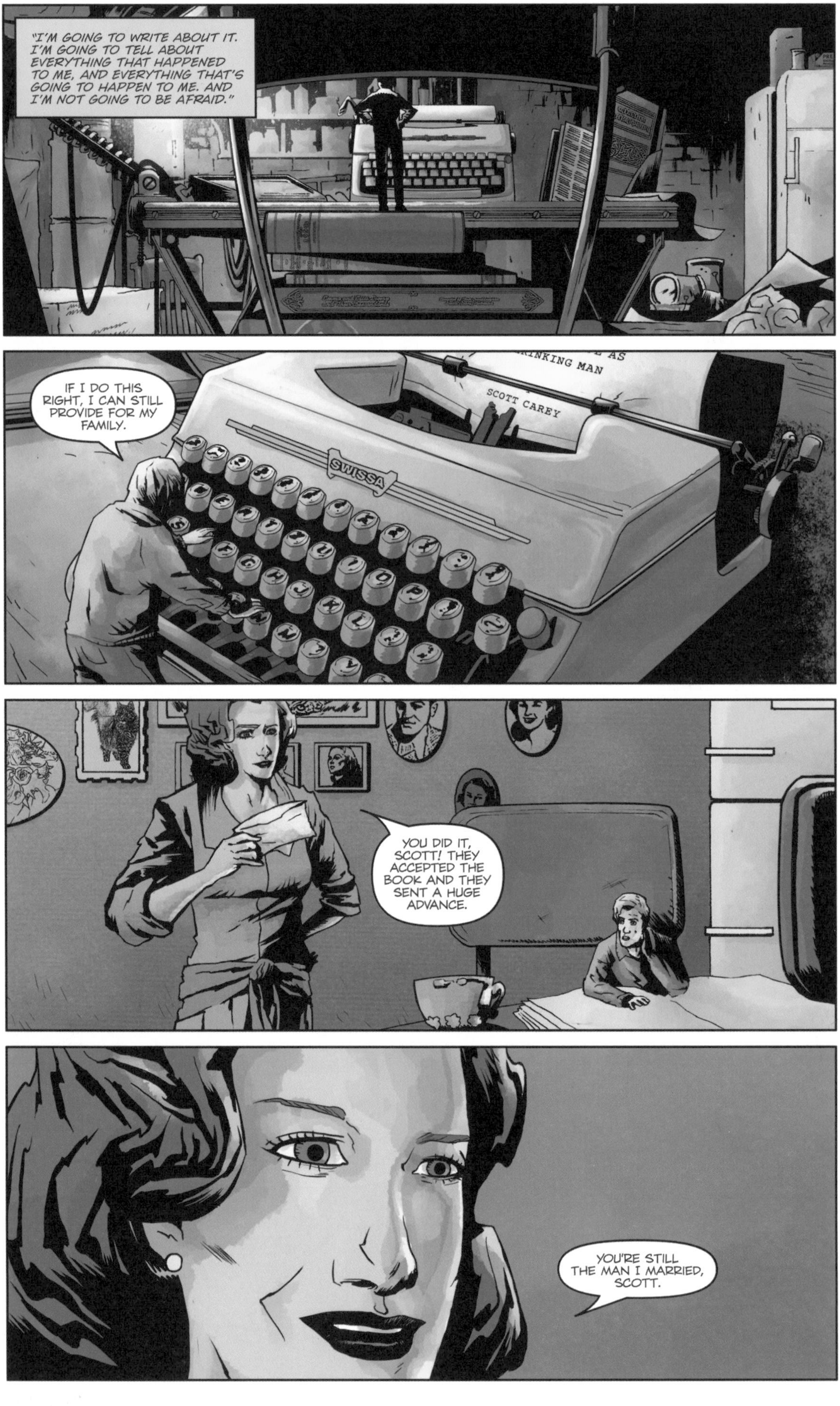
"I'M GOING TO WRITE ABOUT IT. I'M GOING TO TELL ABOUT EVERYTHING THAT HAPPENED TO ME, AND EVERYTHING THAT'S GOING TO HAPPEN TO ME. AND I'M NOT GOING TO BE AFRAID."
SCOTT CAREY
SWISSA
IF I DO THIS RIGHT, I CAN STILL PROVIDE FOR MY FAMILY.
YOU DID IT, SCOTT! THEY ACCEPTED THE BOOK AND THEY SENT A HUGE ADVANCE.
YOU'RE STILL THE MAN I MARRIED, SCOTT.

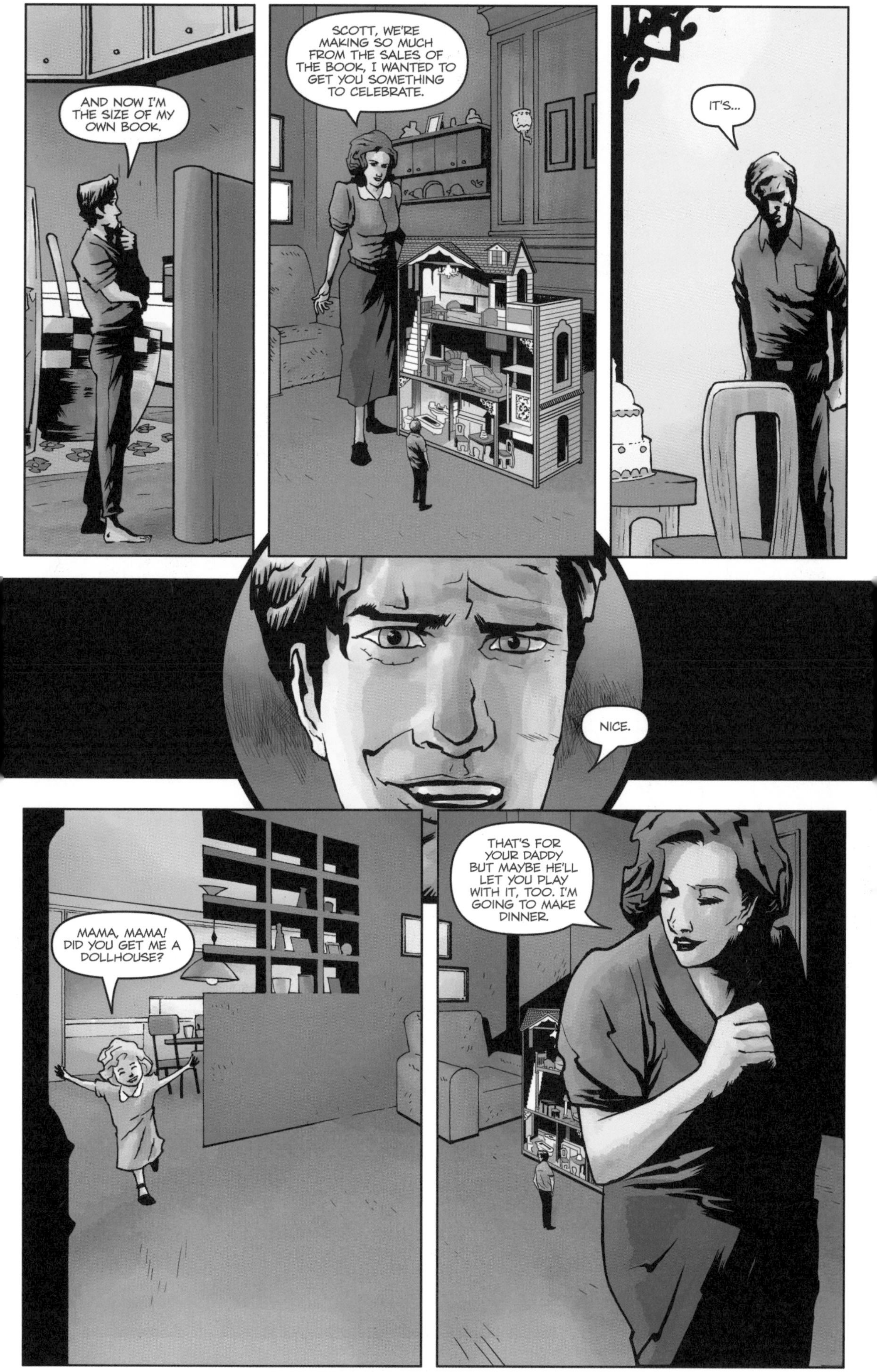

AND NOW I'M THE SIZE OF MY OWN BOOK.
SCOTT, WE'RE MAKING SO MUCH FROM THE SALES OF THE BOOK, I WANTED TO GET YOU SOMETHING TO CELEBRATE.
IT'S...
NICE.
MAMA, MAMA! DID YOU GET ME A DOLLHOUSE?
THAT'S FOR YOUR DADDY BUT MAYBE HE'LL LET YOU PLAY WITH IT, TOO. I'M GOING TO MAKE DINNER.

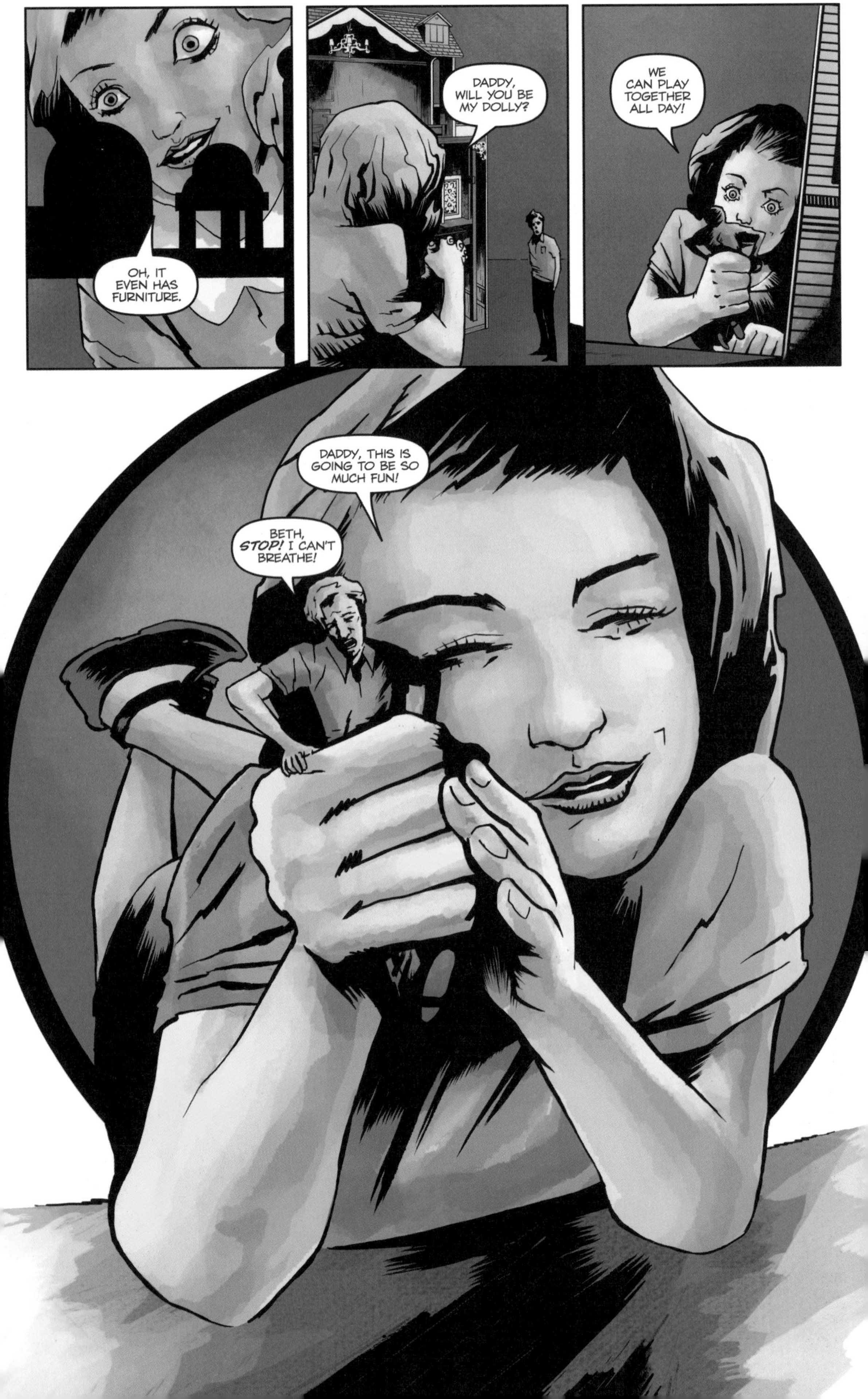
OH, IT EVEN HAS FURNITURE.
DADDY, WILL YOU BE MY DOLLY?
WE CAN PLAY TOGETHER ALL DAY!
DADDY, THIS IS GOING TO BE SO MUCH FUN!
BETH, STOP! I CAN'T BREATHE!

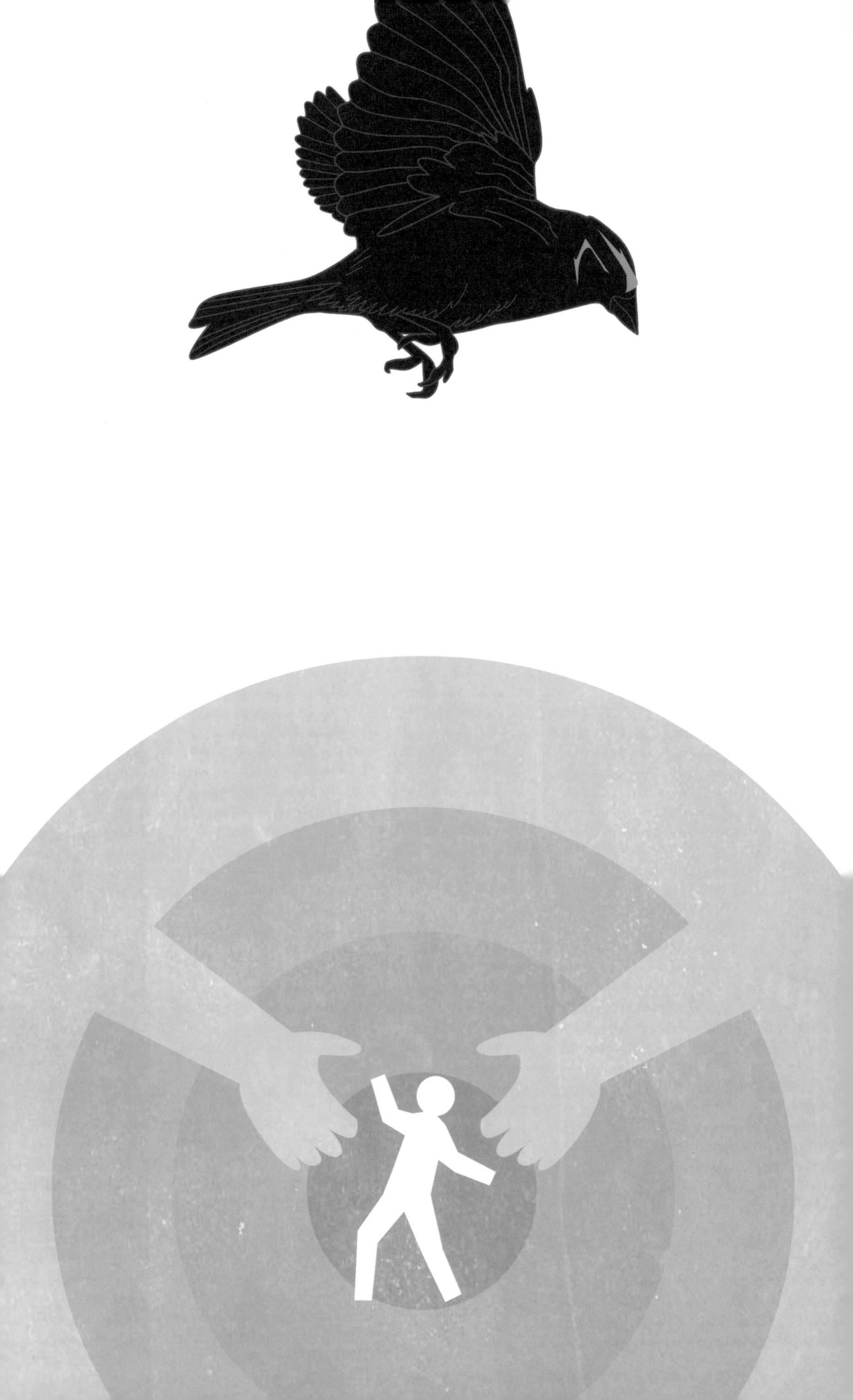

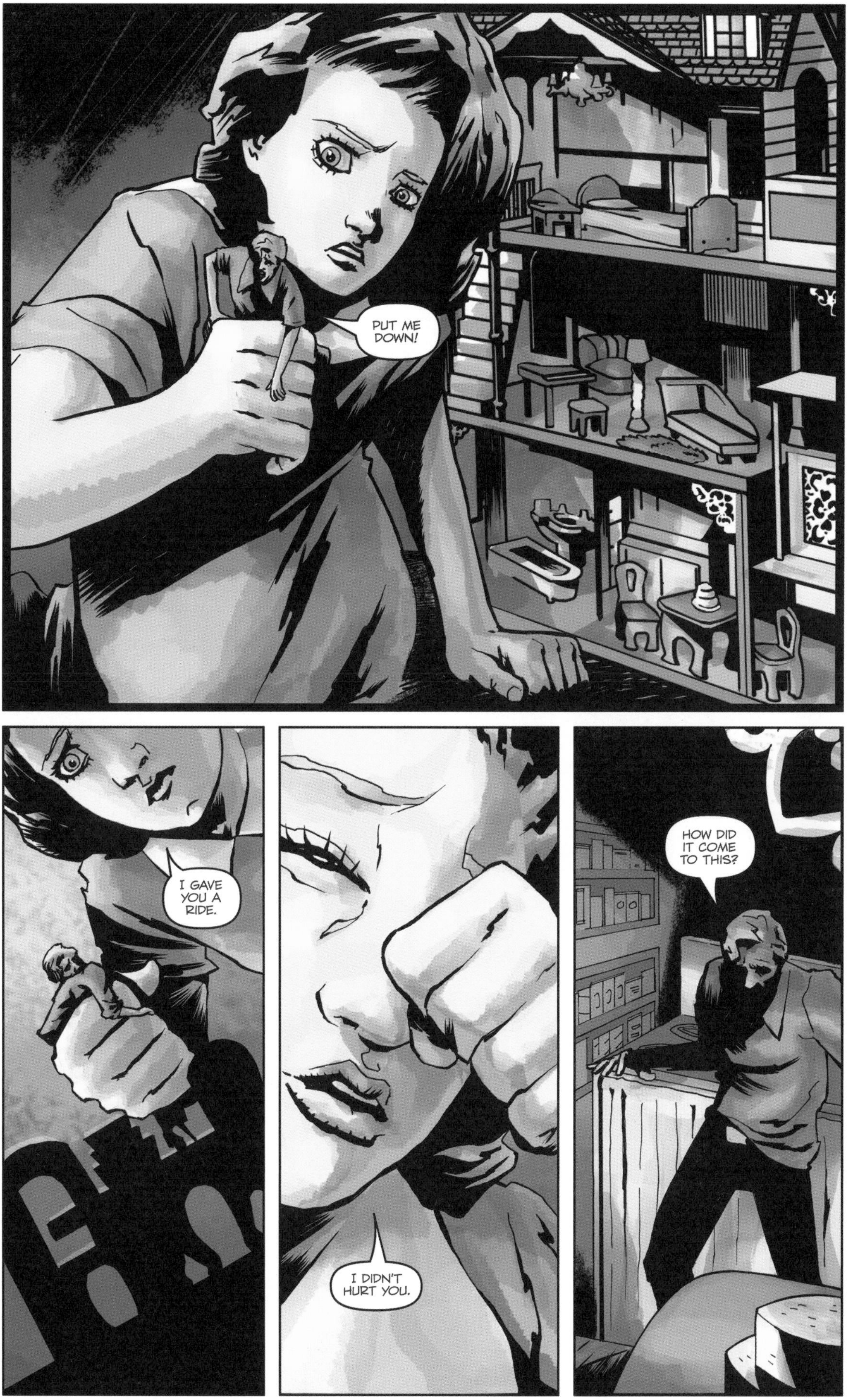
PUT ME DOWN!
I GAVE YOU A RIDE.
I DIDN'T HURT YOU.
HOW DID IT COME TO THIS?

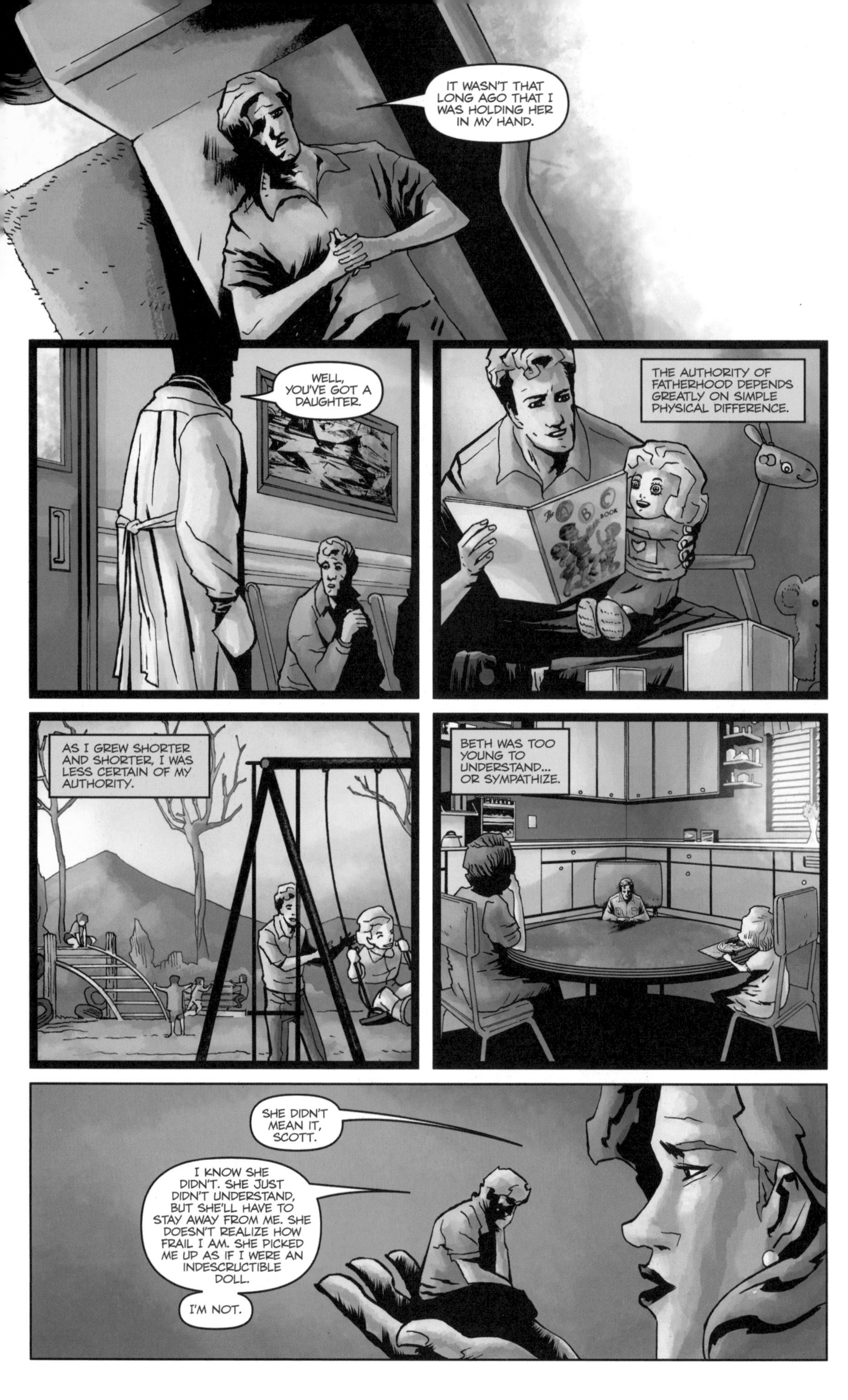
IT WASN'T THAT LONG AGO THAT I WAS HOLDING HER IN MY HAND.
WELL, YOU'VE GOT A DAUGHTER.
THE AUTHORITY OF FATHERHOOD DEPENDS GREATLY ON SIMPLE PHYSICAL DIFFERENCE.
The ABC BOOK
AS I GREW SHORTER AND SHORTER, I WAS LESS CERTAIN OF MY AUTHORITY.
BETH WAS TOO YOUNG TO UNDERSTAND... OR SYMPATHIZE.
SHE DIDN'T MEAN IT, SCOTT.
I KNOW SHE DIDN'T. SHE JUST DIDN'T UNDERSTAND, BUT SHE'LL HAVE TO STAY AWAY FROM ME. SHE DOESN'T REALIZE HOW FRAIL I AM. SHE PICKED ME UP AS IF I WERE AN INDESCRUCTIBLE DOLL.
I'M NOT.

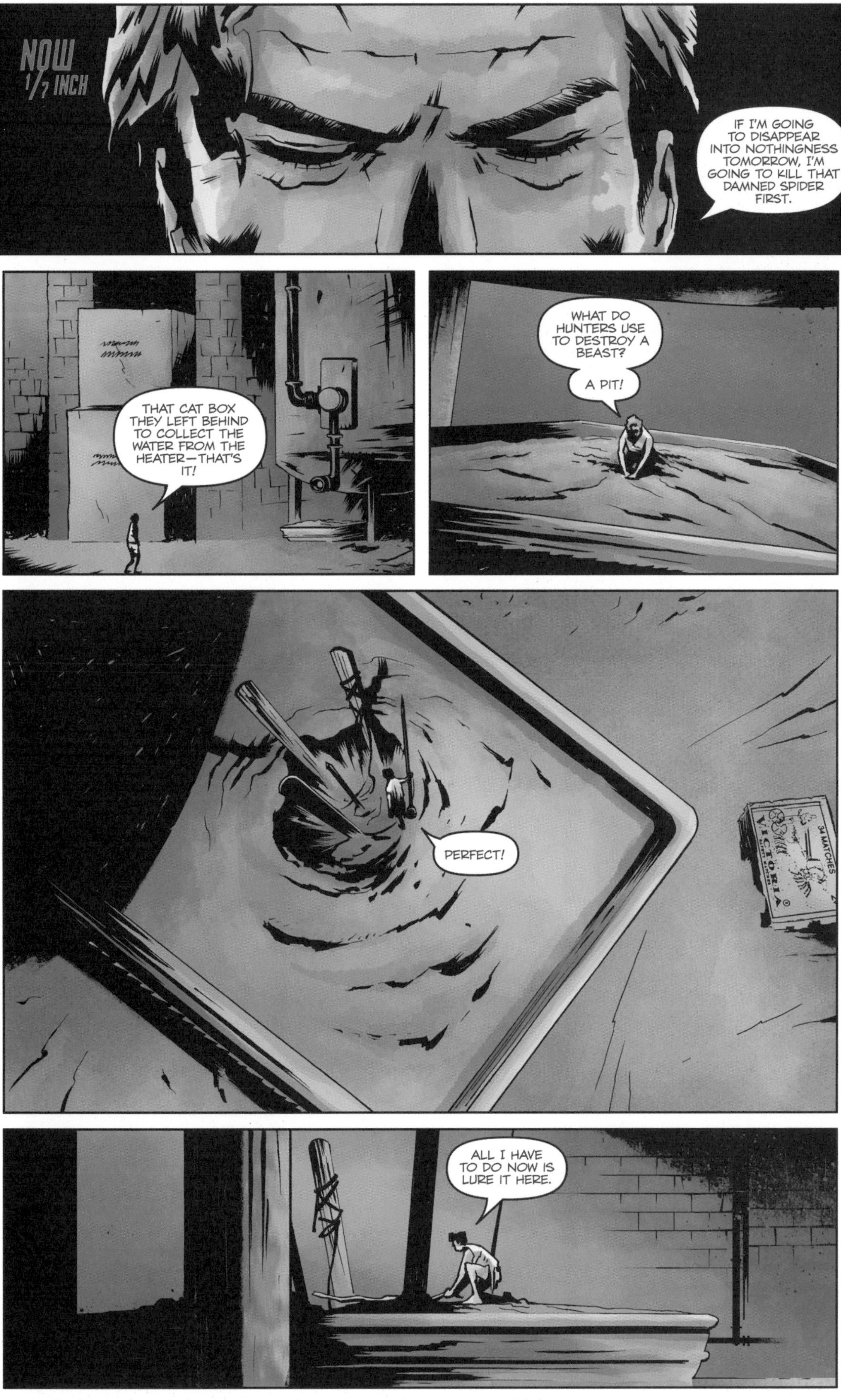
NOW
1/7 INCH
IF I'M GOING TO DISAPPEAR INTO NOTHINGNESS TOMORROW, I'M GOING TO KILL THAT DAMNED SPIDER FIRST.
THAT CAT BOX THEY LEFT BEHIND TO COLLECT THE WATER FROM THE HEATER—THAT'S IT!
WHAT DO HUNTERS USE TO DESTROY A BEAST?
A PIT!
PERFECT!
34 MATCHES
VICTORIA
ALL I HAVE TO DO NOW IS LURE IT HERE.

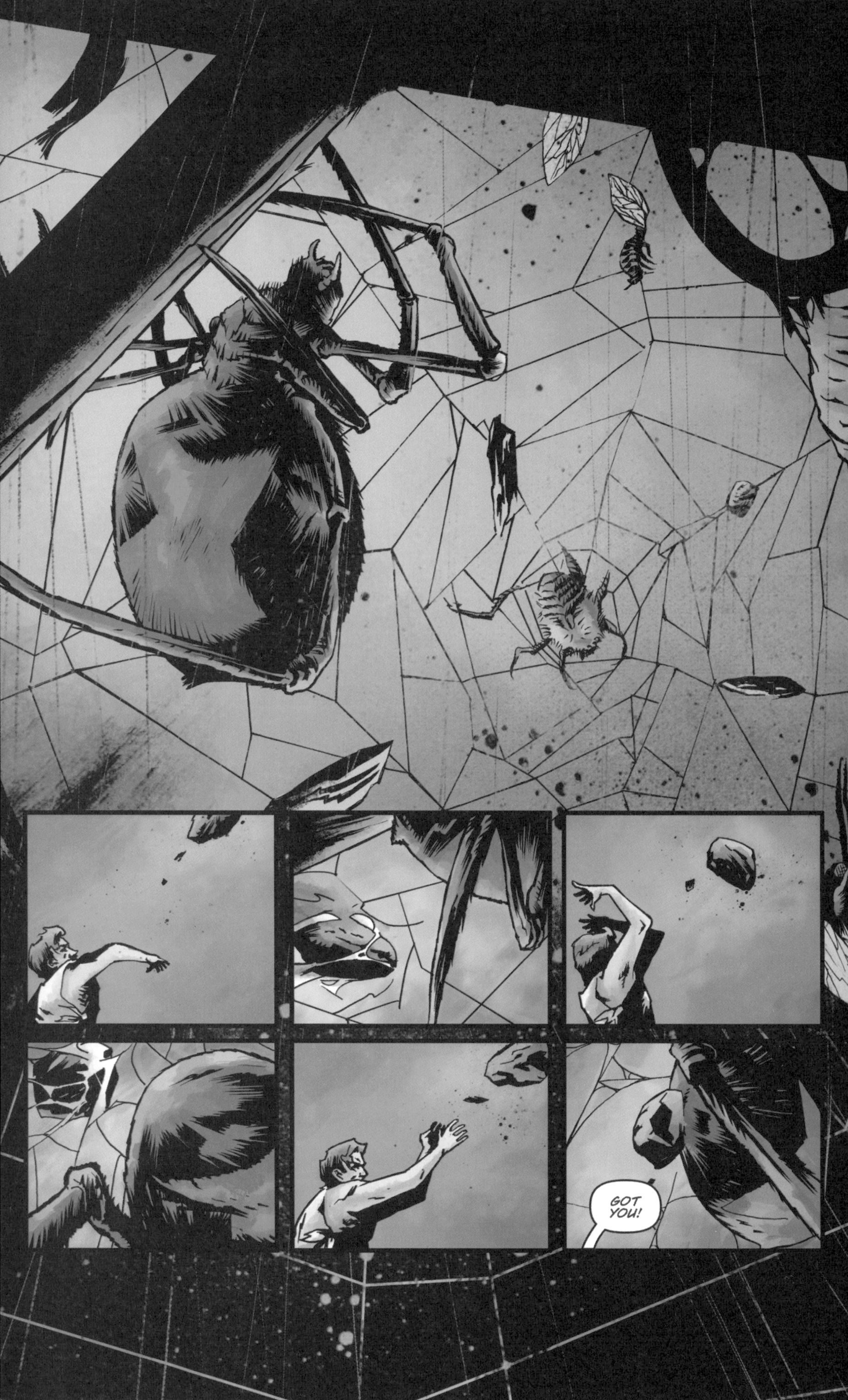
GOT YOU!

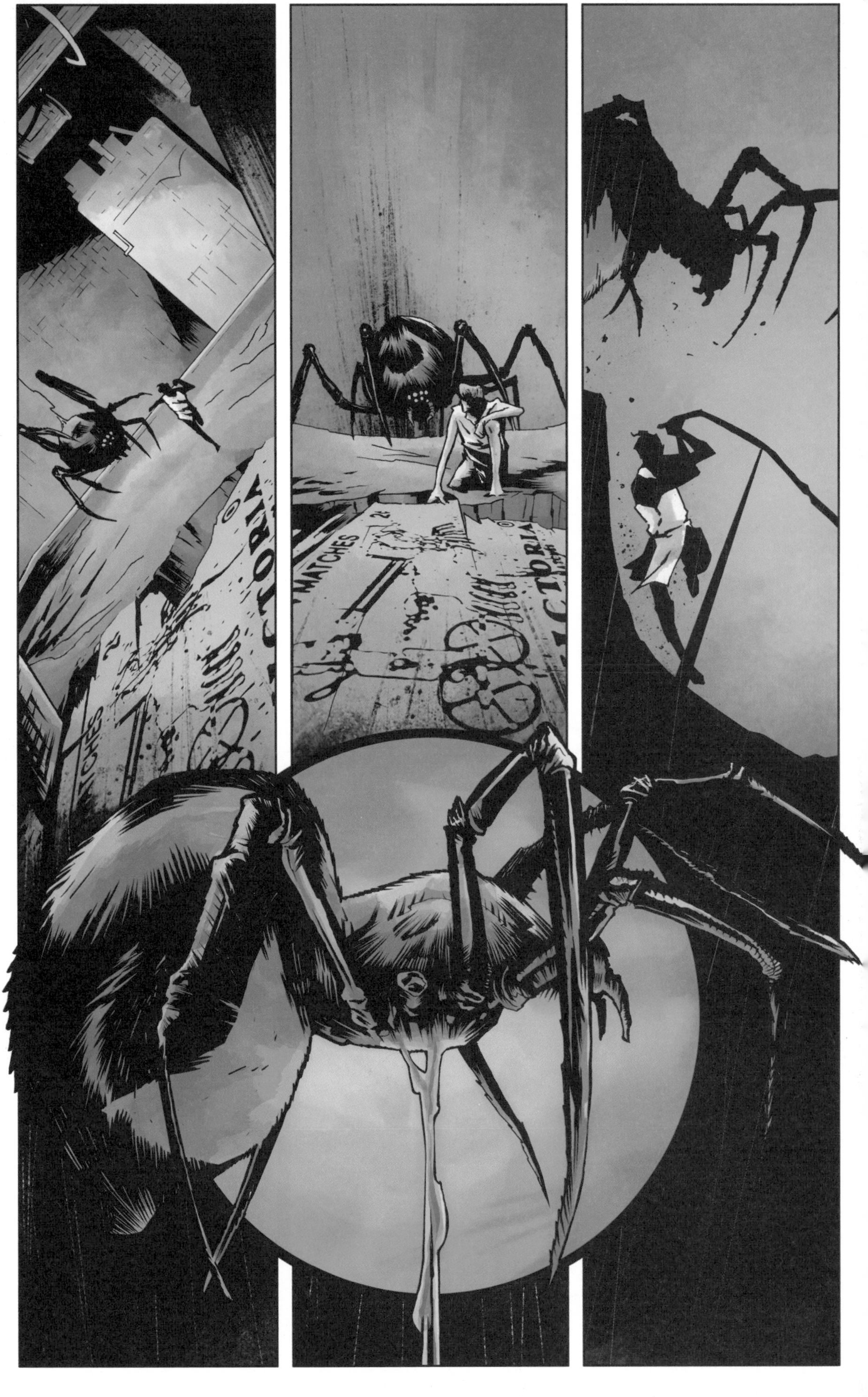
MATCHES
VICTORIA

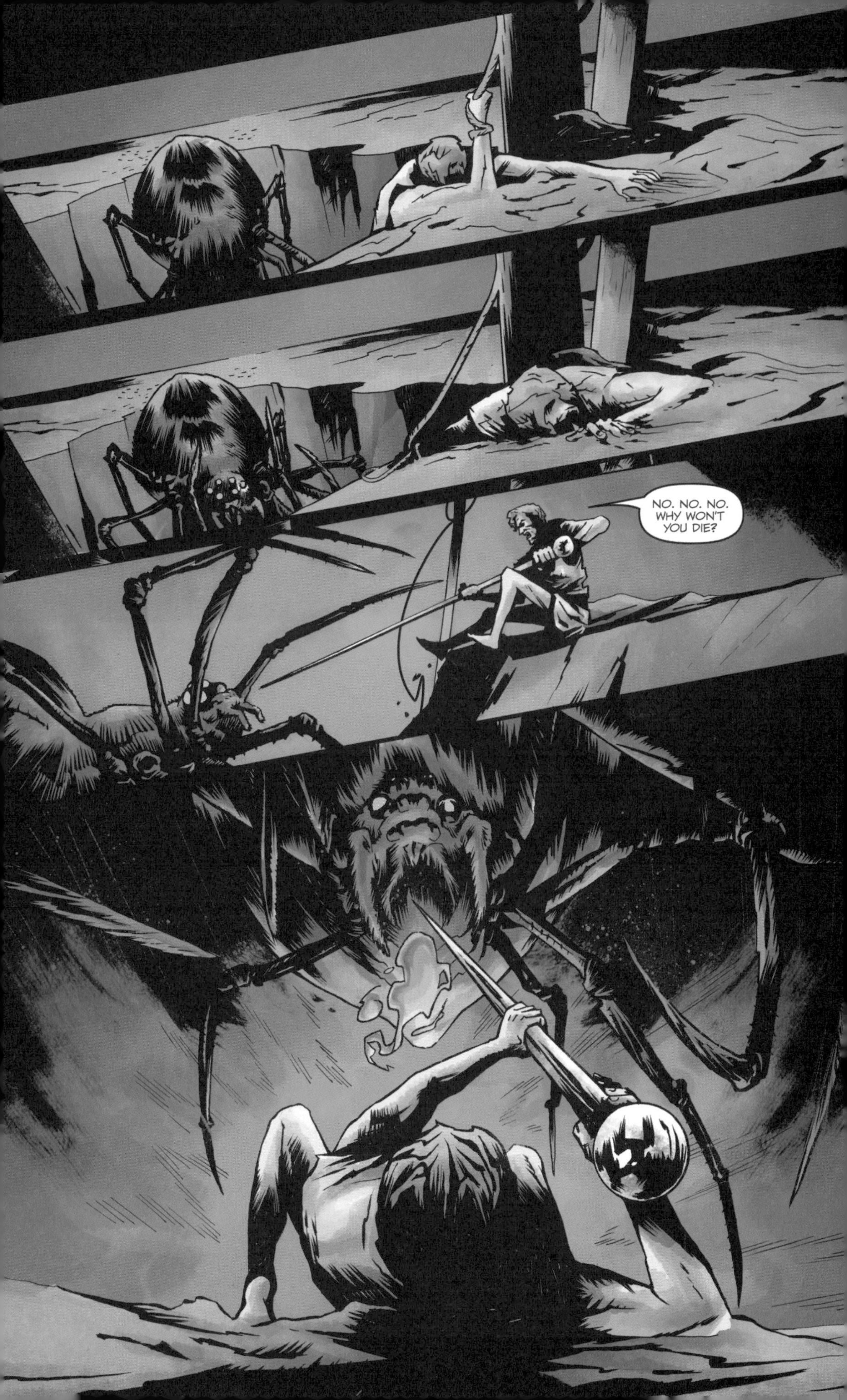
NO. NO. NO. WHY WON'T YOU DIE?

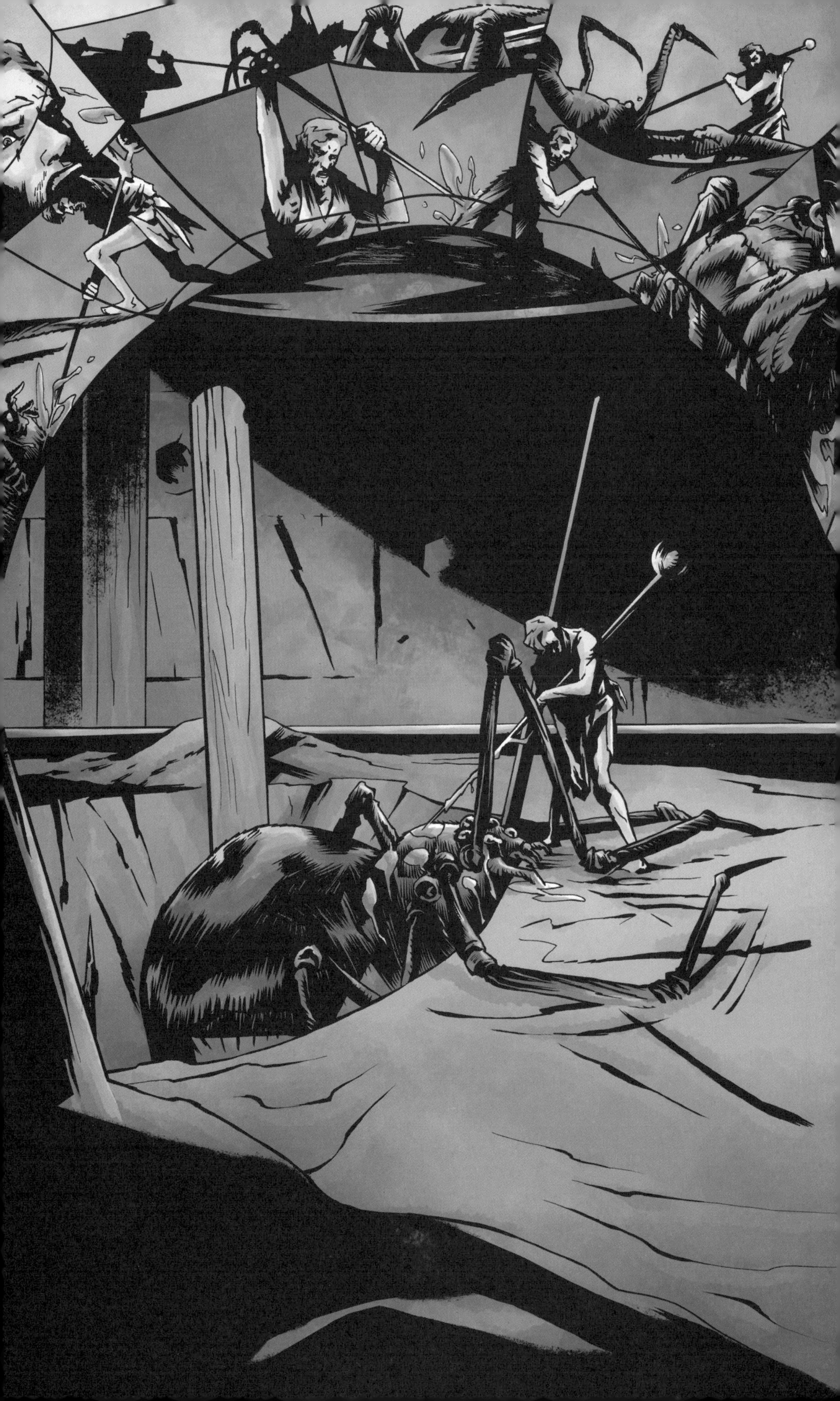

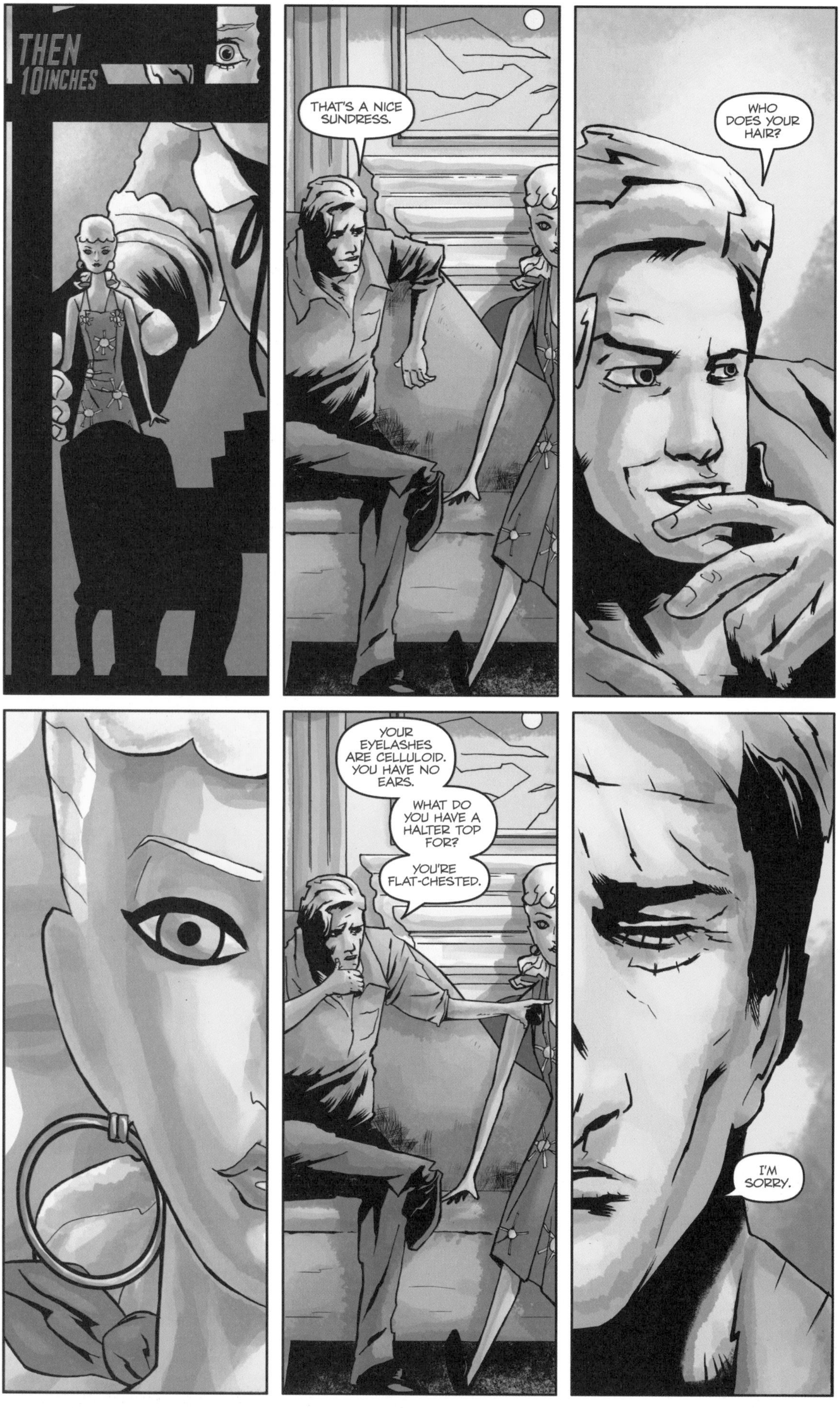
THEN
10 INCHES
THAT'S A NICE SUNDRESS.
WHO DOES YOUR HAIR?
YOUR EYELASHES ARE CELLULOID. YOU HAVE NO EARS.
WHAT DO YOU HAVE A HALTER TOP FOR?
YOU'RE FLAT-CHESTED.
I'M SORRY.

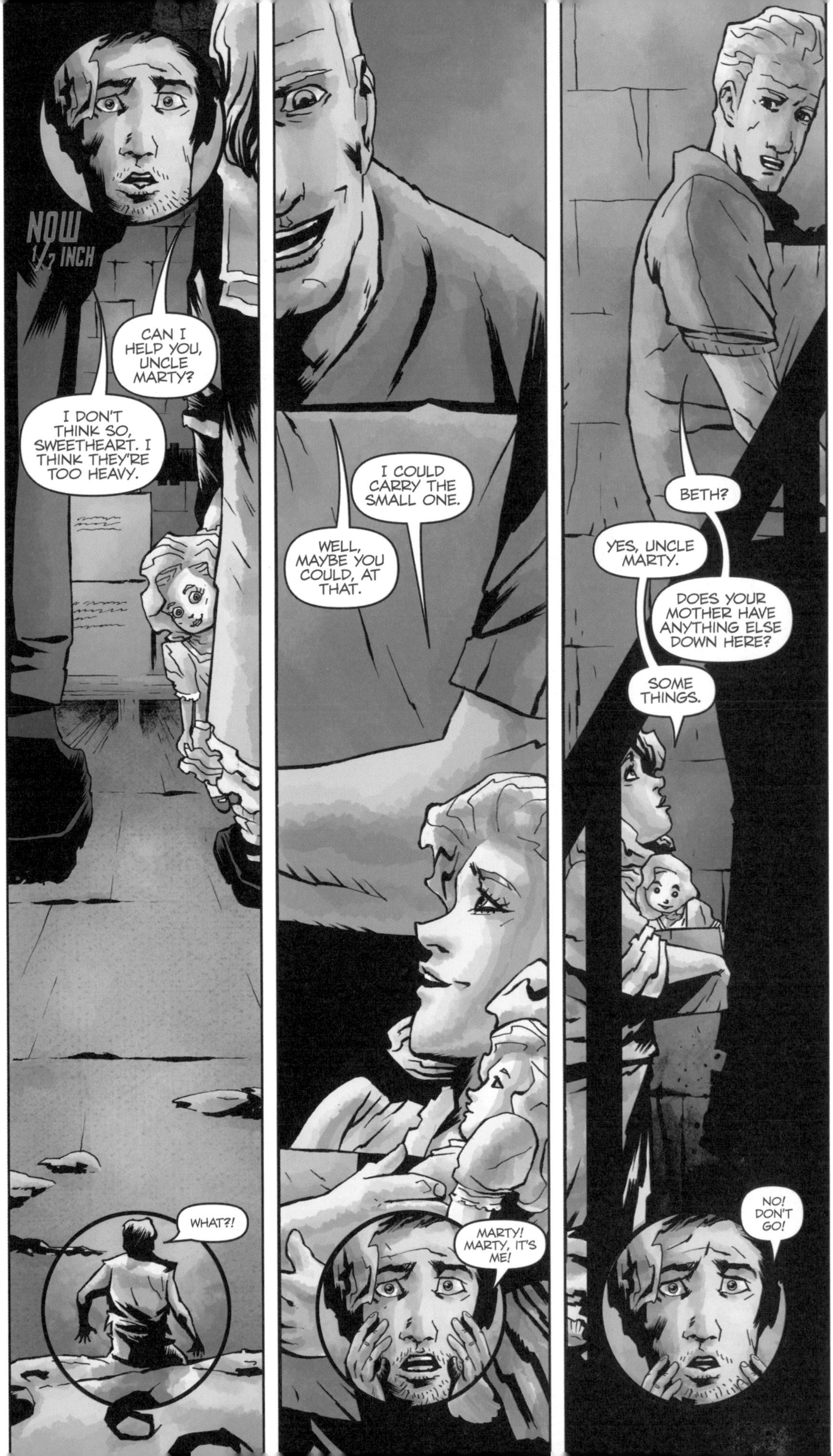
NOW
1/2 INCH
CAN I HELP YOU, UNCLE MARTY?
I DON'T THINK SO, SWEETHEART. I THINK THEY'RE TOO HEAVY.
WHAT?!
I COULD CARRY THE SMALL ONE.
WELL, MAYBE YOU COULD, AT THAT.
MARTY! MARTY, IT'S ME!
BETH?
YES, UNCLE MARTY.
DOES YOUR MOTHER HAVE ANYTHING ELSE DOWN HERE?
SOME THINGS.
NO! DON'T GO!

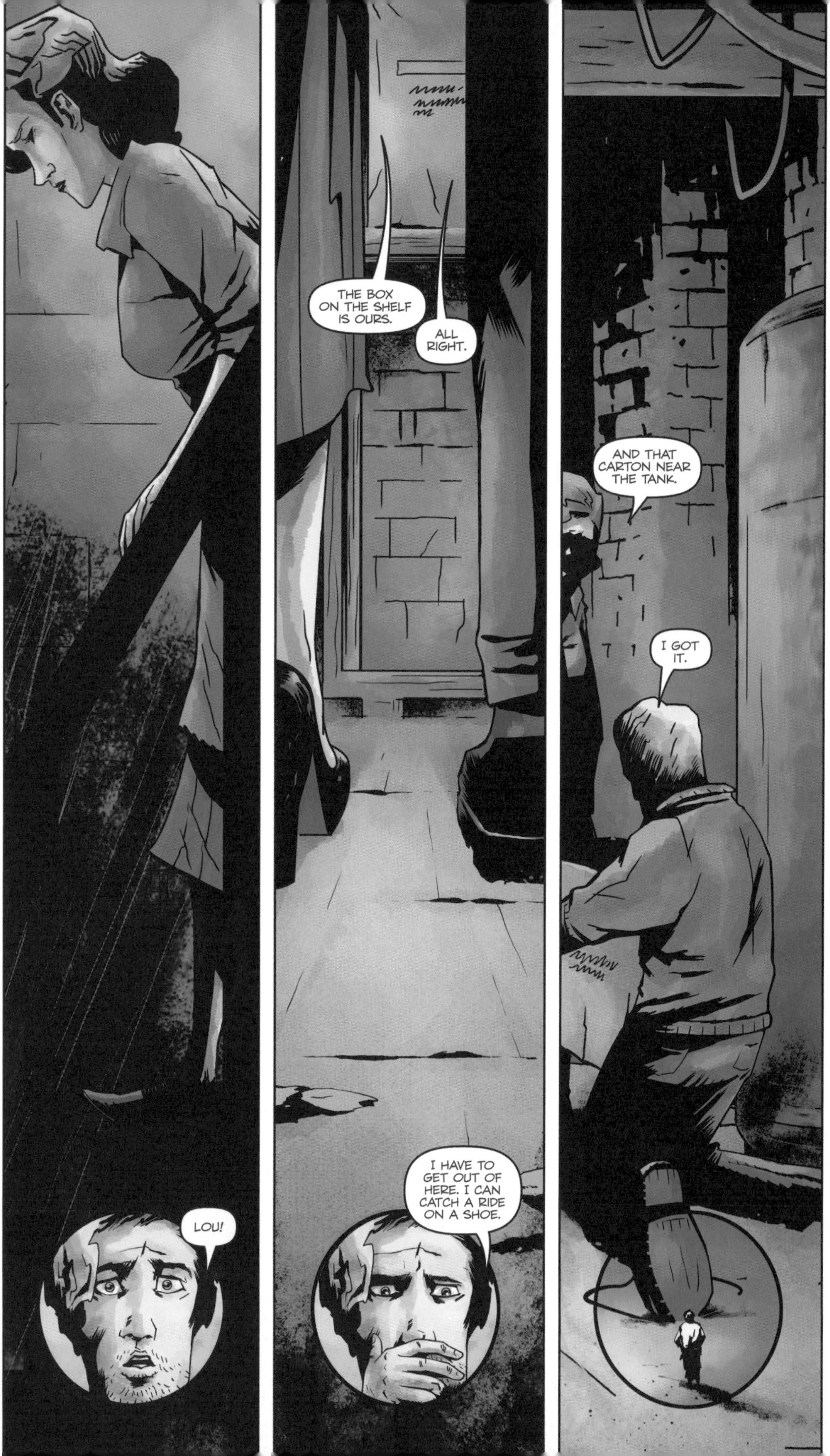
LOU!
THE BOX ON THE SHELF IS OURS.
ALL RIGHT.
I HAVE TO GET OUT OF HERE. I CAN CATCH A RIDE ON A SHOE.
AND THAT CARTON NEAR THE TANK.
I GOT IT.

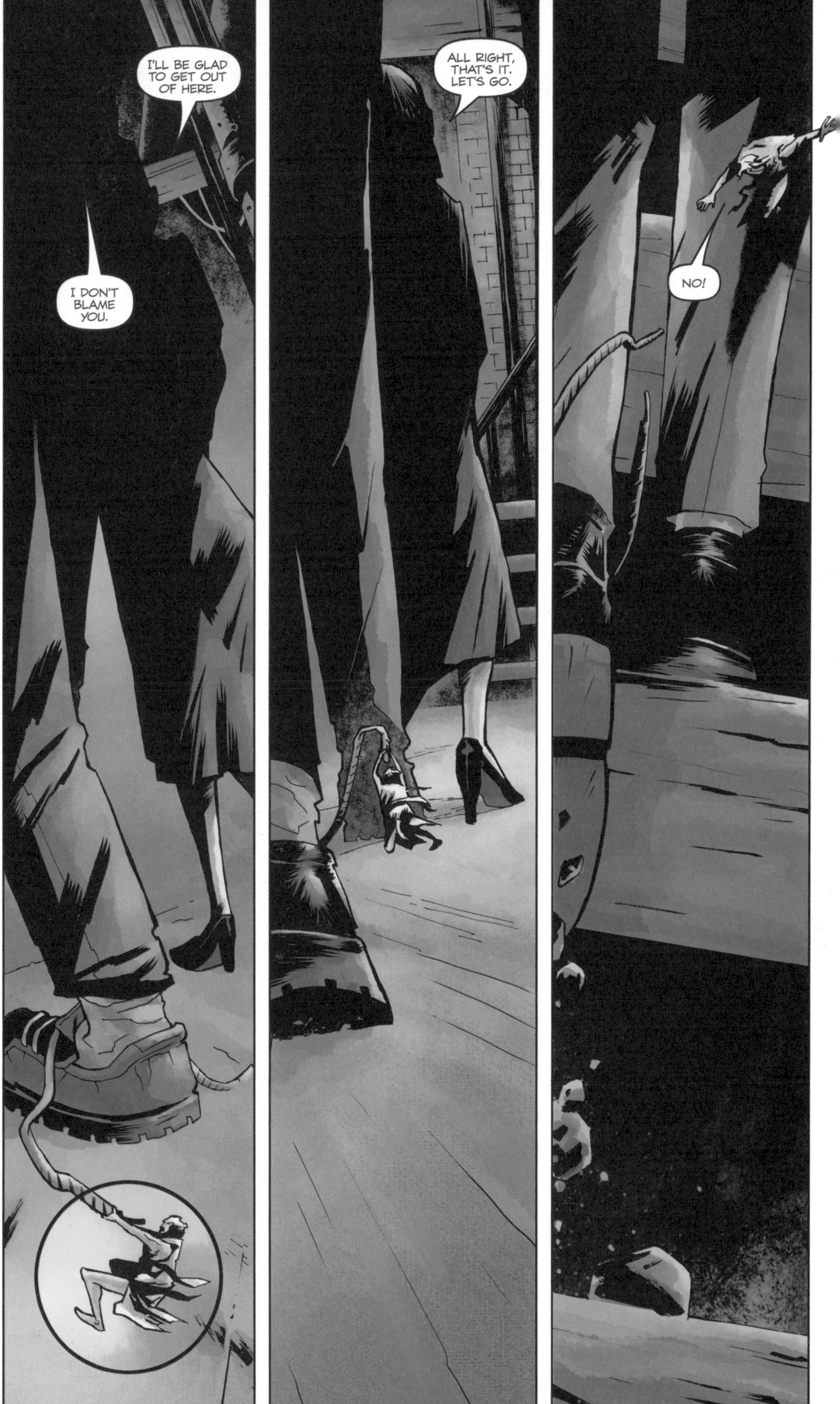
I'LL BE GLAD TO GET OUT OF HERE.
I DON'T BLAME YOU.
ALL RIGHT, THAT'S IT. LET'S GO.
NO!

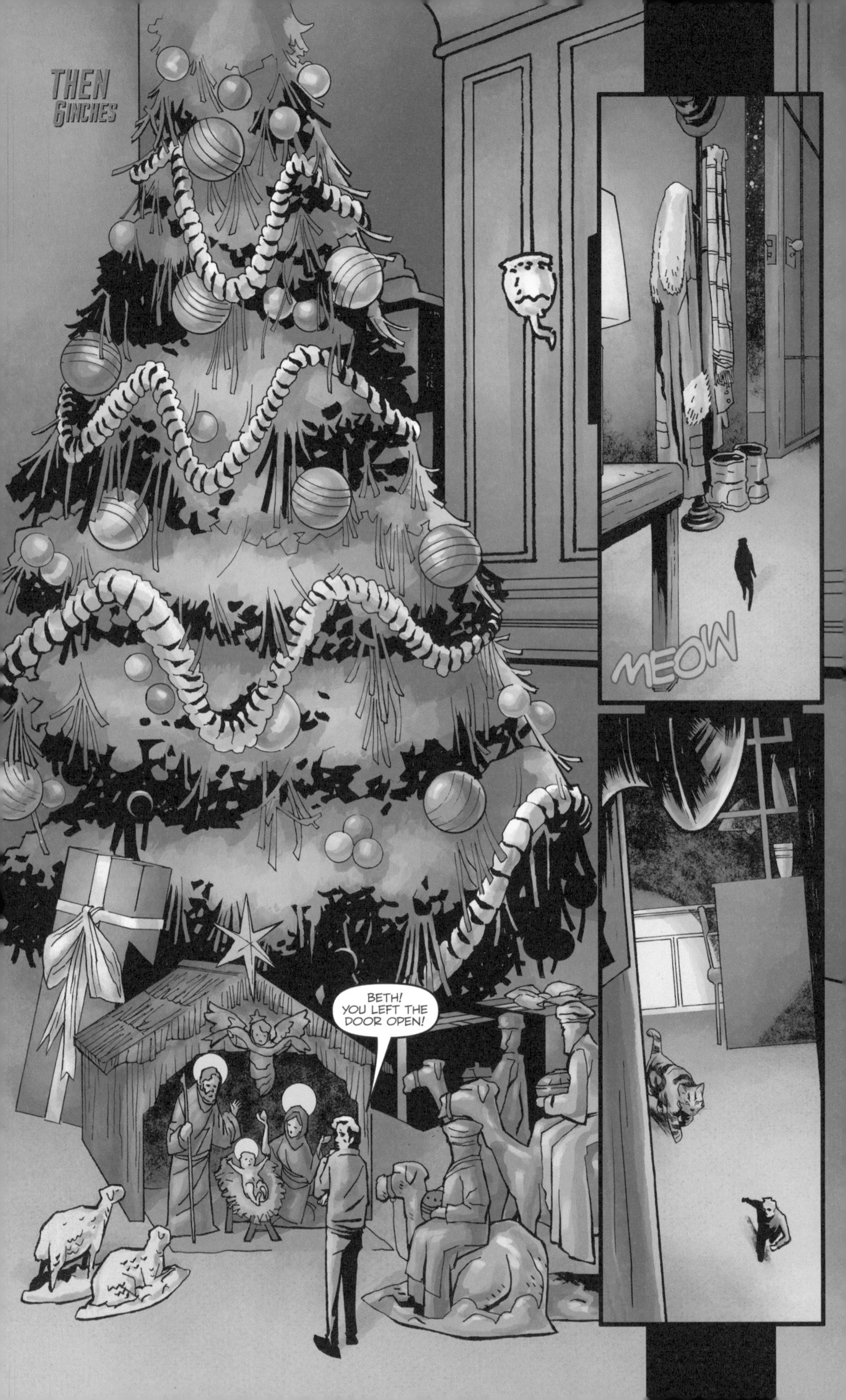
THEN
6 INCHES
BETH! YOU LEFT THE DOOR OPEN!
MEOW

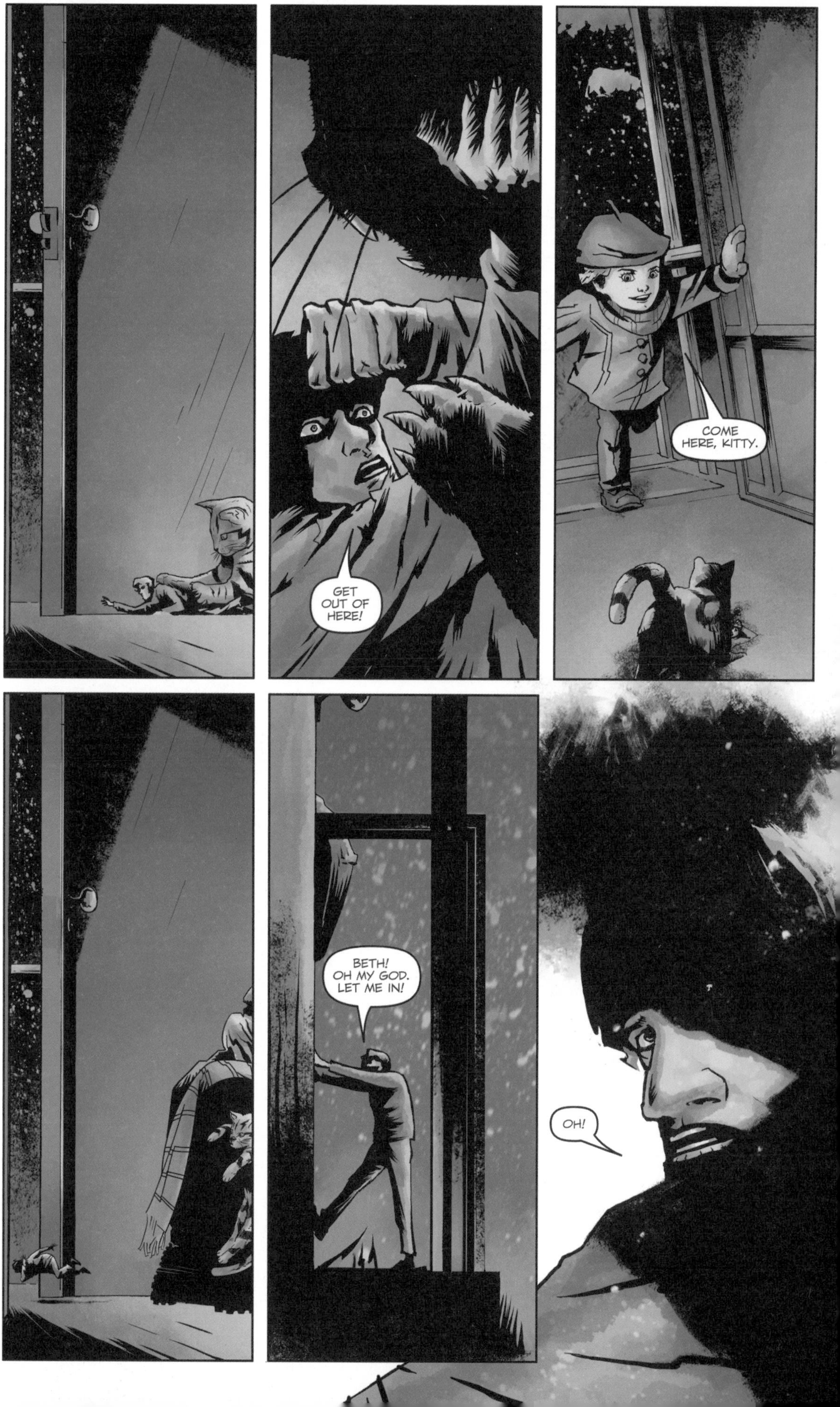
GET OUT OF HERE!
COME HERE, KITTY.
BETH! OH MY GOD. LET ME IN!
OH!

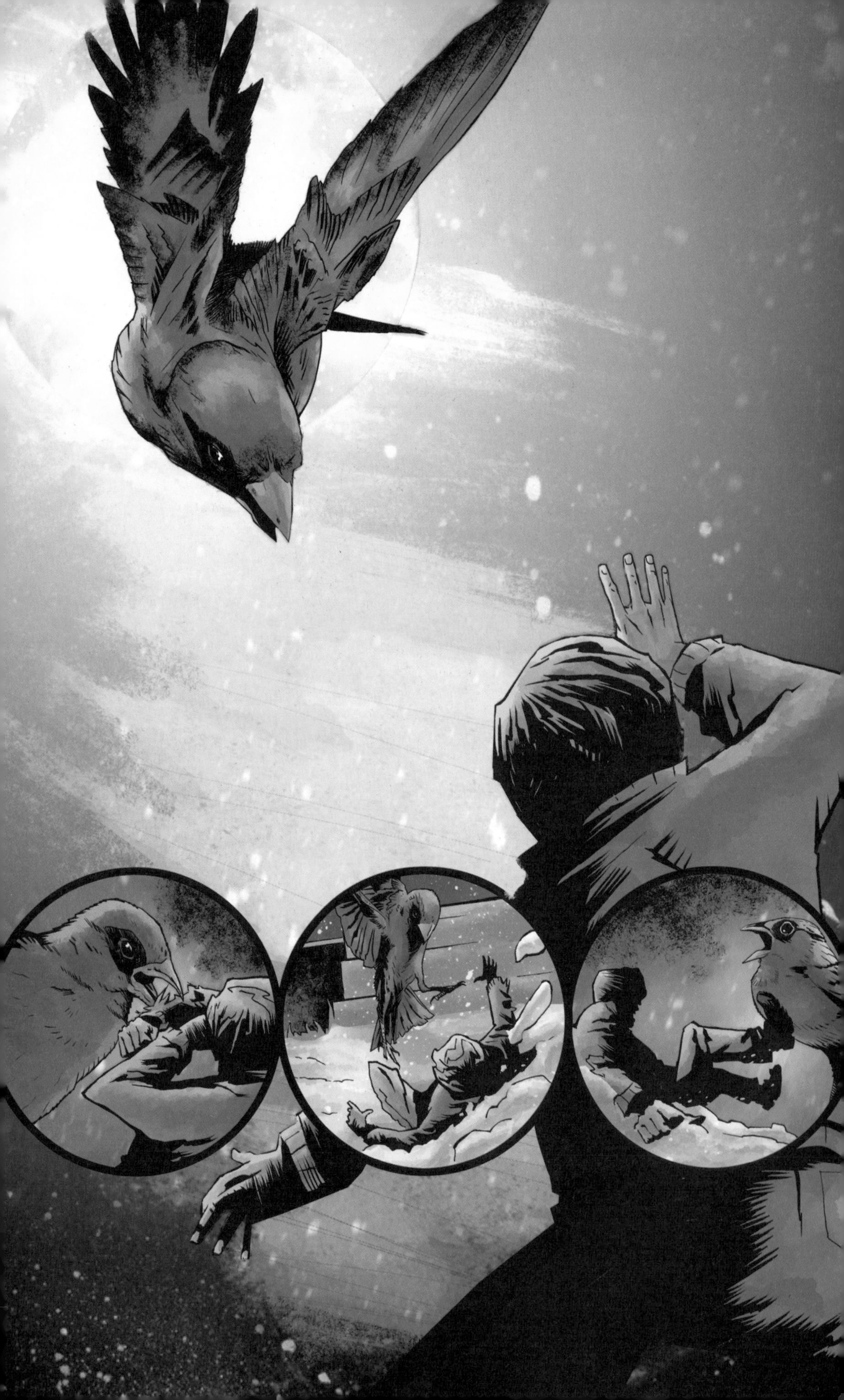

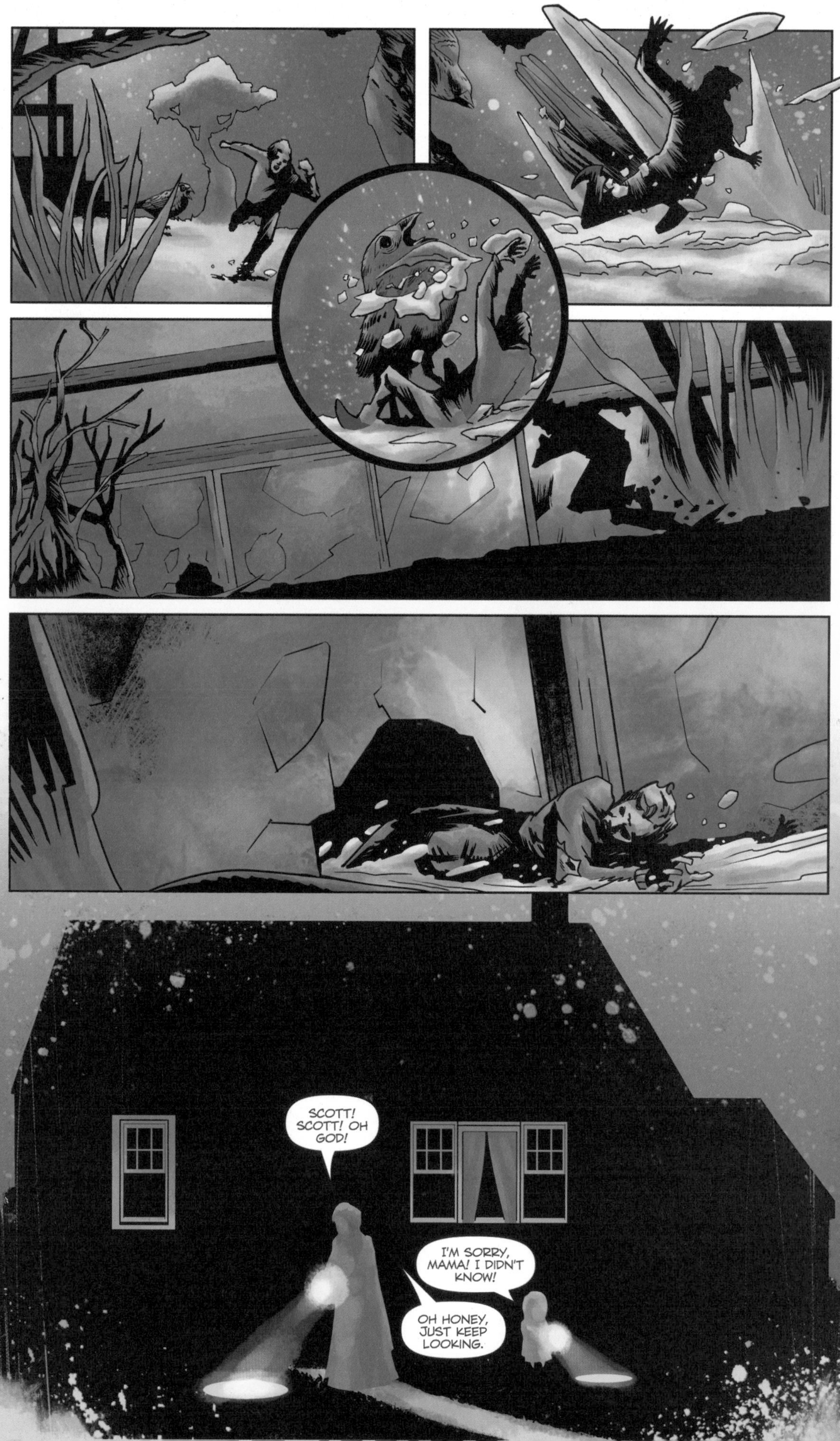
SCOTT! SCOTT! OH GOD!
I'M SORRY, MAMA! I DIDN'T KNOW!
OH HONEY, JUST KEEP LOOKING.

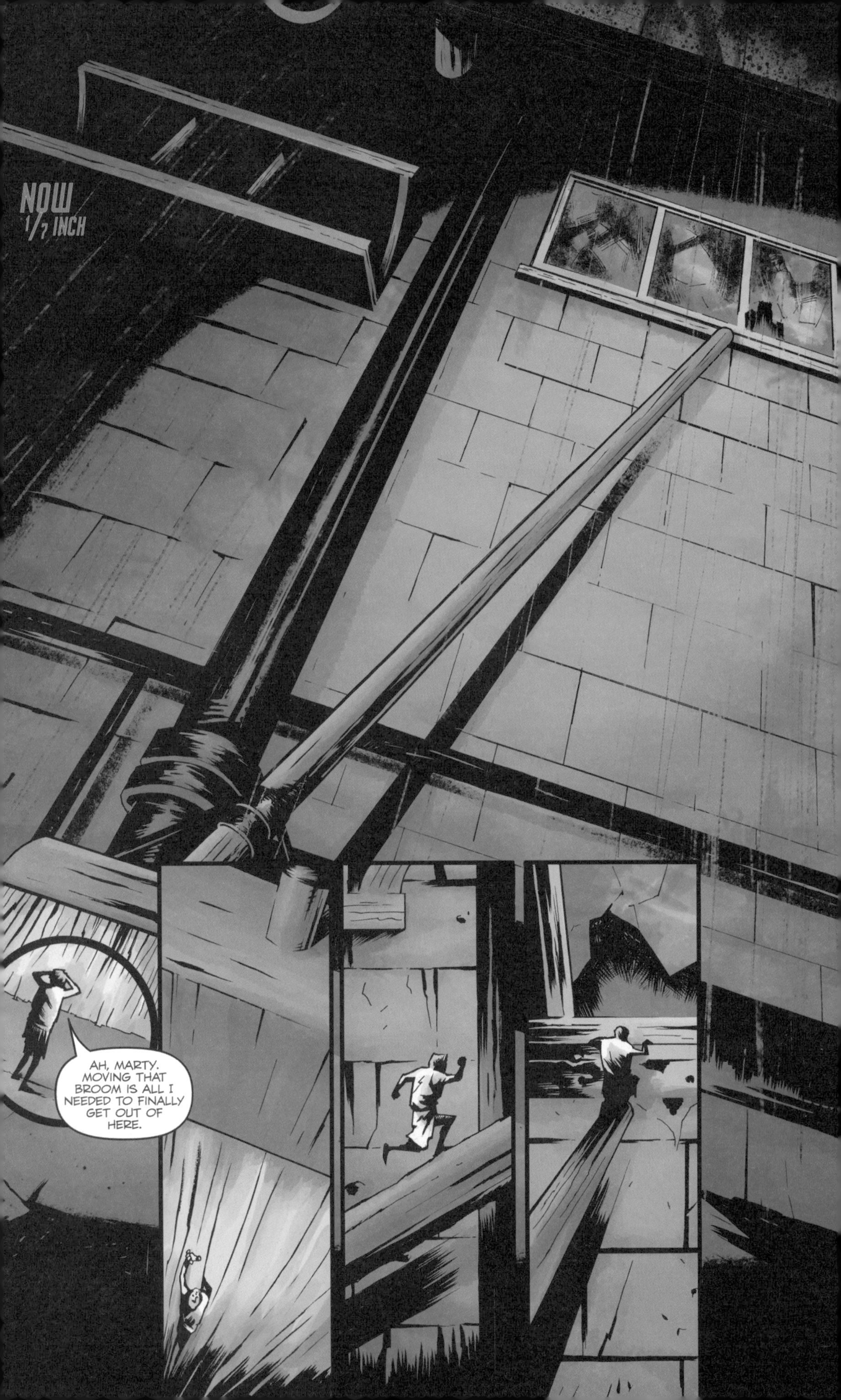
NOW
1/7 INCH
AH, MARTY. MOVING THAT BROOM IS ALL I NEEDED TO FINALLY GET OUT OF HERE.

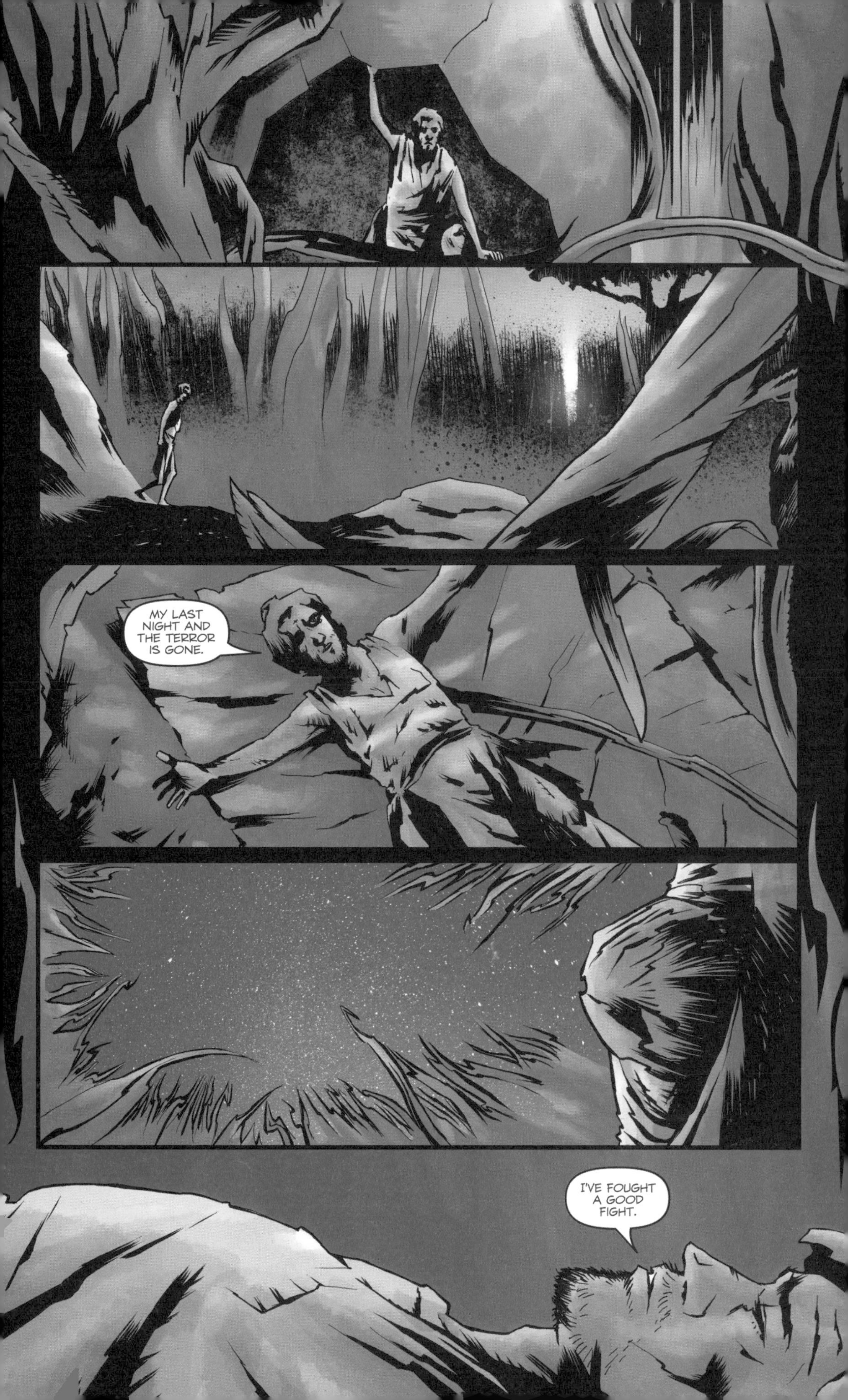
MY LAST NIGHT AND THE TERROR IS GONE.
I'VE FOUGHT A GOOD FIGHT.

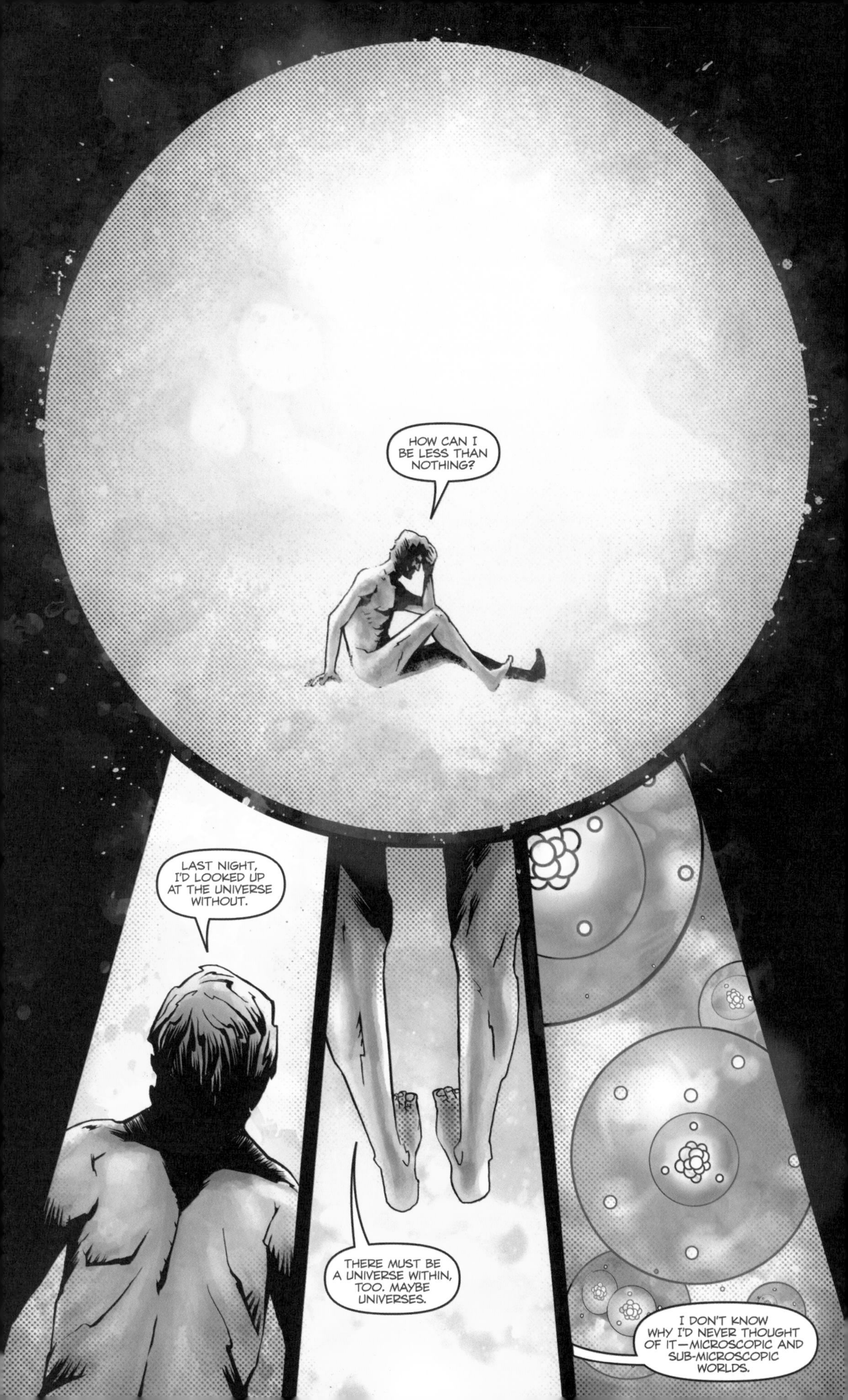
HOW CAN I BE LESS THAN NOTHING?
LAST NIGHT, I'D LOOKED UP AT THE UNIVERSE WITHOUT.
THERE MUST BE A UNIVERSE WITHIN, TOO. MAYBE UNIVERSES.
I DON'T KNOW WHY I'D NEVER THOUGHT OF IT—MICROSCOPIC AND SUB-MICROSCOPIC WORLDS.

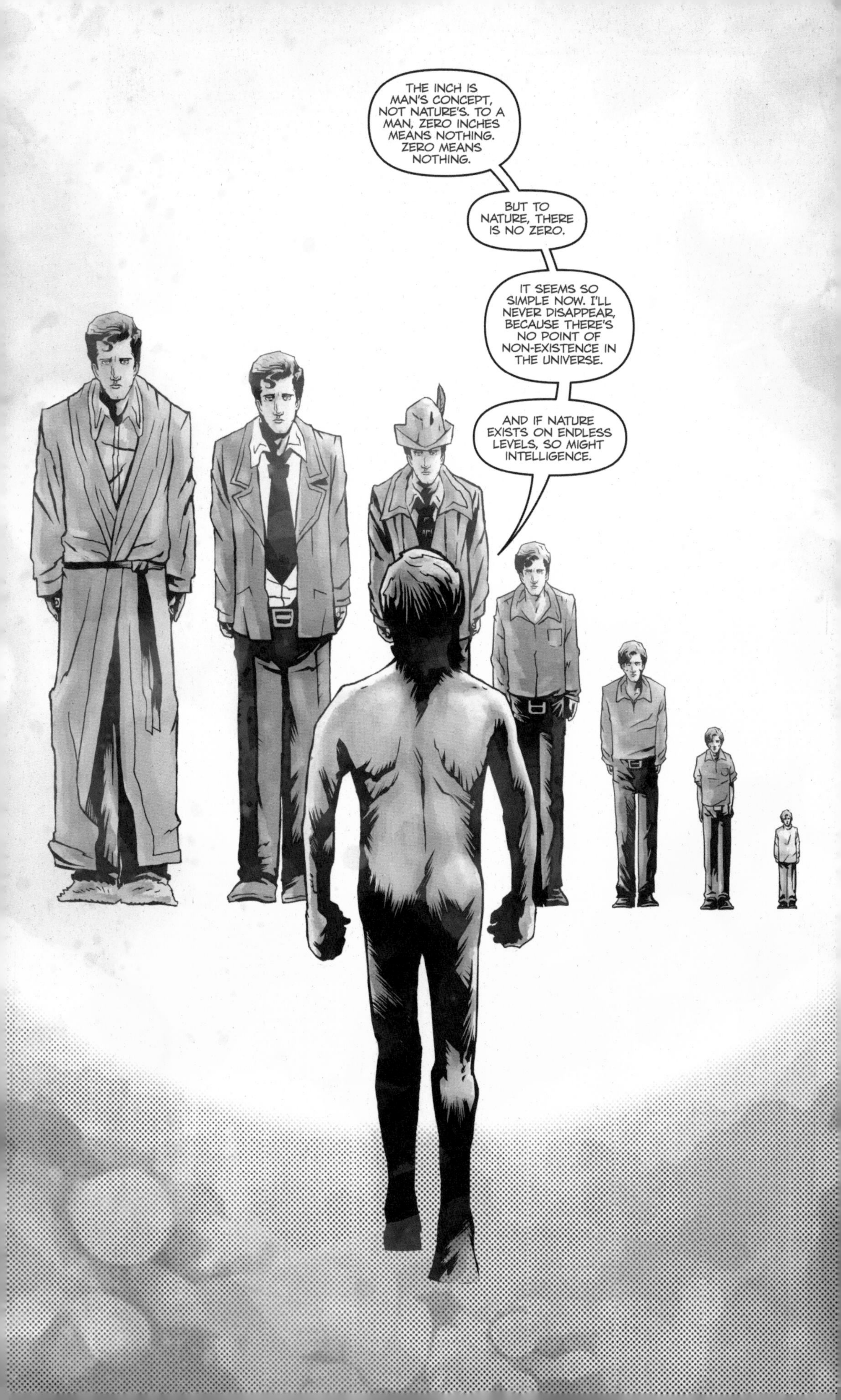
THE INCH IS MAN'S CONCEPT, NOT NATURE'S. TO A MAN, ZERO INCHES MEANS NOTHING. ZERO MEANS NOTHING.
BUT TO NATURE, THERE IS NO ZERO.
IT SEEMS SO SIMPLE NOW. I'LL NEVER DISAPPEAR, BECAUSE THERE'S NO POINT OF NON-EXISTENCE IN THE UNIVERSE.
AND IF NATURE EXISTS ON ENDLESS LEVELS, SO MIGHT INTELLIGENCE.

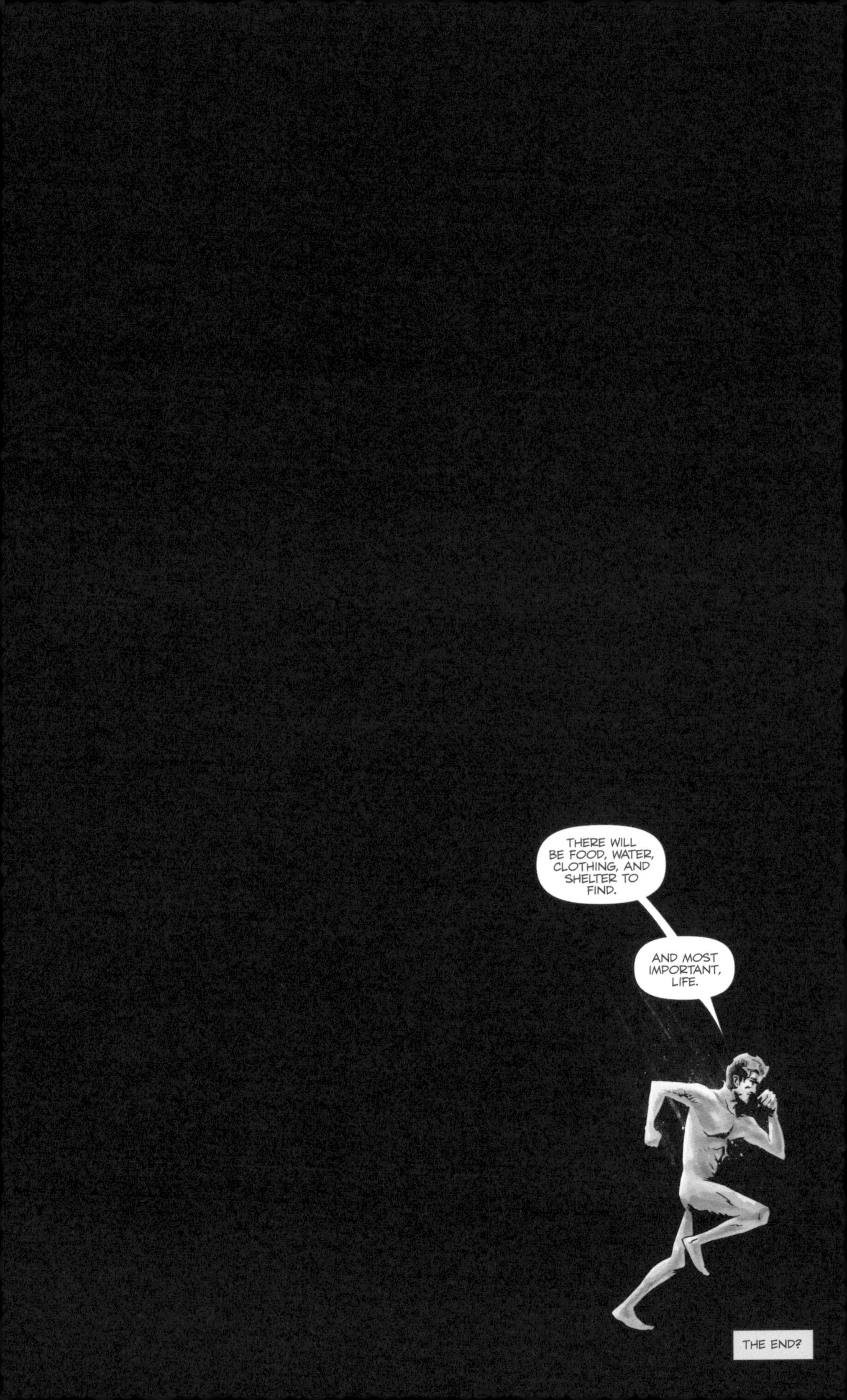
THERE WILL BE FOOD, WATER, CLOTHING, AND SHELTER TO FIND.
AND MOST IMPORTANT, LIFE.
THE END?

AFTERWORD

by DAVID MORRELL

The terrifying novel that inspired the classic motion picture!
"A classic of suspense as poignant as it is frightening— a mix that only Richard Matheson could pull off." —Dean Koontz
RICHARD MATHESON
THE INCREDIBLE SHRINKING MAN

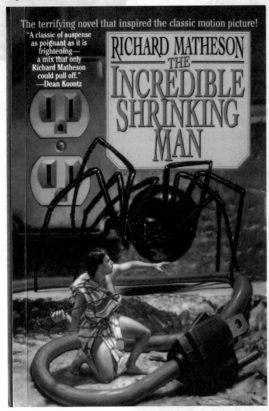

What follows is the entirety of David Morrell's afterword, which was published in the 2001 limited edition printing of Richard Matheson's science-fiction masterpiece, *The Shrinking Man*, and explores the deeper meaning and creation of Matheson's original novel. Enjoy!

Richard Matheson notes in his introduction to his *Collected Stories* that his mother was an orphan before she was ten. In her early teens, she immigrated from Norway to the United States, where "insecure and frightened, thrust into an alien environment" she eventually married a fellow immigrant and fostered in her children an uneasiness with the outside world. Soon she took to religion while her husband took to drink. Three years after Matheson was born in 1926, his parents separated. Subsequently, his mother and older sister raised him.

"I found personal escape in writing," he says. "The creating of a new world of imagination in which I could work out any and all troubles. A therapeutic battlefield on which I could confront my enemies (my anxieties) and—in relative safety—deal with them in socially acceptable ways."

The fantasy he speaks about (most of it based on fear) led him to explore many different types of writing: science fiction (*I Am Legend, The Shrinking Man, Seven Steps to Midnight*), horror (*A Stir of Echoes, Hell House, Earthbound*),* noir suspense (*Someone Is Bleeding, Fury on Sunday, Ride the Nightmare, Passion Play*), combat fiction (*The Beardless Warriors*), metaphysical fantasies (*Bid Time Return, What Dreams May Come*),

---

*For the record, Matheson prefers not to be associated with the term "horror," feeling that it is too suggestive of slasher pictures such as *Friday the 13th*. He believes that the explicitness of that kind of story is contrary to his usual method in which the gooseflesh detail is suggested more than described. In place of being labeled a horror writer, he favors the word "terror," although he admits that this may be only a matter of semantics. *Earthbound*, his most recently published novel of this type, has a complex history that merits an explanation. About a female succubus, "an earthbound spirit, probably the most insidious psychic force," the book uses sexuality as the basis for its fright. Matheson wrote it in the late sixties, cut it by about a hundred pages at the suggestion of his agent, then saw it eviscerated by two editors before it was finally published as a 1982 paperback original from Playboy Press. Matheson was so displeased by the result that he used his Logan Swanson pseudonym. The restored text was eventually published under his own name in England in 1989 and in the U.S. in 1994.

and westerns (*Journal of the Gun Years*, *The Memoirs of Wild Bill Hickok*, as well as several others). A mainstream novel, *Hunger and Thirst*, about a man dying from a bullet wound who recalls the various stages of his troubled life, was the first book Matheson completed but has only recently appeared in print.

At the same time, few writers have been skilled in so many different modes. Not only short stories and novels, but also his scripts for episodic television (his 14 contributions to Rod Serling's *The Twilight Zone*, plus his work for such diverse series as *Have Gun Will Travel*, *Wanted: Dead or Alive*, *Richard Diamond*, *Star Trek*, *Night Gallery*, and *Lawman*, for which he received a Writers Guild of America award), his stand-alone teleplays (*Duel*, which was directed by Stephen Spielberg, *The Night Stalker*, and the mainstream character study of an alcoholic, *The Morning After*, plus many more), and his film scripts (*The Incredible Shrinking Man*, a number of Edgar Allan Poe adaptations for Roger Corman, *The Legend of Hell House*, and *Somewhere in Time*, his moving adaptation of *Bid Time Return*). That doesn't include his non-fiction about paranormal phenomena: *The Path* and *Mediums Rare*.

So much output. So much variety. Although diverse, however, most of Matheson's work has a common theme, which he relates to his difficult childhood and which he describes as the "individual isolated in a threatening world, attempting to survive." Often, his characters are isolated by a drastic shift in reality. In "Disappearing Act," for example, a man discovers that one-by-one his friends, his relatives, his employer, and his wife have disappeared as if they'd never existed. Eventually, he too vanishes, leaving only a diary on a coffee-shop counter. In "The Curious Child," a man panics when his memory increasingly fails him. First he can't remember where he parked his car. Then he can't remember what kind of car it is, where he lives, or even what his last name is. In a *Twilight Zone* script, "A World of Difference," a businessman enters his office one morning, picks up the phone, and is startled to hear someone yell "Cut!" The businessman is told that he's a character in a film, but he insists that he isn't an actor, that he really is the businessman. Dismayed to discover himself burdened by a shrewish wife and studio pressures, he struggles to find a way to return to the pleasant home, wife, and occupation depicted in the script.

But Matheson's most ambitious depiction of someone isolated by altered reality, struggling to survive, is his fourth novel *The Shrinking Man* (1956), in which a veil of radioactive mist causes a man to shrink until specks of sand become boulders and a black-widow spider becomes a giant. Seen strictly as a novel in which the conflict is between large and small, *The Shrinking Man* has several obvious predecessors: Odysseus' encounter with the cyclops, Beowulf against Grendel, St. George against the dragon. In Swift's *Gulliver's Travels*, the title character journeys to a land in which he is a giant among tiny people (who turn out to be vicious) and to another land in which *he* is the tiny person among giants (who turn out to be gentle).

The idea of a story about shrinking has antecedents, also. In 1934, for example, Harry Bates wrote "A Matter of Size" in which a scientist is taken to another planet to contribute to its gene pool. He escapes and returns to earth, only to discover that he is now a couple inches high. In his struggle to stay alive, he uses burned-out matches and hair pins to construct climbing tools that get him up towering stairs. He also has a fierce battle with a giant cat. In 1936, Henry Hasse wrote "He Who Shrank" in which a scientist tests a new substance by injecting it into his assistant. The assistant shrinks to a submicroscopic level in which he descends past electrons moving planetlike around the nuclei of atoms. Occasionally, he lands on electrons which turn out to be inhabited by various types of beings: gossamer-winged sylphs, murderous robots, and stone-age hunters. In time, he lands on an electron which we learn is earth and where he disrupts the Great Lakes before he shrinks further and enters even smaller universes.

Matheson claims that he backed into a career as a science-fiction writer because there were so many magazines of that type when he started in the fifties. Because he hadn't researched the history of the genre, it's doubtful that the stories I've just summarized had an influence on him. Even if they had, however, the influence would have been negative, for "A Matter of Size" and "He Who Shrank" are flatly written and preposterous whereas *The Shrinking Man* brilliantly demonstrates Matheson's primary contribution to the genre: his determination to convince the reader that the story, no matter how far-fetched, is actually taking place.

This has been called (by Matheson's friend and fellow *Twilight Zone* writer, George Clayton Johnson) the "coffee and cakes" approach to scaring people. Matheson showed that a writer didn't have to imitate conventions created by Mary Shelley, Bram Stoker, or H.P. Lovecraft in order to scare readers. As Douglas E. Winter noted, Matheson along with a few other writers such as Robert Bloch and Jack Finney "created the modern landscape of fear." He took fright from Gothic "misty moors and haunted mansions to the American suburbs. He invited terror into our shopping malls and peaceful neighborhoods—into the house next door." There, coffee and cake were being served. We could smell them. We could taste them. Meanwhile something unspeakable was about to smash through the kitchen door.

In *The Shrinking Man*, this realistic approach is achieved in part by its emphasis on sensate description. "He was still shivering. He could smell the dry, acrid odor of the cardboard close to his face, and it seemed as if he were being smothered." Every scene is depicted in that palpable detail. The hero, Scott Carey, is physically present in the extreme. The pain and deprivation he suffers—his scraped hands, his sprained joints, his cuts, his fever, his sore throat, his hunger and thirst—are so vividly communicated that we feel we are in his place.

The Shrinking Man's realism is achieved also by its candid (for its time, amazingly so) treatment of sex. Scott's preoccupation about sex is so constant that references to it have a structural function. Scenes involving it become a way of measuring his torturous descent. The first reference is early in the novel. Five-sevenths-of-an-inch tall, he has been sleeping on a crumpled pink rag, which he suddenly realizes is part of a slip that his wife threw away. Once it had "rested against her warm, fragrant flesh." Frustrated and angry, he kicks at it. But with sex on his mind, he soon comes across a gigantic magazine with an alluring photograph of a young woman leaning over a rock, "a pair of clinging black shorts cut just below the hips." He "could almost feel the curved smoothness of her legs as mentally he ran his hands along them." He fantasizes about the feel of her breasts. Abruptly he recalls a tense evening with his wife in which, four feet tall, he wanted to have sex with her but couldn't bring himself to ask. When his wife finally realized what was bothering him, she reacted with surprise and pity. After an awkward discussion ("I guess it would be rather grotesque."), they finally did have sex, but it was as if the wife were having intercourse with a child.

Scott becomes so small that he goes to bed with a carnival midget (he tells his wife and asks her to drive him home from the midget's trailer the next morning). After that, he becomes a miniature Peeping Tom, staring "rigidly tensed" out a cellar window at his daughter's babysitter lying in the backyard in a bathing suit. When she leans forward to pick up a ball, her breasts slip out. "Oops," she says. Soon he lives in a doll house, where his wife supplies him with a toy female figure "legs spread apart, arms half raised, as though she contemplated a possible embrace." Trying to sleep with it, he "pressed close to her and slipped his arms around her body."

Not all encounters involve women. At one point, he looks so much like a boy that a pervert picks him up when he has car trouble. "Scott jumped up as he sat on the man's thick hand. The man drew it away, held it before his eyes. 'You have injured the member, my boy.'" Later a group of teenage thugs surrounds him. Realizing that he is the famous shrinking man, they call him "Freako" and want to pull down his pants to "see if *all* of him shrunk." He says, "If you want my money, take it." One answers, "Bet ya shrinkin' *butt* we'll take it." (Matheson's italics.)

If Matheson's realism was innovative for science fiction, so was his unusual structure. In this regard, it's useful to compare the novel with the well-known movie adaptation which came out in 1957, a year after the novel. Although Matheson had published three prior novels and dozens of much-praised short stories, his income still wasn't enough to pay the bills (for a time he worked as a machine operator at Douglas Aircraft). Thus when Universal-International wanted to purchase the film rights for *The Shrinking Man*, he refused to agree unless he was hired to write the screenplay (it won a Hugo).** The successful result (in documentary black-and-white, with *Incredible* added to the title) gave him a sufficient reputation in Hollywood that more screen work followed.

For the film, he chose a conventional chronological approach. While on a boating holiday, Scott (played by Grant Williams) is engulfed with an eerie mist. In rapid succession, his clothes become too big for him as does the furniture around him. Medical specialists are mystified until they conclude that the mist, which was radioactive, must have altered some insecticide with which he'd been accidentally sprayed, causing a molecular mutation that shrinks him. This scientific rationale is no more convincing in the movie than it is in the book, by the way. It isn't necessary. We take for granted that the mist was toxic. In 1954, two years before *The Shrinking Man* was published, the United States exploded the world's first hydrogen bomb on Bikini in the Marshall Islands. The blast was a thousand times greater than the atomic bomb dropped on Hiroshima. Radioactive ash struck an American destroyer, three inhabited islands, and a Japanese fishing boat. The ash resembled a huge mist in which something drizzled. As one of the fisherman said, "Some kind of white sand is falling from the heavens." The fisherman was dead in seven months. By the time the film adaptation of Matheson's novel was released three years after the blast, the Cold War had intensified. As the US and the USSR competed to build more and deadlier nuclear weapons, as we worried about strontium-90 and other toxic elements floating around in the atmosphere, it made perfect sense that a radioactive mist engulfed our hero. It's exactly what everyone had been fearing.

Once Matheson gets the explanation out of the way (one of the few places in the movie where the sets look cheap), he proceeds to the movie's point, which is Scott's vulnerability as he gets smaller. While Scott resides in the doll house, the family cat attacks him. He tries to hide in the cellar, becomes trapped down there, and finds himself being stalked by a towering spider. The film's climax is his fight-to-the-death

---

**I've already mentioned that Matheson received a Writers Guild award for his television work. His other awards include the Bram Stoker (Horror Writers Association), the Edgar (Mystery Writers of America), the Golden Spur (Western Writers of America) and the Howard. The latter is named after fantasist Robert E. Howard, the creator of Conan the Barbarian, and is given each year at the prestigious World Fantasy Convention, where on one occasion Matheson was selected for the rare distinction of being called a Grand Master. The Horror Writers Association also gave him that honor.

with it. Subsequently, he becomes so small that he can step between the wires of a screen and enter the back yard, a brave new world where infinite and the infinitesimal are linked and he looks forward to the new adventures that will show him the beauty of the universe.

Character and texture aren't important here. Basically this is a special-effects movie that uses trick sets, split-screen techniques, and process shots to put the viewer in awe of Scott's ordeal in the basement. During the nineteen fifties, the visual illusions were effective but now seem primitive, yet the film still engages the viewer, a tribute to Jack Arnold's speedy direction and the strong situations in Matheson's screenplay. Some of the best aren't in the novel. For example, in the film the hero comes upon a mouse trap, figures out how to spring it without hurting himself, but causes the cheese to flip away and drop down a drain. Later, he is almost washed down the same drain in a flood caused by a ruptured water heater.

As positive as the movie was for Matheson's career, it was negative in this respect— many people who have seen the film think that they know the story and hence haven't bothered to read the book. A pity, because the novel is far more accomplished than the film and has more surprises. The structure is particularly noteworthy. In a stark one-page opening chapter, "First he thought it was a tidal wave. Then he saw that the sky and ocean were visible through it and it was a curtain of spray rushing at the boat." The spray hits him, making him tingle. He towels himself, and the feeling is gone. "It was the beginning."

Wham! The still-unnamed hero is suddenly racing for his life across an alien landscape, pursued by a spider whose "body was a giant, glossy egg that trembled blackly as it charged across the windless mounds." How he got to be in this alien environment we're not told, although we can guess from the title. There's a huge red snake and a great orange mass. A steel-encased flame glares behind him. Thunder shakes the air. The descriptions are maddeningly vague. Only when he eludes the spider for what we gather has been dozens of times, do we learn that the flame in the steel tower is from an oil burner. The thunder is the sound of the fuel igniting. The red snake is a garden hose. The orange structure is a stack of lawn chairs. "And the tanklike cans were used paint cans, and the spider was a black widow." Then comes a hammering single-sentence paragraph: "He lived in a cellar."

Thereafter Matheson shifts to a scene in which Scott (we learn his name casually in the middle of a paragraph) tells his incredulous wife that he just measured his height and he's not six-feet tall anymore. Almost at once, the novel switches back to Scott, a half-inch tall and getting smaller, continuing to fight to survive in the basement. Sometimes his memories make him recall a scene from the past, but often the flashback has no transition. Sometimes there are flashbacks within flashbacks. More, there is no chronology to the flashbacks. They describe disparate events in which he's short, then tall, then really short, then not-so tall. Only a few pages from the book's end do we learn how Scott came to be trapped in the basement. In this universe where big has become small and small has become big, the fractured structure is appropriate—convention no longer applies.

These days, after the fictional experiments of the 1960s, after what was called metafiction which drew attention to the techniques of storytelling, a fractured structure isn't unusual. Indeed some writing classes experimented with creating novels in which each chapter was on a note card. If you shuffled the cards and jumbled the structure, you instantly achieved a new version of the novel whose message was how arbitrary and disjointed life could be. Before 1956, however, few novelists had experimented in this manner. Faulkner's *The Sound and the Fury* (1929) comes to mind. So does Proust's *A la Recherche du Temps Perdu* (1913-1927). The reader no doubt has pre-fifties favorites in which chronology is shattered. But there aren't many, for this type of experimentation didn't gain great interest (mostly among academics) until the last third of the century. From this perspective, *The Shrinking Man* wasn't only innovative within the science-fiction genre; it was ahead of most experimental fiction also.

Not that anyone would try to make a case that Matheson is equal to Faulkner. This is a genre piece. It never pretends otherwise, although it accomplishes its purpose with remarkable technical sophistication. But it is interesting to note that the novel's thematic concerns are very comparable to those of some non-genre "serious" novelists, particularly the French existentialists Albert Camus and Jean-Paul Sartre. At its core, Existentialism links these three statements. There is no God. Everybody dies. It's difficult to find meaning in a universe that consequently seems pointless and absurd. In his influential essay, "The Myth of Sisyphus" (1942), Camus compared our existence to that of the mythic Greek figure, Sisyphus, who was doomed to push a huge boulder up a hill, only to have it crash to the bottom and he would be forced to push it to the top again and again and again. "It is legitimate and necessary to wonder if life has a meaning," Camus said. "Therefore it is legitimate to meet the problem of suicide face to face." His conclusion was that suicide was not a valid course, "that even within the limits of nihilism it is possible to find the means to proceed beyond nihilism." One method that he and Sartre advocated was to find meaning in being what they called "authentic," which basically meant being what *we* wanted to be rather than what *others* wanted us to be. A corollary is that the past and the future shouldn't dictate how we behave in the present. Now is all that matters. We are free to reinvent ourselves with each second, finding meaning in the moment, regardless of the strictures of society and the people around us. In contrast, the worst thing to do is live by default, by going through the motions without any appreciation of existence.

Now consider the theme of *The Shrinking Man*. When we first see Scott in the basement, he is less than an inch tall. He calculates that he has only six days to live. Despair so overwhelms him that he debates letting the spider catch and kill him. "The thing would be out of his hands then. It would be a hideous death, but it would be quick; despair would be ended. And yet he kept fleeing from it, improvising and struggling and existing." In subsequent scenes, his mood worsens. "Poets and philosophers could talk all they wanted about a man's being more than fleshly form, about his essential worth, about the immeasurable stature of his soul. It was rubbish." More and more, he begins to sound like an Existentialist. "He still lived, but was his living considered, or only an instinctive survival?... Was he a separate, meaningful person; was he an individual? Did he matter? Was it enough just to survive? He didn't know." It might be that "he was a pathetic fraction of a shadow, living only out of habit, impulse-driven, moved but never moving, fought but never fighting."

It's worth noting that while the radioactive mist is the literal cause of Scott's shrinking, there are numerous metaphoric causes; the insane international politics that made a radioactive mist all too believable in the fifties, the increasing tension within Scott's marriage, and the economic hardships that would have struck Scott even if he hadn't gotten sick (his brother for whom he works has major business problems, for example). Now, a half-inch tall in the basement, his face is unusually calm for a man "who lived each day with dread and peril. Perhaps jungle life, despite physical danger, was a relaxing one. Surely it was free of the petty grievances, the disparate values of society. It was simple, devoid of artifice and ulcer-burning pressures…. There were no political connivings necessary, no financial arenas to struggle in, no nerve-knotting races for superior rungs on the social ladder. There was only to be or not to be."

As things get worse, however, Scott keeps asking himself, "Why do I go on?… Why do I try so hard? Instinct? Will?… It would have been so much better if his brain had lost its toxic introspections long before. Much better if he could have concluded life as a true bug instead of being fully conscious each hideous, downward step of the way." That thought startles him, making him realize that "so long as he had his mind, he was unique…. His mind could be his salvation, as it had been his damnation." Throwing himself into the search for food, he becomes a version of Sisyphus, repeatedly climbing and descending huge heights. He eventually fixates on the spider as the ultimate goal— not to let it kill him, but to manage the reverse, to kill *it*. "True satisfaction was based on struggle…. He was alive, he was trying. Suicide was a distant impossibility. He wondered how he could ever have considered it."

The spider takes on metaphysical dimensions. It "was immortal. It was more than a spider. It was every unknown terror in the world fused into wriggling, poison-jawed horror. It was every anxiety, insecurity, and fear in his life given a hideous, night-black form." I'm reminded that the early-American Calvinists thought of humanity as bugs so disgusting that they deserved to be consumed by God whom they saw as a vengeful spider. In *The Shrinking Man*'s climax, Scott finally manages to kill the spider. In his victory, he suddenly realizes that he isn't going to shrink into nothingness, that instead he's going to enter a new level of existence. Finding a way into the back yard, he concludes, "How could he be less than nothing?… Last night he'd looked up at the universe without. Then there must be a universe within, too…. He'd always thought in terms of man's own world and man's own limited dimensions. He had presumed upon nature…. But to nature there was no zero. Existence went on in endless cycles…. There was no point of non-existence in the universe." Thus from despair, the hero passes through what amounts to the principles of Existentialism to arrive at a new (indeed mystical) appreciation of reality in which "he stood in speechless awe looking at the new world with its vivid splashes of vegetation, its scintillant hills, its towering trees, its sky of shifting hues…. It was a wonderland." His mind teems with "questions and ideas and—yes—hope again" as he races into his new world. The significant final word is "searching."

I have no way of knowing whether this remarkably textured novel which almost transcends its genre was influenced by Camus' essay. It's interesting that an English translation of his collection, *The Myth of Sisyphus*, appeared in 1955, a year before *The Shrinking Man* was published. But whether Matheson read that book isn't certain. Sometimes ideas are in the air. American writers were very interested in Existentialism during the 1950s. It's possible that Matheson came across these ideas in conversations with friends, or maybe he worked out these ideas on his own. If the latter, I am amazed when I read the following final words of Camus' essay and realize how easily they could have been added to the final page of Matheson's novel with only a few changes (the tense, for example) to keep anyone from suspecting that Matheson hadn't written them. "Each atom of that stone, each mineral flake of that night-filled mountain, in itself forms a world. The struggle toward the heights is enough to fill a man's heart." ∎

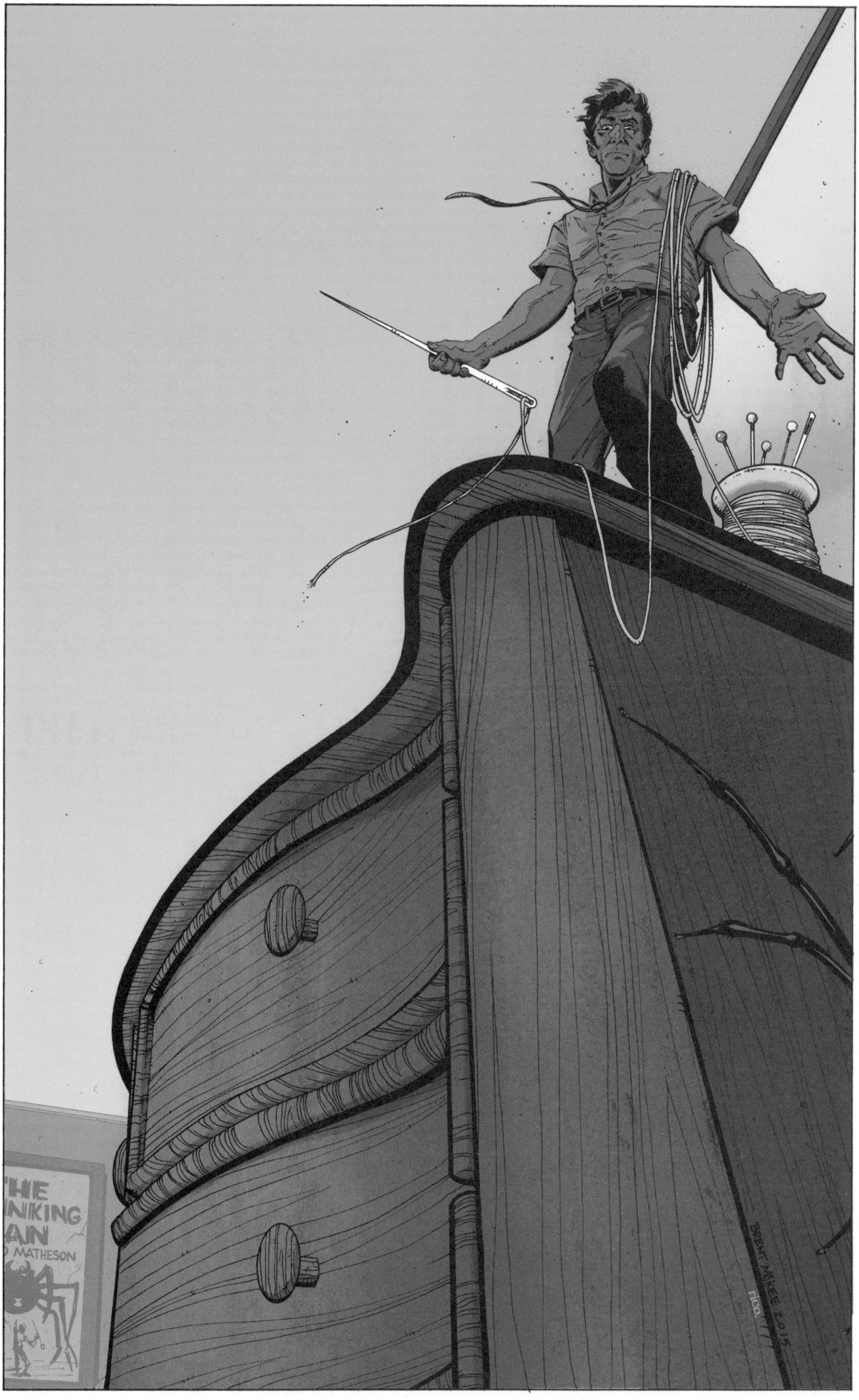
THE
NIKING
AIN
MATHESON
BRENT McKEE 2015
rico.

He fired my imagination by placing his horrors, not in European castles and Lovecraftian universes, but in American scenes I knew and could relate to. "I want to do that," I thought. "I must do that." Matheson showed the way.
—*Stephen King*

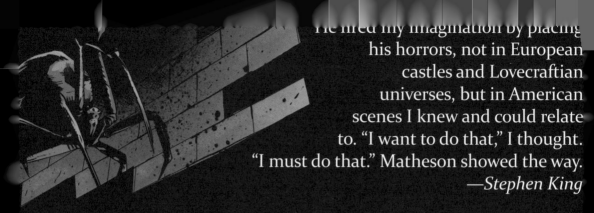

ADAPTING A MASTER

by Ted Adams

As a kid growing up in the '70s and '80s, I revered the work of Richard Matheson. I came to his work via Stephen King's non-fiction overview of the horror genre, *Danse Macabre*, where he describes the influence Matheson had on him. In those days, it wasn't possible to immediately have access to every book ever written and every TV show ever produced. So I spent years hunting used bookstores for Matheson's novels and many hours watching the *Twilight Zone*, hoping to see episodes written by him.

When IDW published Steve Niles and Elman Brown's adaptation of *I Am Legend* in 2003, I was extremely proud to be Matheson's publisher. It was the start of IDW publishing many of the writers who made me want to be a publisher in the first place—a list that now includes Robert Bloch, Clive Barker, Anne Rice, Richard Stark, Philip Jose Farmer, George R. R. Martin, H.P. Lovecraft, and Stephen King.

Since publishing *I Am Legend*, which collected comics originally published by Eclipse Comics, we went on to create all-new adaptions of *Hell House*, four short stories in our prophetically named *Doomed* magazine, and most recently, *Duel*.

My day job as IDW's CEO and Publisher keeps me pretty busy so I don't have as much time to write as I'd like, but when we started discussing the idea of adapting *The Shrinking Man*, I knew I'd have to find the time to do the adaptation myself.

Not only is it my favorite of Matheson's novels, I'd recently read it aloud to my son, Sam, and I thought it would be fun for us to work on the adaptation together. Sam ultimately decided

I AM LEGEND
RICHARD MATHESON

HELL HOUSE
RICHARD MATHESON

DOOMED
DOOMED PRESENTS
ASHLEY WOOD

IDW
MATHESON
RYALL
GARRES
MATHESON
ROAD RAGE
DUEL

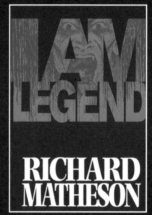

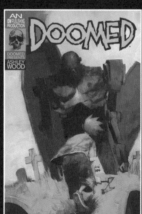

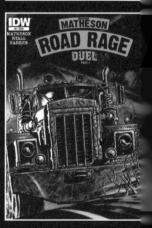

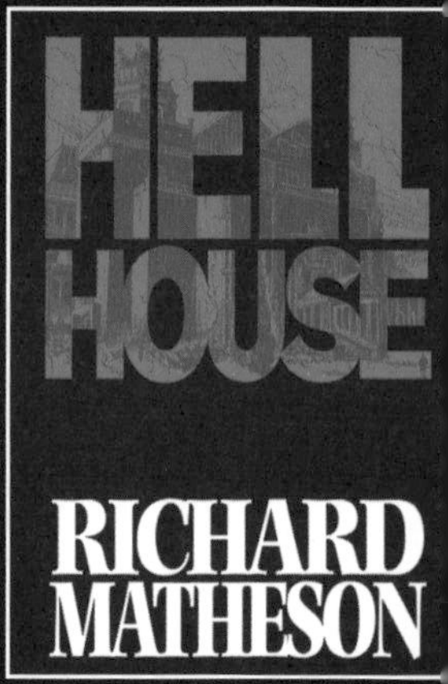

that he didn't want to take a credit on the book for his work but I wanted to share some of our process on breaking down the story.

The novel cuts back and forth between Scott's adventures in the basement when he is fully shrunk and the scenes that explain how he got there, and we kept that structure for the comic.

We used the latest paperback edition and started by figuring out how many pages we needed for each chapter. As you'll see here, we decided that Chapter One could be a single page with 4 panels. You can also see that wherever possible, we used Matheson's dialogue. The only scenes where we really had to create some dialogue are the ones where Scott's alone in the basement. Because these parts of the book are all an internal dialogue in Scott's head, and thought balloons are no longer *en vogue* in comics, we added some dialogue to help tell the story.

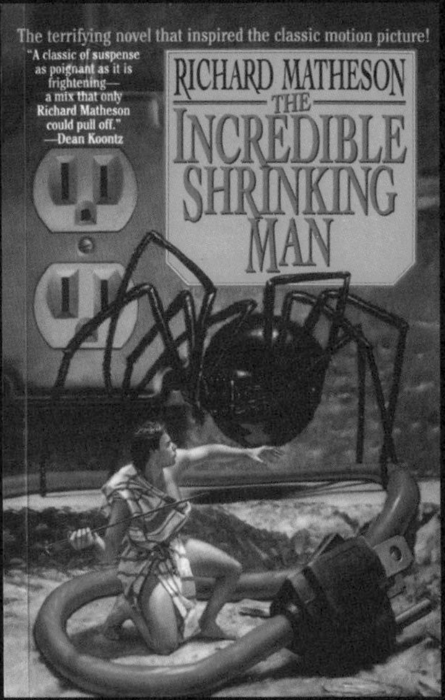

The terrifying novel that inspired the classic motion picture!
"A classic of suspense as poignant as it is frightening—a mix that only Richard Matheson could pull off." —Dean Koontz
RICHARD MATHESON
THE INCREDIBLE SHRINKING MAN

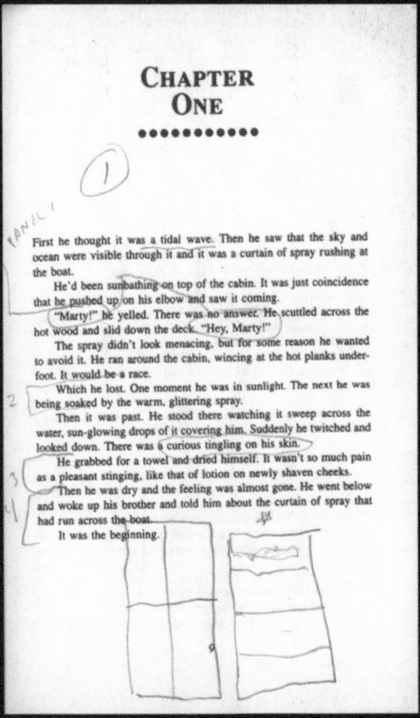

CHAPTER ONE

First he thought it was a tidal wave. Then he saw that the sky and ocean were visible through it and it was a curtain of spray rushing at the boat.

He'd been sunbathing on top of the cabin. It was just coincidence that he pushed up on his elbow and saw it coming.

"Marty!" he yelled. There was no answer. He scuttled across the hot wood and slid down the deck. "Hey, Marty!"

The spray didn't look menacing, but for some reason he wanted to avoid it. He ran around the cabin, wincing at the hot planks underfoot. It would be a race.

Which he lost. One moment he was in sunlight. The next he was being soaked by the warm, glittering spray.

Then it was past. He stood there watching it sweep across the water, sun-glowing drops of it covering him. Suddenly he twitched and looked down. There was a curious tingling on his skin.

He grabbed for a towel and dried himself. It wasn't so much pain as a pleasant stinging, like that of lotion on newly shaven cheeks.

Then he was dry and the feeling was almost gone. He went below and woke up his brother and told him about the curtain of spray that had run across the boat.

It was the beginning.

9

For the scene that's on Page 4 of our comic, we needed to be able to include a lot of dialogue to explain what's happening to Scott. Three panels of three characters sitting around a table could be visually dull so we decided to spin the point of view in each panel. You can see again here that the dialogue on this page comes right from the novel.

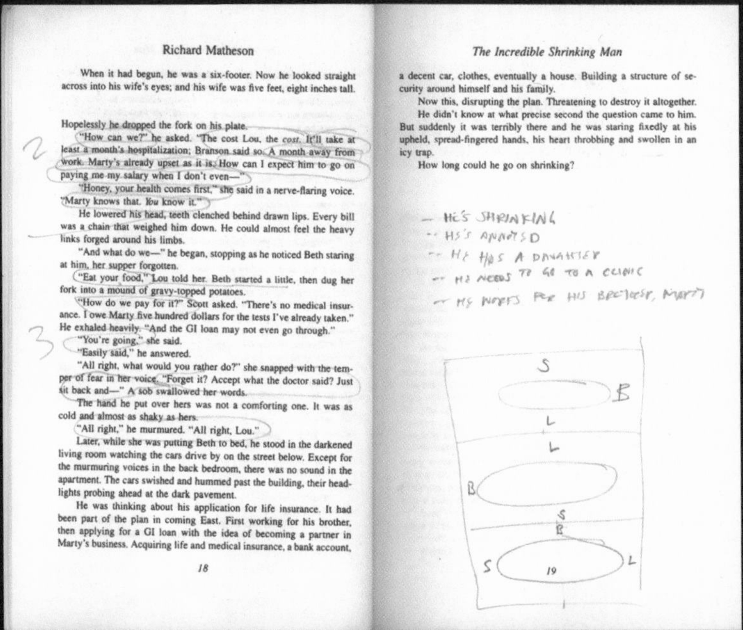

Richard Matheson

When it had begun, he was a six-footer. Now he looked straight across into his wife's eyes; and his wife was five feet, eight inches tall.

Hopelessly he dropped the fork on his plate.

"How can we?" he asked. "The cost Lou, the *cost*. It'll take at least a month's hospitalization; Branson said so. A month away from work. Marty's already upset as it is. How can I expect him to go on paying me my salary when I don't even—"

"Honey, your health comes first," she said in a nerve-flaring voice. "Marty knows that. *You* know it."

He lowered his head, teeth clenched behind drawn lips. Every bill was a chain that weighed him down. He could almost feel the heavy links forged around his limbs.

"And what do we—" he began, stopping as he noticed Beth staring at him, her supper forgotten.

"Eat your food," Lou told her. Beth started a little, then dug her fork into a mound of gravy-topped potatoes.

"How do we pay for it?" Scott asked. "There's no medical insurance. I owe Marty five hundred dollars for the tests I've already taken." He exhaled heavily. "And the GI loan may not even go through."

"You're going," she said.

"Easily said," he answered.

"All right, what would you rather do?" she snapped with the temper of fear in her voice. "Forget it? Accept what the doctor said? Just sit back and—" A sob swallowed her words.

The hand he put over hers was not a comforting one. It was as cold and almost as shaky as hers.

"All right," he murmured. "All right, Lou."

Later, while she was putting Beth to bed, he stood in the darkened living room watching the cars drive by on the street below. Except for the murmuring voices in the back bedroom, there was no sound in the apartment. The cars swished and hummed past the building, their headlights probing ahead at the dark pavement.

He was thinking about his application for life insurance. It had been part of the plan in coming East. First working for his brother, then applying for a GI loan with the idea of becoming a partner in Marty's business. Acquiring life and medical insurance, a bank account,

18

The Incredible Shrinking Man

a decent car, clothes, eventually a house. Building a structure of security around himself and his family.

Now this, disrupting the plan. Threatening to destroy it altogether.

He didn't know at what precise second the question came to him. But suddenly it was terribly there and he was staring fixedly at his upheld, spread-fingered hands, his heart throbbing and swollen in an icy trap.

How long could he go on shrinking?

— HE'S SHRINKING
— HE'S ANNOYED
— HE HAS A DAUGHTER
— HE NEEDS TO GO TO A CLINIC
— HE WORKS FOR HIS BROTHER, MARTY

19

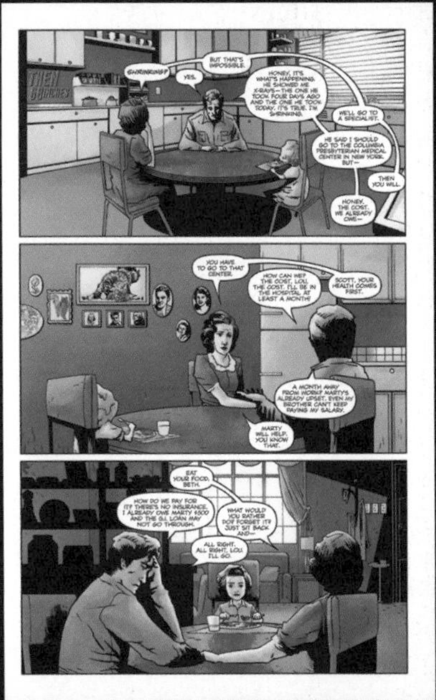

SHRINKING?
YES.
BUT THAT'S IMPOSSIBLE.
HONEY, IT'S WHAT'S HAPPENING. HE SHOWED ME X-RAYS—THE ONE HE TOOK FOUR DAYS AGO AND THE ONE HE TOOK TODAY. IT'S TRUE. I'M SHRINKING.
WE'LL GO TO A SPECIALIST.
HE SAID I SHOULD GO TO THE COLUMBIA PRESBYTERIAN MEDICAL CENTER IN NEW YORK. BUT—
THEN YOU WILL.
HONEY, THE COST. WE ALREADY OWE—
YOU HAVE TO GO TO THAT CENTER.
HOW CAN WE? THE COST, LOU, THE COST. I'LL BE IN THE HOSPITAL AT LEAST A MONTH!
SCOTT, YOUR HEALTH COMES FIRST.
A MONTH AWAY FROM WORK? MARTY'S ALREADY UPSET. EVEN MY BROTHER CAN'T KEEP PAYING MY SALARY.
MARTY WILL HELP. YOU KNOW THAT.
EAT YOUR FOOD, BETH.
HOW DO WE PAY FOR IT? THERE'S NO INSURANCE. I ALREADY OWE MARTY $500 AND THE G.I. LOAN MAY NOT GO THROUGH.
WHAT WOULD YOU RATHER DO? FORGET IT? JUST SIT BACK AND—
ALL RIGHT. ALL RIGHT, LOU. I'LL GO.

Mark's art throughout the comic is terrific—great storytelling in the action scenes and expressive characters in the scenes where we learn what's happening to Scott. We were lucky to have him as our artist and I'm looking forward to seeing what he'll do next for IDW.

I'm proud of the work we've done here and I hope Matheson would have approved of our adaptation. But, what I hope more than anything is that this comic encourages you to pick up and read the actual novel. Any time you spend with Matheson's work is time well spent, and *The Shrinking Man* has a lot of themes that resonate with a modern audience.

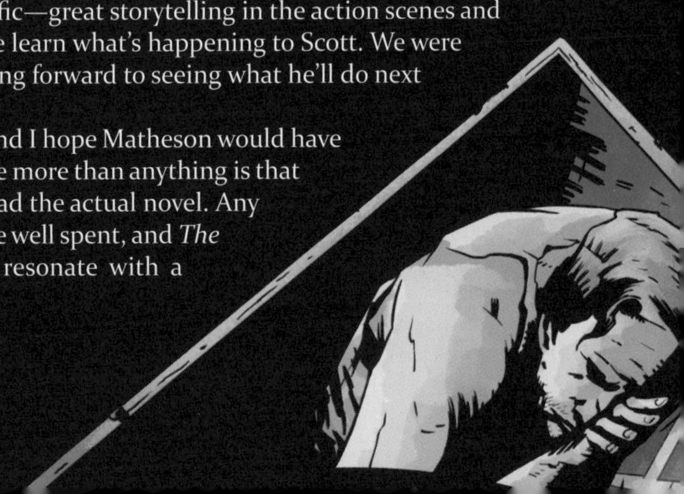

MATHESON AND MOVING PICTURES

by Ted Adams

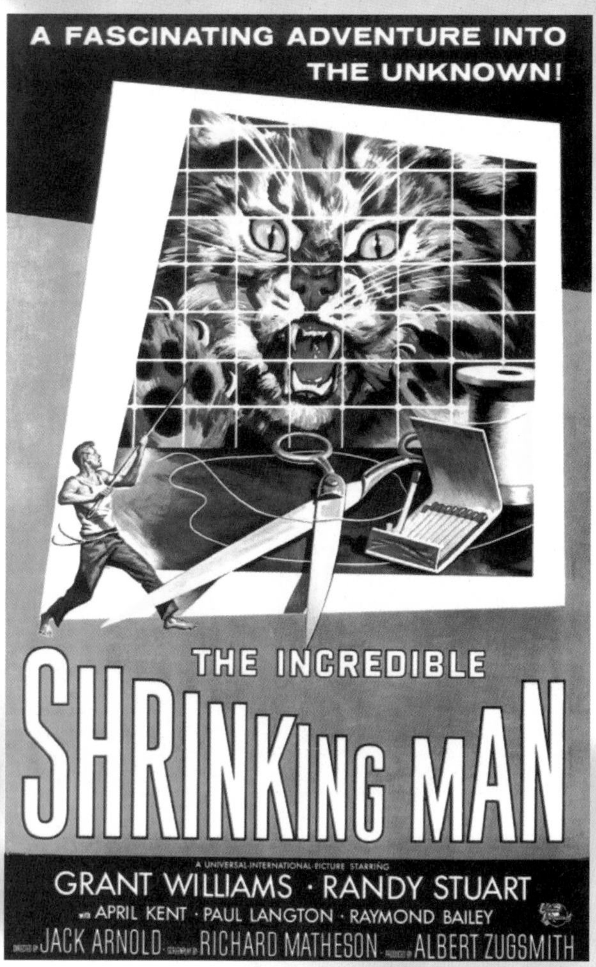
A FASCINATING ADVENTURE INTO THE UNKNOWN!
THE INCREDIBLE
SHRINKING MAN
A UNIVERSAL-INTERNATIONAL PICTURE STARRING
GRANT WILLIAMS · RANDY STUART
APRIL KENT · PAUL LANGTON · RAYMOND BAILEY
JACK ARNOLD · RICHARD MATHESON · ALBERT ZUGSMITH

I realized when researching this article that my first experience with Matheson's work was at the Universal Studios theme park in the 1970s. I was there on a vacation with my family and, way back then, the backlot tour included a stop where you disembarked the studio bus and walked around the backlot. That area had huge props that kids were allowed to crawl all over. I didn't realize it at that time but those props were from the 1957 Universal Studios movie adaptation of *The Shrinking Man* that Matheson himself wrote.

Before sitting down to write the comic book adaptation of *The Shrinking Man*, I thought it would be helpful to see how Matheson himself adapted his material for another medium. The movie holds up well and the effects, done long before any kind of computer graphics, are effective. Little of Scott's sexual frustration is addressed in the movie, for obvious 1950s-era reasons, but the existential crisis of what it means to be a man who is shrinking away is handled nicely, and the action scenes are fun.

This was Matheson's first screenwriting experience and he went on to have a long career in Hollywood. His filmography includes hundreds of hours of movies and TV shows including *Duel* (directed by Steven Spielberg) and many classic episodes of *Star Trek* and *Twilight Zone*.

In his introduction to the 2001 limited edition version of *The Shrinking Man* published by Gauntlet Press, Matheson says:

> While living in Los Angeles from 1951 – 1954, I made various attempts to get script assignments—none of which succeeded. I came to the conclusion that the only way I would ever get such an assignment, would be to sell Hollywood a novel and demand the right to write the screenplay.
>
> This is the way it worked out. I had an agent in Los Angeles named Al Manuel who submitted the manuscript of *The Shrinking Man*...
>
> I telephoned Al Manuel and discovered that I could, indeed, do the script. I'm sure they figured it would be an unsatisfactory first draft, which they could have re-written by one of their contract writers.
>
> Fortunately, it did not work out that way. The script got me started in the movie business. To make use of Oliver Onions' title, I was ready for "The Beckoning Fair One."

Matheson's script ended up in the very capable hands of director Jack Arnold, who—before tackling *The Shrinking Man*—had already brought to the screen the sci-fi classics *It Came From Outer Space*, *Creature From the Black Lagoon*, and *Tarantula*. In *Starlog* magazine #11, Ed Naha describes how Arnold handled the special effects.

For the first shrinking scenes, actor Grant Williams was surrounded by oversized furniture, scaled to make him look slightly shorter than his normal-sized six-foot height. As the character of Carey slowly decreased in size, the furniture on the sets increased in stature. During the final scenes, Grant Williams was surrounded by some of the most amazing oversized sets ever constructed for a film. Giant blocks of cheese, fantastic scissors, mammoth coffee cans, spools of thread, needles, mousetraps, pencils, pieces of cake.

But director Arnold knew that the audiences would soon catch on if only differently scaled sets were used. To add to the believability of it all, he resorted to both process shots and split screen setups when shrinking Scott was shown in the same frame as "normal-sized" people. The same type of effects were used during his battles with the cat and the spider giants but Arnold added over-sized props of animal limbs to give extra "oomph" to the encounters. The essence of the film's power, in fact, rested in the total believability of Scott's problem on the part of the audience. Matheson and Arnold achieved total realism both in dialogue and in visuals.

Matheson was asked by William P. Simmons, in an interview published by *Cemetery Dance* magazine, whether or not he liked the movie and he responded, "For years I didn't like it. It was not appropriate, I thought. But over the years I realized that it was very unusual for its time. The ending, the whole approach, was unusual. And, actually, it is excellent. Grant Williams did a bang up job playing the man."

Matheson also wrote an unproduced treatment for a sequel to *The Incredible Shrinking Man*. The *Fantastic Shrinking Girl* (or *Fantastic Little Girl*) that would have seen Louise Carey discover a way to shrink herself so she could be reunited with Scott. If you'd like to read what could have been, Gauntlet Press has published the treatment (along with two others) in *Unrealized Dreams*. More information can be found on their website: gauntletpress.com.

MORE MATHESON FROM IDW

HELL HOUSE
RICHARD MATHESON

Hell House
TPB • $19.99 • ISBN: 978-1-60010-263-9

RICHARD MATHESON'S
I AM LEGEND
adapted by
STEVE NILES
AND
ELMAN BROWN

I Am Legend
HC • $24.99 • ISBN: 978-1-93238-208-2
TPB • $19.99 • ISBN: 978-1-93323-921-7

ALL-NEW INTRODUCTIONS BY JOE HILL AND STEPHEN KING
ROAD
JOE HILL STEPHEN KING RICHARD MATHESON
RAGE

Road Rage
HC • $24.99 • ISBN: 978-1-61377-282-9
TPB • $19.99 • ISBN: 978-1-61377-780-0

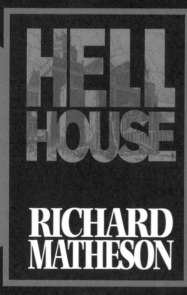

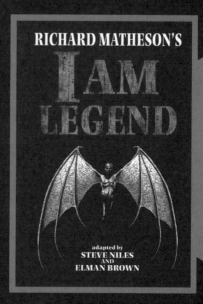

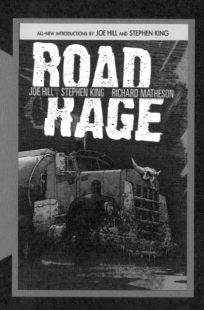